Comparative social policy

Theory and research

PATRICIA KENNETT

Open University Press
Buckingham • Philadelphia

Open University Press
Celtic Court
22 Ballmoor
Buckingham
MK18 1XW

email: enquiries@openup.co.uk
world wide web: www.openup.co.uk

and
325 Chestnut Street
Philadelphia, PA 19106, USA

First Published 2001

A catalogue record of this book is available from the British Library

ISBN 0 335 20123 7 (pb)   0 335 20124 5 (hb)

Library of Congress Cataloging-in-Publication Data
Kennett, Patricia, 1959-
    Comparative social policy: theory and research/Patricia Kennett.
        p. cm. – (Introducing social policy)
    Includes bibliographical references and index.
    ISBN 0-335-20124-5 (hb) – ISBN 0-335-20123-7 (pbk.)
    1. Social Policy.   2. Welfare state.   I. Title.   II. Series.

HN17 5 K459 2001
361.61–do21   00-065238

Typeset by Type Study, Scarborough, North Yorkshire
Printed in Great Britain by Biddles Limited, Guildford and Kings Lynn

For my family

Contents

List of boxes and tables

Notes on contributors

Ben Oakley lectures in the field of Development Studies at the University of Bristol.

Nicola Yeates is a lecturer in the School of Sociology and Social Policy, Queen's University of Belfast, Northern Ireland.

Series editor's foreword

Welcome to the first volume in the Introducing Social Policy series. The series itself is designed to provide a range of well-informed texts on a wide variety of topics that fall within the ambit of social policy studies.

Although primarily designed with undergraduate social policy students in mind, it is hoped that the series – and individual titles within it – will have a wider appeal to students in other social science disciplines and to those engaged on professional and post-qualifying courses in health care and social welfare.

The aim throughout the planning of the series has been to produce a series of texts that both reflect and contribute to contemporary thinking and scholarship, and which present their discussion in a readable and easily accessible format.

It is entirely appropriate that the first volume in the series should be concerned with cross-national perspectives in social policy. Over the past 20 years the study of social policy has been enriched and extended by the comparative perspective which has moved the study of welfare influences, arrangements and outcomes beyond the confines of one country or nation-state in isolation.

This emphasis is reflected in the contents of Patricia Kennett's book. But her contribution to the series is also more distinctive since she engages with the process – as well as the outcomes – of cross-national social policy research, and with the implementation of an integrated approach to comparative social policy. That leads her to discuss issues around citizenship, gender and development, as well as globalization, the role of the nation-state and supra-national governance.

Patricia Kennett has provided an exciting contribution to comparative social policy studies which successfully integrates the results of recent research with an informed discussion of the research process itself.

David Gladstone, University of Bristol

Acknowledgements

Much of the content of this book has developed as part of my teaching activities in the School for Policy Studies at the University of Bristol. I would like to thank colleagues with whom I have taught a number of units, as well as the students who have commented on the course content.

The research for Chapter 5 was carried out with financial support from the Sir Robert Menzies Centre for Australian Studies and the Japan Endowment Committee Foundation. I am grateful to them both for their support.

I would like to thank Ben Oakley and Nicola Yeates for their contribution to this volume, and David Gladstone, the series editor, for his very helpful comments on various drafts of the book.

List of abbreviations

AFDC	Aid to Families with Dependent Children
CAP	Common Agricultural Policy
CEC	Commission of the European Communities
CIS	Commonwealth of Independent States
DATPERS	Dalit and Tribal People Electronic Resource Site
DONGO	donor non-governmental organization
ECHPS	European Community Household Panel Survey
EEC	European Economic Community
ELFS	European Community Labour Force Survey
EMU	economic and monetary union
ERDF	European Regional Development Fund
EU	European Union
Eurostat	Statistical Office of the European Union
FDI	foreign direct investment
FEANTSA	European Federation of National Organizations Working with the Homeless
GATS	General Agreement on Trade and Services
GATT	General Agreement on Tariffs and Trade
GBM	Green Belt Movement
GDI	gender-related development index
GDP	gross domestic product
GEM	gender empowerment measure
GNP	gross national product
GONGO	governmental non-governmental organization
HDI	human development index
HIPCs	heavily indebted poor countries
HPI	human poverty index
IDS	Institute for Development Studies

IFIs	international financial institutions
ILO	International Labour Organization
IMF	International Monetary Fund
LDC	less developed country
LIS	Luxembourg Income Study
NGO	non-governmental organization
NIC	newly industrialized country
NTIA	National Telecommunications and Information Administration
ODA	official development assistance
OECD	Organization for Economic Cooperation and Development
OPEC	Organization of Petroleum Exporting Countries
PAR	participatory action research
PES	principal economic status
PLA	participatory learning and action
PPP	purchasing power parity
PRA	participatory research appraisal
QUANGO	quasi-autonomous non-governmental organization
RRA	rapid rural appraisal
SAF	Structural Adjustment Facility
SAP	structural adjustment programme
TNC	transnational corporation
TRIPS	Trade-Related Intellectual Property Rights
UN	United Nations Organization
UNCHS	United Nations Centre for Human Settlements (Habitat)
UNCTAD	United Nations Conference on Trade and Development
UNDP	United Nations Development Programme
Unesco	United Nations Educational, Scientific and Cultural Organization
Unicef	United Nations Children's Fund
WHO	World Health Organization
WTO	World Trade Organization

Introduction

The changing context of social policy

The expansion of the **welfare state** across Western Europe following the Second World War occurred in the context of full (male) employment, increasing affluence and an extension of social rights for the majority of the population. The prevailing discourse of this period was that the state had a central role to play in ensuring that citizens enjoyed a certain minimum standard of life, economic welfare and security as a matter of right. National welfare regimes helped to underpin a global system of interacting national economies characterized by mass production and mass consumption. This model of institutionalized, bureaucratic provision and social rights was perceived as the inevitable outcome of a 'modern' or developed society. More recently, the dismissal of the post-war consensus and social Keynesianism and the increasing influence of **transnational** factors in the policy-making arena have been accompanied by higher levels of unemployment, increasing inequality and a renegotiation of the social contract between the state and the individual. These changes have contributed to a rethinking of the theoretical and analytical traditions of the welfare state as well as a fundamental reappraisal of the assumption embedded in social policy research. It is in this context that this book explores the conceptual and analytical challenges for cross-national social policy research and considers the strategies and approaches that may contribute to an understanding of the complexity of contemporary social change.

Nation, state and welfare in cross-national research

More than ever, the world in which we live is a fluid and dynamic environment. Social, cultural and economic manifestations are imported and exported across borders. People flow between countries and there has been a proliferation of international organizations such as the **General Agreement on Tariffs and Trade** (GATT), the **World Bank**, the **European Union** (EU) and the **International Monetary Fund** (IMF), and an increase in the number of transnational companies which have no specific national base. Chapter 1 explores these and other key aspects of **globalization**, and considers the political and ideological developments of recent decades that have facilitated the process. The expansion of capitalist social relations, the end of the ideological opposition between East and West, the emergence of a 'transnational governance', and the discrediting and demise of Keynesian macro-economic management and its replacement by a neo-liberal agenda emphasizing deregulation, privatization and free trade are all elements of a new era of global capitalism which are said to have undermined the post-war social democratic commitment to the welfare state and limited the autonomy of the **nation-state**. Chapter 1 will argue that we need to understand and appreciate the globalizing processes taking place but must remain sensitive to differences between nations as well as similarities. Global processes interact with nation-states in a way which reflects the political, cultural and institutional dimensions of individual countries. At the present time the nation-state is a useful unit of analysis even though there are a variety of global processes occurring. It is still central, along with other providers, to the delivery and administration of welfare. The reconfigured international order is still primarily one of politically constructed nation-states which provide the administrative units and much of the infrastructure through which social policy is implemented and delivered. Policy provision is not simply about meeting the needs and demands of international capital to provide services and infrastructure at the lowest possible cost. The nation-state remains an arena of contestation, where social struggles and social rights are won and lost and where governments strive for national legitimacy.

The discussion in Chapter 1 will conclude with an exploration of the European Union's drive towards the harmonization of social policy and its impact on the links between the state, welfare and social policy. These links vary throughout EU countries and reflect the particular profile of individual nations, for example the strength of the trade union movement, political parties, gender relations, religion, culture and tradition. Thus, causal relationships and the outcome of processes are specific to cultural and political forms and, as such, the particularities of individual nations take on real significance. Each brings with it a historical and cultural context within which specific patterns of institutional and organizational arrangements are embedded. A fundamental challenge for those undertaking cross-national research is to grasp the relationship and dynamic between domestic political factors and supranational institutions in the formulation of social policy. The chapter considers briefly a range of approaches for understanding the dynamics of global decision-making and draws on the social dimension of the EU to explore the character of global governance as well as the extent to which we can talk of supranational social policy instruments and provision (Deacon *et al.* 1997).

Clarifying concepts in cross-national social policy analysis

The current context of cross-national research is one that requires an integrated social policy framework (Gough 2000). This integrated framework needs to look beyond the boundaries of the state not only in terms of transnational activities, but also in terms of the mixed economy of welfare within different societies. As Rose (1991) argues, analysis between states requires

> an understanding of what happens within states, for national governments respond to national electorates as well as to international pressures. More than that, national governments impose constraints upon what can and cannot be done internationally. Before we can understand interaction between nations we must understand what goes on within them, and relate that knowledge across national boundaries through the use of generic political concepts.
>
> (Rose 1991: 462)

Chapter 2 is primarily concerned with the *process* of cross-national social policy analysis. It outlines the distinctive features of this type of research as well as the various definitions and interpretations of this approach. While Crow (1997) has emphasized the importance of micro-comparisons between groups and localities *within* societies, these studies fall outside the scope of this volume in which the terms comparative and cross-national are used interchangeably and refer to the explicit, systematic and contextual analysis of one or more phenomena in more than one country.

Issues of definition are central to understanding and exploring social phenomenon and in the construction of an integrated social policy framework. Thus, a particular concern of **comparative, cross-national analysis** (explored in Chapter 2) is the construction and implementation of robust and appropriate concepts. The difficulties of using concepts such as nation, country and society in cross-national research are highlighted by Crow (1997), who argues that

> the boundaries of nation states have become increasingly attenuated . . .
> It can no longer be assumed that people sharing a particular geographical space will also have the common social ties and culture by which 'society' has conventionally been defined.
>
> (Crow 1997: 10)

However, the concept of society should be utilized not in the sense of an isolated, impermeable 'bounded unit', but as 'constituted by multiple, overlapping networks of interaction' (Mann 1993: 738, cited in Crow 1997: 16). This principle can also be applied to the study of social policy and the 'welfare state'. While recognizing that there is no agreed definition of the term 'social policy', Baldock *et al.* (1999: xxi) define it as 'a deliberate intervention by the state to redistribute resources amongst its citizens so as to achieve a welfare objective'. The welfare state is a term which has been widely used to denote the extensive involvement of government in a range of activities to provide social services and promote social well-being through a set of social and economic policies. Schottland (1967) suggests that it is also useful to identify the welfare state as a *legal state* whereby statutory rights entitle citizens to a range of services. This approach, according to Rodgers (2000), sees the welfare state as

> performing an administrative function within the general apparatus of the state charged fundamentally with ensuring the defence of the statutory rights whilst also delineating the limits of legal obligations on individuals and social agents to meet welfare responsibilities within society.
>
> (Rodgers 2000: 8)

Alber *et al.* (1987) have expressed concern at the limitations of the traditional social policy perspective in cross-national research which has tended to concentrate only on state programmes and has utilized measures such as social spending levels or programme coverage to capture welfare output. According to the authors, this has often resulted in reducing the 'welfare state' to one or two highly aggregated indices. They argue that

> boundaries between state and non-state functions are problematic in ways that confound comparative research. Further, the interplay of public and private institutions around issues of social protection has become so complex that the isolation of state welfare expenditure as the object of study makes little sense theoretically.
>
> (Alber *et al.* 1987: 561)

It is important to understand the structure of welfare, its composition and the complex and changing patterns of relationships between different producers. The state is not the sole institution to provide welfare in a society; it derives from a multiple of sources.

Baldock *et al.* (1999) have suggested the concept of **welfare system** which they define as

> the range of institutions that together determine the welfare of citizens. Amongst these are the family and the community networks in which it

exists, the market, the charitable and voluntary sectors, and the social services and benefits provided by the state.

(Baldock et al. 1999: xxi)

Specific national mixes and webs of welfare will vary. More specific examples will follow in later chapters but even at a general level it is possible to begin to explore the mosaic of variation across countries. It could be argued that in Britain and the USA, there has been greater scope for the private sector to promote welfare than in Germany, for example, where the voluntary sector has an institutionalized and established role. In Australia the labour market plays a key role and this model has been characterized as 'the wage-earner's welfare state' (Castles 1985). The role of the family, and in particular women, is also central to the production of welfare across societies. However, not only do family forms vary, but also the extent to which the family, and more specifically women, are considered the 'natural' providers of welfare varies from country to country (Sainsbury 1996). Welfare systems can be predicated on the family or kinship network as welfare providers with religious and philosophical beliefs and values reinforcing 'compulsory altruism' (Land and Rose 1985) or what Hill (1996: 5) refers to as 'webs of interlocking obligations and emotions'. Other commentators argue that the emphasis should not be on welfare state, but on welfare society (Robson 1976; Rein and Rainwater 1981; Rodgers 2000). For Rodgers, the notion of welfare society encapsulates the 'undertheorized relationship between state-sponsored welfare programmes and their reception by and impact on society, both at the level of individual behaviour and of social and community relations' (Rodgers 2000: 9). It is these broader conceptualizations of nation, state and welfare which are utilized in this book as the most appropriate for cross-national social policy analysis. Ball *et al.* (1989) and Esping-Andersen (1990) have both emphasized adopting the 'broader view' in comparative analysis and have cautioned the researcher on analysing concepts in isolation and failing to recognize their interconnectedness and mutual determination. What is certain is that comparative research which focuses exclusively on government social provision can be misleading and may well obscure the complex webs of welfare that emerge in different societies rather than expose them. Thus, cross-national social policy analysis is as much about appreciating relationships across policy areas and between the range of different providers in the national context as it is about recognizing and integrating a global perspective into comparative research.

It is also about understanding that values and interpretations of phenomenon vary from society to society and change over time. The chapter looks at the evolving debates around poverty and disadvantage, and homelessness to show how social 'problems' are constructed and how their meanings and significance are manipulated through policies, definitions and units of measurement. The increasing availability of international and comparative data sources has expanded opportunities for cross-national social policy research. However, as Chapter 2 argues, it is vital that the data are utilized and interpreted critically and cautiously and, where possible, qualified by more in-depth statistical and empirical research.

Approaches to cross-national analysis

The recognition of the need for a broader perspective in cross-national comparative studies has been accompanied by shift in theory and analysis. Theoretical frameworks provide different ways of obtaining or producing different types of knowledge. According to Rosamond (2000), what is written about welfare is grounded in a particular set of assumptions about the way the world operates:

> Knowledge is not neutral. We gather it according to agreed rules that change over time and which, in turn, influence the sorts of questions we ask . . . different theoretical perspectives produce and reproduce different types of knowledge. Each theory begins with a 'basic image' of social reality (ontology) upon which is built a theoretical superstructure including established ways of gathering knowledge (**epistemology**).
> (Rosamond 2000: 5, 7)

Chapter 3 will trace the development of some of the most influential perspectives which have sought to explain the growth of the welfare state. The main focus of the chapter is on approaches to cross-national social policy analysis. However, the discussion takes a broader approach in the belief that assumptions and explanatory frameworks do not emerge in isolation but often draw upon, extend or refute alternative perspectives. Thus, the key aims of this chapter are to show how first, theoretical perspectives do not emerge independently but are historically embedded in particular social and intellectual contexts, and second, how different perspectives articulate and utilize particular frameworks and conceptual tools.

In relation to comparative, cross-national social policy research, Mabbett and Bolderson (1999) have identified three broad categories of comparative social research. At one end of the spectrum there are studies which test hypotheses using large-scale regression analysis of macro-economic and social indicators. This type of research is often based on a general model of development or modernization and utilizes quantitative data (for example Wilensky 1975; Alber 1983). While this approach enables the exploration of a large number of countries and seeks to avoid many of the cultural and linguistic problems involved in cross-national research, this type of research has been criticized for failing fully to 'provide the keys to understanding, explaining and interpreting' (Ragin 1987: 6) and sacrifices depth for breadth. At the other end of the spectrum are micro-studies which are more likely to utilize in-depth, qualitative techniques and to emphasize cultural sensitivity and specificity, agency and reflexivity in the policy and research process.

Regime theory represents mid- or meso-level cross-national analysis and is exemplified in the work of Esping-Andersen (1990). His work has made a major contribution to cross-national research in that his analysis identifies the form and content of particular developed, western regimes, as well as the pattern of processes of social relations which have emerged in particular national regimes. The use of welfare state typologies in cross-national analysis has become extremely popular with few studies failing to make some connection between the countries under discussion and regime types. Reference to the various typologies has almost become a shorthand for taken-for-granted assumptions about the nature of welfare within the clusters of countries associated with the various regimes (Abrahamson 1999). Nevertheless, the approach has stimulated substantial debate regarding the **ethnocentrism** permeating cross-national research. It has also brought issues of gender and **patriarchy** to the fore in comparative analysis. Women are at the core of the reconstruction of the welfare state in that they form a large share of the population involved in the newly emerging (social) service industries and organizations, they form the majority of clients and they also do the servicing work in the 'community' (Balbo 1987). Thus, they have a central role to play in the construction and manipulation of the political and welfare agenda.

Each of the approaches mentioned above has its own strengths and weaknesses and conceptual tools through which ways of seeing, articulating and understanding social phenomena are articulated. There is an increasing recognition that cross-national research should be multi-method, utlizing a process of triangulation. Denzin (1978: 291) defines triangulation as 'the combination of methodologies in the study of the same phenomenon', thus potentially drawing on the strengths of each of the above categories to capture the complex patterns and outcomes of a 'mixed economy of welfare' and the role of non-state elements in welfare provision. It can also contribute to establishing a framework for overcoming the 'false segregation' between developed/developing, North/South or First/Third World countries in cross-national analysis.

The implications of these categorical distinctions between parts of the world are explored in Chapter 4. The chapter will establish how these distinctions came about and their relationship with theory construction, the research process and policy. Dissatisfaction with traditional development thinking and the Eurocentric paradigms applied to the countries of the South have provided an opportunity for re-evaluating analysis and research strategies. This chapter will evaluate the potential of recent innovative research strategies for exposing the complexity and multifaceted nature of development, contributing to strategies for change, and facilitating cross-national comparative research across categorical boundaries.

Fragmentation, differentiation and social exclusion

The development of the welfare state in Western Europe following the Second World War was accompanied by expectations that social disadvantage would be eradicated. In Britain, full employment combined with universal access to education, health services and pensions were the centre-pieces of post-war development and certainly contributed to an improvement in living standards for the bulk of the population. Eastern Europe and the former Soviet Union also made great advances during the 1950s and 1960s, with life expectancy increasing from 58 to 66 years for men, and from 63 to 74 for women, and infant mortality rates reduced by half. Indeed, the majority of the population in Western Europe are still enjoying some of the highest living standards in the world, and there have been substantial, if fragmented, improvements in developing countries as discussed in Chapter 3.

However, more recent debates about disadvantage have been concerned with the changing face of poverty, patterns of social differentiation and in some cases a reversal of the progress in human development recorded in the 1960s. In the countries of Eastern Europe and the former Soviet Union as well as Sub-Saharan Africa, for example, social indicators indicate a decline in life expectancy and an increase in infant mortality rates as well as an increase in the numbers living in absolute poverty. Castells (1998) has attempted to identify and distinguish between the various types of social differentiation evident in contemporary society, some of which are outlined in Box I.1.

Box I.1 Definitions of social differentiation

- **Inequality** refers to the differentiated appropriation of wealth (income and assets) by different individuals and social groups, relative to others.
- **Polarization** is a specific process of inequality that occurs when both the top and the bottom of the scale of income or wealth distribution grow faster than the middle, thus shrinking the middle and sharpening social differences between the two extreme segments of the population.

- **Poverty** is an institutionally defined norm concerning a level of resources below which it is not possible to reach the living standards considered to be the minimum norm in a given society at a given time.
- **Social exclusion** Castells (1998: 73) sees as a process 'by which certain individuals and groups are systematically barred from access to positions that would enable them to [construct] an autonomous livelihood within the social standards framed by institutions and values in a given context'. By autonomous, what he means is 'socially constrained autonomy'. Obviously a worker or self-employed person is not autonomous. They are reliant on an employer or on their customers or clients for their livelihood. So 'socially constrained autonomy' can be contrasted with people's inability to organize their own lives within the constraints of the social structure because of their lack of access to resources that are deemed necessary to construct their limited autonomy.
- **Perverse integration** refers to the criminal economy. By criminal economy Castells (1998) means income-generating activities that are normatively declared to be crime and which form part of the burgeoning global criminal economy which is characteristic of informational capitalism. Processes of social exclusion and the inadequacy of policies of social integration leads to perverse integration into the criminal economy.

Source: Castells 1998

There are important differences between these categories but clearly there are links between them and there is also overlap. Castells (1998: 71) points out, 'it is obvious that all these definitions (with powerful effects in categorizing populations, and defining social policies and resource allocations) are statistically relative and culturally defined, besides being politically manipulated'. However, they do begin to highlight and clarify the diversity of social differentiation. Box I.2 gives some indication of the increasing inequality between rich and poor and the uneven distribution of the opportunities of globalization.

Chapter 5 highlights the interaction between the nature and content of the 'social contract' and the drawing of the boundaries of inclusion and exclusion in Australia, Britain and Japan. It utilizes the concept of **citizenship** to undertake critical cross-national analysis. The focus of the chapter is on the social relations of gender, ethnicity and class to show how the boundaries of social rights vary from country to country, between different groups and change over time. All three countries have experienced a renegotiation of the boundaries of citizenship and a reassessment of the balance between rights and obligations. This chapter explores the implications of the reconstructed

---

Box I.2   Increasing inequality and fragmentation

- The world's 200 richest people more than doubled their net worth in the four years to 1998, to more than $1 trillion. The assets of the top three billionaires are more than the combined gross national product (GNP) of all 43 least developed countries and their 600 million people.
- The distance between the richest and poorest countries was 3 to 1 in 1820, 35 to 1 in 1950 and 72 to 1 in 1992.
- In 1993 just ten countries accounted for 84 per cent of global research and development expenditure.
- Organization for Economic Cooperation and Development (OECD) countries, with 19 per cent of the global population, have 76 per cent of global trade in goods and services, 58 per cent of foreign investment and 91 per cent of all internet users.

Source: United Nations Development Programme (UNDP) 1999

---

social contract as it coincides with the impact of economic restructuring and global integration.

There is evidence of increasing inequality and polarization in the distribution of wealth as the opportunities of globalization are unevenly distributed between nations and people. The final chapter in this book will consider the challenges for cross-national social policy research in terms of developing and operationalizing conceptual and theoretical frameworks which capture the multiple dimensions of these disparities within the newly emerging global political economy.

Globalization, supranationalism and social policy

Introduction

An understanding of contemporary social phenomena can be achieved only through a consideration of global processes that are impacting on the everyday experiences of individuals. Since the mid-1970s a series of global transformations have impacted on contemporary capitalist development, as economic, political, social and cultural activities are said to have created a set of new conditions from the past. These changes have made cross-national research even more relevant as the parameters of social policy have been expanded to include not only a domestic but also a supranational frame of reference (Deacon *et al.* 1997). As we seek to make sense of the new environment a full understanding of developments in any particular country is now, more than ever, possible only if set, not only in the context of developments in other countries, but also in a wider, global perspective.

This chapter explores the implications for social policy and the welfare state of increasing globalization and the erosion of the political, economic and ideological conditions within which the modern welfare state emerged after the Second World War. It will begin with a discussion of the key elements of globalization and their implications. Taken-for-granted assumptions associated with the globalization thesis – such as the 'shrinking' of the state and the 'inevitable' race to the bottom as welfare states are dismantled and nations compete for comparative advantage in the global marketplace – will be assessed. The final section will focus on the EU to explore the changing dynamics between welfare, the nation-state and the supranational policy-making arena. Thus, the overall focus of this chapter will be the critical assessment of first, the nature and extent of the decline of the solidaristic welfare state, second, the role of the state and **supranational governance** in the formulation of social policy, and third, the prospects for cross-national social policy research. Box 1.1 gives an indication of the range of processes, activities and key actors contributing to a 'globalized world' and the range of issues to be explored critically in this chapter.

The shaping of a globalized world

The concept of globalization is multifaceted, incorporating economic, cultural, technological, social and political dimensions. From an economic perspective, the focus of attention is the growth of international trade and transactions. However, as Dickens (1992) explains, the development of a global economy is a process rooted in history. The beginnings of the world economy were evident first in the expansion of trade during the period from

---

Box 1.1 Elements of globalization and the key actors on the global stage

Economic

- Volume and intensification of international financial transactions
- Expansion of capitalism
- **Transnational corporations** (TNCs) and their increasing share of world trade
- Developments in information and communications technology

Social and cultural

- Fragmentation and polarization
- Global consumer culture
- 'Socialization' of global politics (for example environment, human rights)

Ideological

- Neo-liberal and free-market global hegemony

Political and institutional

- Expansion of democracy
- Increasing influence of international organizations (**IMF, World Bank, World Trade Organization** (WTO))
- Growth of **international non-governmental organizations**
- Erosion of the functions of the state
- **Supranational governance**

1450 to 1640, but during the nineteenth century the process of industrialization greatly accelerated the expansion of world trade and transformed its
character. The nature and geographical pattern of world trade at this time
was one in which the core (initially Britain during the period of Pax Britan-
nica) exported manufactured goods throughout the world and imported raw
materials especially from the colonies. Exports of textiles were followed in
the second half of the nineteenth century, by heavy manufacturing goods,
such as iron and steel. According to Hirst and Thompson (1992: 360),
'Britain, as hegemon, carried the burden of the open international economy,
much as the US was to do during the Bretton-Woods era'. The world economic system which emerged after 1945 represented 'a new beginning' (Dickens 1992: 13), and reflected the political realities of the post-war period and
the division between East and West, as well as the experiences of the 1930s
characterized by protectionism and slump. It was a period of 'increased
internationalisation of economic activities and of the greater interconnectedness which have come to characterise the world economy' (Dickens 1992:
16). The immediate post-war period saw a gradual consolidation of a world
economic order based on the IMF, the World Bank and GATT, with the USA
as one of the only major powers not severely damaged by the ravages of war,
able to succeed in establishing a hegemonic 'Pax Americana'.

It was not until the 1970s, following the breakdown of the Bretton Woods
system of fixed exchange rates, that a new era of globalization began to
reshape relations between nations, economies and people. In contrast to
previous periods in history, the current conditions of restructuring have not
yet seen the emergence of one specific national hegemony, but instead the
emergence of competing economic blocs. Scott and Storper (1992) argue
that economic development in the new global context is made up of a set of
specialized regional production systems, each with its own closed system of
intra-regional transactional arrangements and local labour market activities.
On the other hand these individual regions are entwined in a worldwide web
of international linkages, investment flows and population migration. The
economic global hierarchy is being redefined with regional hegemonies of
North America, Asia and Europe reflected in attempts to create a North
American Free Trade Area, a European Economic Space and an Asian Pacific
Community.

Capitalism, democracy and deregulation

Within this worldwide web of international linkages, global capital has now
become the dominant form of capitalist organization. This process has been
accommodated through the expansion of capitalist markets. Capitalism has
become practically the only economic system as centralized socialism, as a
separate economic system, has practically ceased to exist. The demise of

Communist regimes has been evident in Central and Eastern European countries where the magnitude and speed of political and economic change occurring at the end of the 1980s took the world by surprise. Despite national variations in the demise of Communist rule, the goals of establishing pluralist political systems and market-oriented economies have been cornerstones in the transition processes that have taken place in the region (Welsh 1994). Throughout Central and Eastern European countries, the switch to a market economy was 'almost universally perceived as the recipe for curing their problems of economic efficiency' (Lambert 1991: 20). Even in China where the political structures of centralized socialism are still in place, the economic system has become more and more integrated with capitalism. In China the international isolation of the 1960s and early 1970s was replaced by a policy of 'openness' to the west and was followed by a programme of reform. As China entered the 1970s, productivity and growth were low, standards of living of the population had been falling and popular confidence in the ruling party was all but non-existent. These circumstances were a marked contrast to developments in the East Asian newly industrialized countries (NICs), which was an influential factor in China's initiative of economic modernization strategies and limited political liberalization, in the hope that the country might emulate the economic development enjoyed by Japan, Singapore, South Korea, Taiwan and Hong Kong.

The deregulation of financial markets in the 1980s meant that most of the restrictions on capital flows were removed in OECD countries. The deregulation of financial markets in developing countries has been somewhat slower. However, with the encouragement of the IMF and the World Bank, a number of countries have opened their capital markets (Argentina, Mexico, Thailand) or liberalized trade (India reduced its tariffs from an average of 82 per cent in 1990 to 30 per cent in 1997) (UNDP 1999). These developments have been accompanied by a substantial, if uneven, increase in the volume of foreign direct investment (FDI). It reached $400 billion in 1997, seven times the level in real terms in the 1970s. Industrial countries received 58 per cent of that $400 billion, developing countries 37 per cent and the transition economies of Eastern Europe and the Commonwealth of Independent States (CIS) received only 5 per cent of foreign direct investment. In addition, just twenty countries received more than 80 per cent of the foreign direct investment in developing and transition economies in the 1990s, while for nine countries net flows were negative (UNDP 1999). International bank lending grew from $265 billion in 1975 to $4.2 trillion in 1994. Cross-border mergers and acquisitions have increased, with 58 transactions in 1997 that exceeded $1 billion each. Large mergers and acquisitions have been concentrated in financial services, insurance, telecommunications and the media (UNDP 1999).

Transnational corporations, mobile capital and the 'race to the bottom'

Global capitalism creates spatially dispersed systems of production in which firms are integrated across, rather than within, national boundaries. Economic activity has become more internationalized, in terms of increasing geographical spread across national boundaries. It has also become more global in the sense of more advanced and complex forms of internationalization and integration with transnational corporations (TNCs), for example, gaining an increasing share of world trade. TNCs accounted for 7 per cent of world gross domestic product (GDP) in 1997, and increased their share of world exports from one-quarter towards the end of the 1980s to one-third in 1995. As shown in Table 1.1, many of the larger multinational corporations have sales greater than the GDP of many countries.

Thus the expansion of world trade has been underpinned by the burgeoning overseas investment of TNCs. This accelerated during the 1980s

Table 1.1 Top corporations with sales totalling more than GDP of many countries in 1997

Country or corporation	*GDP or total sales (US$ billion)*
General Motors	**164**
Thailand	154
Norway	153
Ford Motor	**147**
Mitsui & Co	**145**
Saudi Arabia	140
Mitsubishi	**140**
Poland	136
Itochu	**136**
South Africa	129
Royal Dutch/Shell Group	**128**
Marubeni	**124**
Greece	123
Sumitomo	**119**
Exxon	**117**
Toyota Motor	**109**
Wal Mart Stores	**105**
Malaysia	98
Israel	98
Colombia	96
Venezuela	87
Philippines	82

Note: Bold is used for corporations
Source: Taken from *Human Development Report* (UNDP 1999: 32)

when information technology and the deregulation of foreign exchange markets in the industrialized countries allowed the TNCs to increase their competitiveness by manufacturing in the most advantageous places. This process has been referred to as the 'hypermobility of quicksilver capital' (Swantson 1993: 63), in which increasingly mobile capital is able to span the globe in search of the lowest cost production sites and to take advantage of the specificities of conditions of production such as cheap labour, lack of unionization or the availability of particular skills (Massey 1992). This thesis is, to some extent, premised on the notion that the primary motivation for global capital is to maximize production and profit by searching out economies with low wages and minimal social costs. The inevitable result is a downward shift in wages and working conditions across the globe. However, according to Mishra (1999: 95) the erosion of working conditions, wages and welfare 'may be considered as one among a range of feasible responses to greater economic internationalisation of global competition'. As Garrett (1998: 72) points out, the mobility of global capital has not resulted in policy **convergence** and a 'race to the bottom' whereby 'governments competing for mobile resources race to dismantle their welfare states'. As discussed earlier, the majority of foreign direct investment flows are within OECD countries where the extent of state involvement in the welfare of its citizens and the power relations between organized labour and the state varies enormously. Garrett (1998) contrasts the social democratic corporatist regimes where

> governments wish to derive the benefits of market integration, but they also seek to shield those most vulnerable with extensive public provision of social services and income transfers. Under more 'market-liberal' regimes, in contrast, the dampening effects of the public economy against market generated risk and inequality are being eroded.
>
> (Garrett 1998: 86)

However, there is no indication that those countries with greater state intervention or stronger labour movements have been particularly disadvantaged in their attempts to capture global capital. The case of Germany (discussed in more detail in this chapter and others) according to Mishra (1999) shows that

> a dynamic and competitive economy is quite compatible with a well-regulated labour market, centralized collective bargaining, high wages, good working conditions and strongly entrenched workers' rights. Indeed, these conditions make for co-operative labour relations and consensus-based implementation of workplace processes which have proven highly effective in terms of efficiency and competitiveness.
>
> (Mishra 1999: 95)

Technology, distribution channels and infrastructure are important elements of the global marketplace, as is an educated, skilled and healthy workforce. Markets also require social and political stability. Contrary to the conventional view that 'markets are allergic to all forms of interventionist government, and react in knee-jerk fashion to any such policies with capital flight' (Garrett 1998: 95), government intervention can be compatible with globally competitive markets.

International institutions and non-governmental organizations

Other major institutional actors on the world stage today include an array of international institutions as well as an increasing number of **international non-governmental organizations**. Many of these organizations have become particularly influential in the lives of the poor, particularly in developing countries and the transition economies of Eastern and Central Europe. The extent to which these organizations are able to shape national economic and social policies, either explicitly or implicitly, is debatable but there can be little doubt that international organizations have penetrated the sphere of the nation-state more deeply than before. While Deacon *et al.* (1997: 3) attribute this to the 'socialization of global politics', as international organizations have become increasingly concerned about social and environmental issues, Mishra (1999) suggests that they are mainly concerned with 'helping to extend and consolidate the hegemony' of neo-liberal capitalism and promoting 'a free market ideology with a minimum of social protection' (Mishra 1999: 8). The following discussion will explore the development of some of the key international organizations, consider their relationship with nation-states and assess the implications for social policy.

The majority of international institutions in existence today were formed after the Second World War and were broadly concerned with establishing and maintaining international cooperation. In the mid-1940s representatives from 50 countries established the **United Nations Organization (UN)** system and its institutional structure made up of a diverse range of 'specialized agencies' and regional commissions covering the economic and social activities of the UN. The UN system has a very wide remit from activities for refugees and disasters to promoting economic order. It has increasingly been involved with the poorest countries in the world. Mishra (1999) regards the concerns of the UN and its affiliated agencies as mainly humanitarian rather than economistic, focusing on the promotion of social and labour rights. The International Labour Organization (ILO) is also concerned with the rights of workers and on improving working conditions throughout the world by requiring member countries to submit to the covenants laid down by the organization, although there are no mechanisms in place to enforce compliance. It is a tripartite organization, bringing together employers, labour unions and governments. By 1994 the ILO had passed 170 conventions relating to various aspects of working conditions. However, as Hoekman and Kostecki (1995: 263) point out, these are adopted by governments at their discretion: 'The United States, for example, had accepted less than two dozen ILO conventions as of 1994'.

The 1944 Bretton Woods Conference also established the International Monetary Fund with an essentially macro-economic mandate to concentrate on helping countries 'pursue sound macroeconomic policies aimed at sustained economic growth' and to provide 'temporary balance of payments financing to members to help them to correct their external payments difficulties' (IMF 1998). The IMF has sustained its macro-economic mandate and, until recently, has not been explicitly concerned with issues of social policy and social development. It has been the World Bank, established along with the IMF to facilitate international monetary cooperation, which has had greater involvement in social issues and social policy (for a fuller discussion see Deacon *et al.* 1997). While the IMF has had no direct mandate to concern itself with social policy issues, along with other intergovernmental organizations such as the OECD and the **Group of 7 (G7)** countries, there is an acceptance that social policy has a role to play in achieving 'desirable' economic goals. The OECD (established in 1961) is largely concerned with economic growth and the extension and maintenance of world trade particularly among the richer, industrialized countries. It has exerted strong pressure on nations for deregulation, privatization and 'flexibility'. Deacon *et al.* (1997) suggest that the OECD has recently altered its position from one in which welfare was perceived as a burden to one in which there is a recognition of the efficacy of 'limited but effective action by the state' (OECD 1993: 41, cited in Deacon *et al.* 1997: 71). For the IMF, however, the preferred strategy is one of establishing a short-term safety net (Deacon *et al.* 1997), in other words residual and selective, stringently targeted social provision.

From its inception the institutional basis of the new framework for international capital, excluding (as it did) agricultural producers from negotiations, represented the almost exclusive interests of developed industrial countries since it was mostly industrial goods that would benefit from the agreement. Although more than 70 countries moved from colonial status to political independence with many achieving economic growth rates higher than ever before during the 1960s, there was growing concern that 'while developed countries made great strides in the post-war years, the less developed countries mostly faltered, with the gap between the two widening dramatically' (Adams 1993: 41). The International Development Association was established in 1960 to expand the flows of concessional finance to poor countries, the UN Conference on Trade and Development (UNCTAD) in 1964 to concentrate on the negotiation of trade and development issues

(UNDP 1999), and the founding of the **Group of 77** (**G77**) (named on the basis of the number of signatories to a declaration of common aims) provided a forum for developing countries to express their concerns in relation to economic issues and multilateral negotiations (Schiavone 1997).

The General Agreement on Tariffs and Trade was established in 1947 to initiate a programme of multilateral negotiation for the mutual reduction of tariff and non-tariff barriers and the improvement of the practices of international trade. By 1995 the total number of countries who were members of GATT had reached 128. In the same year the GATT was incorporated within the World Trade Organization in an attempt to strengthen dispute settlement and surveillance mechanisms. The WTO administers multilateral trade agreements negotiated by its members: GATT, the General Agreement on Trade and Services (GATS) and the Agreement on Trade-Related Intellectual Property Rights (TRIPS). The TRIPS Agreement means that virtually all knowledge-based production is now subject to intellectual property protection, including agriculture and medicine.

The basic underlying philosophy of the WTO, according to Hoekman and Kostecki (1995: 1), is that 'open markets, non discrimination, and global competition in international trade are conducive to the national welfare of all countries'. Recently the WTO has begun to recognize the environmental dimensions of its strategies and to take seriously the goals of the ILO in relation to the improvement of labour standards. Hoekman and Kostecki (1995: 235) concede that the GATT 'was basically a club that was primarily of relevance to OECD countries' and that 'developing countries were for a long time effectively second class members of the GATT-based trading system' (Hoekman and Kostecki 1995: 244). However, they regard the increasing global significance of the WTO combined with the greater liberalization of trade policies of many developing countries (often following the advice of the IMF and the World Bank) as an opportunity for the countries of the South to play a much greater role in the global arena in the future. Yet the unevenness of global integration discussed earlier in this chapter and the erosion of a 'common voice' among developing countries might also suggest that those countries that are not yet linked into global markets and institutions could be left further behind, thereby reinforcing economic stagnation and polarization.

For Biersteker (1998) international institutions have become increasingly intrusive in individual nation-states. He argues that 'The IMF, the World Bank, the World Trade Organization and regional institutions [such as the EU] have increased the frequency, the depth and the scope of their intervention' (Biersteker 1998: 20). The best known instrument of the IMF and the World Bank is the Structural Adjustment Facility (SAF) set up in March 1986 in order to provide balance of payments assistance to low-income developing countries on concessional terms. The IMF and the World Bank are now heavily involved in Central and Eastern European countries as well as the republics of the former Soviet Union. The substance and impact of structural adjustment programmes (SAPs) in developing countries are discussed more fully in Chapter 4, but it is in the face of increasing criticism regarding the negative effects of these programmes, particularly in the countries of the South, that the World Bank (and to a lesser extent the IMF) has become more concerned with softening the impact of some of the SAPs.

Much of the criticism of the negative impacts of SAPs in developing countries came from non-governmental organizations (NGOs) which have come to have major influence at the global level, particularly in the countries of the South but also in the North (discussed more fully in Chapter 4). International NGOs like Oxfam and Greenpeace have flourished, with the number increasing from 176 in 1909 to 28,900 by 1993. Biersteker (1998: 20) argues that they are 'no longer just "thinking globally and acting locally", but many are beginning to act globally as well'. The *Human Development Report* (UNDP 1999) points to their role in maintaining pressure on national governments, international agencies and corporations to protect human rights and environmental standards. Organizations such as Amnesty International operate on a global scale, drawing attention to particular issues and concerns and putting pressure on states accused of human rights violations. NGOs such as Greenpeace and Friends of the Earth have been particularly active in environmental matters and have been successful in influencing international environmental negotiations. And in the field of humanitarian intervention and international relief, NGOs distributed over 10 per cent of all public development aid in 1994 'surpassing the volume of the combined UN system ($6 billion) excluding the international financial institutions' (Biersteker 1998).

The shaping of the global political economy during the 1980s and 1990s has involved, therefore, the expansion of capitalist relations, the intensification of global trade and the growth and increasing influence of international organizations in the development of national social policies. It has also involved the expansion and penetration of telecommunications systems and information technology into the social, cultural and economic spheres of societies and peoples around the world. The next section will assess the extent to which we could be said to be living in a 'global village'. It will consider the implications of the spread of information technology in terms of its capacity to empower and include as well as its potential to reinforce fragmentation within and exclusion from society for those countries and people who are not 'wired in'.

Culture and communication: globalization or polarization?

The growth and pervasiveness of mass media and communication is said to have been particularly influential in both the economic and cultural spheres and in the creation of the 'global village' in which 'the peoples of the world are incorporated into a single world society, global society' (Albrow 1996: 9). Worldwide telecommunications systems link individuals and organizations in complex networks of information exchange. Banks, insurance companies, stock markets and multinational companies are now linked by these systems that permit instantaneous exchanges of information and the rapid movement of currency and capital from one country to another.

Harvey (1989) has recognized the impact of the growth of global forms of communication in the cultural and economic spheres and has referred to the compression of time and space which has dramatically affected the codes of social values and meaning, as spatial barriers have been removed. Giddens (1990: 64) refers to the process of time–space distanciation whereby 'the modes of connection between different social contexts or regions become networked across the earth's surface as a whole'. Lyotard (1984) has also emphasized the role of the media in shaping the languages of self and society in capitalist states. According to Harvey (1989: 287): 'Advertising and media images have come to play a very much more integrative role in cultural practices and now assume a much greater importance in the growth dynamics of capitalism'. For Jameson (1984) we have moved into an area in which the production of culture itself:

> has become integrated into commodity production generally: the frantic urgency of producing fresh waves of ever more novel seeming goods at ever greater rates of turnover, now assigns an increasingly essential structural function to aesthetic innovation and experimentation.
>
> (Jameson 1984: 56)

Between 1980 and 1991 world trade in goods with a cultural content (literature, music, visual art, cinema, television and radio equipment for example) almost tripled from $67 billion to $200 billion. Over a 15 year period (1980 to 1995) the number of television sets per 1000 people worldwide almost doubled. The number of Internet users rose from 100,000 in 1988 to more than 143 million users in mid-1998. The number is expected to exceed 700 million by the end of 2001 (World Bank 1999). The UNDP (1999) points out that smaller, local industries are being pushed out of the global cultural market which is increasingly dominated by producers and products from the USA. There is concern that US dominance is eroding diversity and encouraging the spread of cultural homogeneity. In addition, the relationship between the media, the markets and global culture promotes the notion of global consumer culture which emphasizes the individual, the self as a consumer and a potential market for western consumer goods – a global culture to accompany a global economy looking for niche markets. In this context 'global culture' could be seen as little more than a sugar-coated version of global imperialism, in which the visions conveyed in the images of 'global culture' reinforce the desirability of a white face, of capitalist consumerism and western values. As Bauman (1990: 23) asserts, 'in post-modern practice, liberty boils down to consumer choice. To enjoy it, one must be a consumer first. This condition leaves out millions' in market-dominated societies where poverty disqualifies from participation.

However, the full impact of mass media and telecommunications on local cultures is difficult to determine given the contradictory processes occurring. While the trends discussed above might suggest the imposition of a global consumer culture, information technology has also become of increasing significance in local struggles and initiatives. Technological advances in communication networks have the potential to facilitate the maintenance of language and cultural differences, through satellite and multilingual radio and television channels. As the World Bank (1999) indicates, communication networks can 'empower small players' by breaking down the barriers of size, time and distance. They highlight a number of examples including the case of the Dalit and Tribal People Electronic Resource Site (DATPERS) in India which works to expose the plight of 250 million low-caste people by coordinating international human rights campaigns and providing information to the community. HealthNet, described in Box 1.2, also provides the opportunity for fast, reliable information exchange.

Box 1.2 HealthNet

This is a networked information service supporting health-care workers in more than 30 developing countries, including 22 in Africa. It uses radio- and telephone-based computer networks and a low-earth-orbit satellite. Slower than the internet, it is also cheaper and accessible in areas with no telecommunications infrastructure.

The network provides summaries of the latest medical research, email connectivity and access to medical libraries. Doctors in Central Africa used it to share information on the 1995 outbreak of the Ebola virus. Burns surgeons in Mozambique, Tanzania and Uganda use it to consult one another on reconstructive surgery techniques. Malaria researchers at a remote site in northern Ghana use the system to communicate with the London School of Hygiene and Tropical Medicine.

HealthNet's communications system also supports ProMED mail, created by the programme for Monitoring Emerging Diseases. A moderated, free email list started in 1994, it now has more than 135 countries – and thousands more over the Web – who report, discuss and request assistance for outbreaks of emerging infectious diseases. The aim of ProMED is fast reporting – of cholera in the Philippines, E. coli in Japan, Delta hepatitis in the upper Amazon, dengue fever in Malaysia, yellow fever in Switzerland and Ebola in Gabon. The speed of communication – often quicker than official channels, yet just as reliable

– translates into faster assistance, earlier warnings to neighbouring countries and greater awareness among health workers.

Source: SatelLife 1998 in World Bank (1999: 59)

However, as Table 1.2 shows, the spread of global communications is extremely polarized. It is concentrated in the USA and other OECD countries and is much less apparent in other regions of the world.

Even with the extensive penetration of electronic access in the USA a recent report referred to the persistent and widening 'digital divide' between certain groups in the USA (NTIA 1998). There is a widening gap between those at upper and lower income levels and since 1994 in the USA Blacks and Hispanic households have come to lag even further behind the White population in their levels of personal computer (PC) ownership and on-line access. White households are more than twice as likely (40.8 per cent) to own a PC than Black (19.3 per cent) or Hispanic households and rates for on-line access are nearly three times higher for White (21.2 per cent) as for Black (7.7 per cent) or Hispanic (8.7 per cent) households. The 'least connected' are those Black and Hispanic households living in rural or central city locations (see Table 1.3). In addition, female-headed households are particularly unlikely to have on-line access (6.4 per cent), compared to dual parent households (27 per

Table 1.2   Internet users worldwide, 1998

	Regional population (as a percentage of world population)	*Internet users (as a percentage of regional population)*
USA	4.7	26.3
OECD (excl. USA)*	14.1	5.9
Latin America and the Caribbean	6.8	0.8
South-East Asia and the Pacific	8.6	0.5
East Asia	22.2	0.4
Eastern Europe and the CIS	5.8	0.4
Arab states	4.5	0.2
Sub-Saharan Africa	9.7	0.1
South Asia	23.5	0.04
World	100	2.4

Note: *The Czech Republic, Hungary, Mexico, Poland, the Republic of Korea and Turkey are included in the OECD and not in the regional aggregates.

Source: Based on data supplied by Nua 1999, Network Wizards 1998b and IDC 1999
Taken from Figure 2.4 in *World Development Report* (World Bank 1999: 63)

Table 1.3 Percentage of US households with on-line services by race/origin by US, rural, urban and central city areas, 1997

	US	Rural	Urban	Central city
White not Hispanic	21.2	15.6	23.5	23.3
Black not Hispanic	7.7	5.5	7.9	5.8
Other not Hispanic	25.2	16.1	26.4	23.5
Hispanic	8.7	7.3	8.9	7.0

Source: NTIA 1998: 26

cent) or male-headed households (11.2 per cent) in the same areas (NTIA 1998).

The typical Internet user worldwide is male, under 35 years old, with a college education and high income, urban based and English speaking. The network society, according to the *World Development Report*,

> is creating parallel communications systems: one for those with income, education and – literally – connections, giving plentiful information at low cost and high speed; the other for those without connections, blocked by high barriers of time, cost and uncertainty and dependent on outdated information.
>
> (World Bank 1999: 63)

The *World Development Report* points not to convergence and inclusion within the 'global village' but rather to the 'increasing concentration of income, resources and wealth among people, corporations and countries' (World Bank 1999: 3). While the quality of life and average living standards have improved for the majority of the population, evidenced by better access to educational opportunities and health care and increased life expectancy (Castells 1998; UNDP 1999), there is evidence of increasing inequality and polarization in the distribution of wealth not only between but also within countries. Using the stringent poverty line set by the World Bank, one-third of the developing world's population – 1.3 billion people – live on incomes of less than $1 per day. Since the end of the 1980s this number has increased by 1 million and is still growing. In the transition economies of Eastern Europe and the CIS there have been dramatic changes in the distribution of national wealth and income. Income inequality (as measured by the Gini coefficient)[1] increased from an average of 0.25–0.28 in 1987 to 0.35–0.38 in 1995, with Russia and Ukraine experiencing the greatest increase (0.24 to 0.48 and 0.23 to 0.47 respectively) and Hungary and Poland the least (0.21 to 0.23 and 0.26 to 0.28). In Eastern Europe and the CIS, 120 million people live below the World Bank poverty line for this region of US$4 per day (UNDP 1999). While these figures may be representative of a short-term response to the turbulence of the transition process, they nevertheless reveal that a substantial (and ever increasing) proportion of the population are experiencing real hardship.

Contrary to the trends established over previous decades, almost all OECD countries experienced an increase in wage inequality during the 1980s except Italy and Germany. The greatest increase in earnings inequality has been in Britain and the USA. In contrast to the post-war period there now seems to be a much greater acceptance of higher levels of unemployment, inequality, poverty and insecurity (Beck 1992). The remainder of this chapter will consider the backcloth against which this ideological and policy shift has occurred and through which the 'Keynesian welfare state' was discredited and constructed as an obstacle to economic prosperity and global integration. It will assess the extent to which processes of globalization are leading to a neo-liberal convergence in social policy regimes and a 'downsizing of the social state' (Mishra 1999: 37) and to the emergence of a supranational social policy and a 'global governance'.

An ideological shift: from Keynesianism to neo-liberalism

The political and ideological context of globalization emerged in the 1980s. It was most apparent with a major shift in the orientation of economic thinking and policy-making and a fundamental 'breakdown of the economic policy consensus that had brought in its train more than two decades of almost uninterrupted economic growth and prosperity in the industrial North' (Weiss 1991: 144). The main pillar of the post-war consensus in many western, developed nations was faith in the ability of governments to maintain rates of economic growth consistent with full employment at stable prices by managing aggregate demand, using essentially Keynesian tools. The consensus was underpinned by the expansion of prosperity to a large share of the population through the operation of the market and supply strategies. It was accompanied by the emergence and spread of a social security system providing unemployment benefits, health, education, retirement pensions and other social benefits to the general population. Demand management and the social security system went hand in hand, the latter complementing the former in playing the role of automatic stabilizer in the maintenance of steady non-inflationary growth (Weiss 1991: 146).

In contrast, the essence of the new approach of the 1980s involved a dismissal of Keynesian aggregate demand policies, the assertion of the benefits of supply-side economics, and the obsolescence of the notion of full employment. A fundamental restructuring of the 'industrial settlement' established in many of the older western nations involving large-scale manufacturing and high-paid, skilled and semi-skilled (male) workers was underway. The changes evident in the economic and social relations of western capitalism have been said to represent the emergence of 'new times'. These 'new times' have been characterized in a number of ways, most influentially perhaps as a transition from Fordism to post-Fordism. The form of capitalism which had been dominant throughout the post-war period in most older industrial countries – Fordism – was, according to Tickell and Peck (1992),

> an industrial system based upon the mass production of standardized goods coupled with steadily-growing mass consumer markets and regulated by Keynesian macroeconomic management.
>
> (Tickell and Peck 1992: 190)

Fordism was based on an urban-industrial 'middle-mass', wage-earning society. Full employment was secured through Keynesian demand-side management while institutionalized collective bargaining facilitated the regulation of demands within the limits consistent with full employment. An emphasis on the 'family wage', the promotion of men as the breadwinners, women's domestic labour, and in Britain the part-time employment of working class women, made possible the way production and consumption were organized. According to Hilary Rose (1986):

> It is in this context that we see the historic achievement of the welfare state – an accommodation between capital and a male-dominated labour movement reached its maturity in the post-war years in North West Europe. This particular achievement which offered substantial gains for the working class did so, none-the-less, at the price of the continued subordination and dependency of women.
>
> (H. Rose 1986: 81)

Similarly, the post-war welfare settlement depended upon women's unpaid caring work in the home and reinforced both this and their economic dependency. Thus, as Williams (1994) argues, the 'universalism' of many post-war services and benefits were based on the norm of the white, British, heterosexual, able-bodied Fordist man and often excluded women and black people upon whose labour it depended.

A crisis in the Fordist mode of capitalist development occurred during the 1970s particularly in North America and Western Europe. Stagflation, rising unemployment and spiralling oil prices triggered a phase of profound global restructuring. This has been accompanied by a decline in manufacturing, increases in service employment, the concentration of economic control in multinational firms and financial institutions, a substantial change in the patterns of state intervention and a reorientation of the welfare state. The Fordist system, based on mass production, consumer durables, capital goods and Keynesian welfare capitalism was abandoned as the institutional arrangements of the post-war period were increasingly perceived as barriers and impediments to the deployment of new methods of production and consumption, while labour contracts and social legislation inhibited effective competition within nation-states and in the increasingly important international markets. Williams (1994) also stresses that it is important to understand the restructuring of the welfare state not only as a neo-liberal response to the crisis of Fordism, and a shift away from mass monolithic forms to prepare the ground for a post-Fordist economy, but also as a reflection of challenges and accommodation to a balance of power especially around class, race and gender.

By the mid-1970s the political rhetoric encompassing deregulation, **privatization**, the efficiency of the 'free market' and rolling back the frontiers of the state had become the global economic discourse influencing both national and international policies. Jessop (1994) identified a shift to what he called a 'Schumpeterian Workfare State'. This referred to a restructuring and a reorientation of the economic and social functions of the Keynesian welfare state, and the assertion of a neo-liberal strategy to marketize social relations, to create an enterprise culture in which individuals could embrace a market-oriented society. The extent and speed of the restructuring of relations between the state and civil society has varied between countries. It was most evident in Britain during the Thatcher era but similar processes occurred elsewhere (the USA, Germany and New Zealand for example). Although the political complexion of central governments has changed, for the most part there has not been a marked difference in terms of the policy agenda. In a British context, according to Marquand (1998), this is an indication that New Labour 'has turned its back on Keynes and Beveridge' (quoted in Dean 1999: 221).

This is not to imply that all nations have travelled in the same direction. The retrenchment and reorientation of welfare have been universal phenomena but the precise form between countries has varied significantly. Lash and Urry (1987) have conceptualized an era of 'disorganized' capitalism, as 'organized' capitalism has come to an end. They draw on the experiences of five societies – Britain, France, the USA, Germany and Sweden – as representing differential development. They assert that the nature and extent to which a nation was 'organized' will reflect the pace at which capital will 'disorganize'. In Britain, particularly after the victory of the Thatcher government in 1979, government strategy according to Krieger (1991: 53) involved 'a co-ordinated assault with electoral appeals, policy agenda, and a discourse united to reconstitute common sense, redefine the nation, and shatter traditional Labourist-collectivist solidarities'. The structural and institutional reforms regarding trade unions, the welfare state and supply-side economics and individualism have been more far reaching than in Germany for example. Germany, considered the ideal of organized capital, is predicted to disorganize more slowly and hesitantly than the other nations under consideration, if at all. The very strength of the institutional arrangements through which the state sought to distance itself from the political domain after the Second World War has prevented any substantial dismantling of the forms established during that time, as the voluntary sector, the Church and the trade unions have become strong, influential and entrenched interest groups. Craft and industrial workers have maintained their numerical position in the labour force and remain a dominant class force. However, some change in the balance of power between capital and labour has occurred and negotiations focusing on the introduction of a new flexibility in the organization of the labour market have become the focus of class struggle. Elements of the neo-liberal strategy have penetrated the framework of cooperative federalism as some of the rights of trade unions have been eroded, the non-profit housing sector has been deregulated and notions of status differentials, rather than citizenship have been strengthened in relation to social rights (Kennett 1998). Nevertheless, the key institutions of this corporatist welfare system are still firmly in place.

The state, the economy and social policy

It is in the context of this ideological shift, the retrenchment and reorientation of welfare and the growing importance of supranational actors that processes of globalization have been said to have contributed to the erosion of the functions of nation-states and deprived national governments of their ability to establish and maintain an autonomous welfare model. According to Deacon *et al.* (1997)

> The social policy of a country or locality is no longer wholly shaped (if it ever was) by the politics of the national government. It is increasingly shaped . . . by the implicit and explicit social policies of numerous supranational agencies, ranging from global institutions like the World Bank and the IMF, through supranational bodies such as the OECD and the European Commission, to supranational non-governmental agencies like OXFAM.
>
> (Deacon *et al.* 1997: 10)

As functions have been diverted both transnationally and subnationally, Mishra argues that 'a resurgent globalization is increasingly blurring the economic boundaries of the nation-state' (Mishra 1999: 12). Biersteker (1998: 21) argues that there have been profound changes in the relationship between states and the global economy, with most states having moved 'from an inward-orientated focus on the domestic economy (from import substitution industrialization or Keynesian counter-cyclical policies focused on the national level) to a preoccupation with export orientation and national competitiveness'. He asserts that

> while states and their publics are still preoccupied with their national welfare (or standing), the means to attain advancement are increasingly

perceived to be through greater participation in the world economy not through insulation from it.

(Biersteker 1998: 21)

Sassen (1991: 167) argues that 'the nation-state is becoming a less central actor in the World'. In a similar vein, Ohmae (1992) states that

the global economy follows its own logic and develops its own webs of interest, which rarely duplicate the historical borders between nations. As a result, national interest as an economic, as opposed to a political reality has lost much of its meaning.

(Ohmae 1992: 183)

For Jessop (1992) there can be little doubt that the nation-state has been and is subject to various changes leading to what he calls a process of 'hollowing out'. He suggests that some state capacities are being transferred to pan-regional, pluri-national or international bodies. Others are being devolved to the regional or local level within the nation-state or are being subsumed within the emerging horizontal, regional or local networks which bypass central states and link regions or localities in several societies. There has been an intensification of competition between urban regions in order to capture increasingly mobile resources, jobs and capital. With the growing importance of international competition in the global marketplace, which had played a fairly minor role in the Fordist 1950s and 1960s, major cities now take on 'world city function' (Short and Kim 1999), and act as centres of economic, social, cultural and structural change as the arena is created in which cities promote innovation and entrepreneurialism in order to secure competitive advantage (Harvey 1989).

While there can be little doubt that states are adapting to new conditions, as Costello et al. (1989: 55) argue, 'the nation-state should be recognized for what it is: the single most powerful mechanism of legal and organizational powers for economic intervention'. Jessop concedes that even though he sees the capacities of the state to project power, even within its own national borders, becoming ever more limited as powers are displaced upward, downward and, to a lesser extent, outward, it nevertheless 'remains crucial as an institutional site and discursive framework for all political struggles, and it even keeps much of its sovereignty' (Jessop 1992b: 9). The nation-state still plays a crucial role in that the interactions between the domestic and the international policy-making frameworks are separate, with interactions resembling a 'billiard ball' type scenario (Glynn 1992). In other words 'international events do not directly penetrate or permeate the domestic economy but are refracted through national policies and processes' (Hirst and Thompson 1992: 359). Mishra (1999) argues that the welfare state developed as and still remains very much a national enterprise and a vital mode of economic and political organization (Silver 1993) within the emerging global hierarchy.

The proliferation of transnational corporations has been the dominant vehicle for the internationalization of capital, yet as Pooley (1991) points out:

> production takes place in solitary sites even in a world of co-ordinated supply and multinational investment. The state enforces norms of behaviour between capital and labour, and the state is responsible for the basic infrastructure supporting production.
>
> (Pooley 1991: 71)

TNCs have been the staunchest defenders of the nation-state, encouraging coordination of national regulation, and it is their ability to exploit national differences, both politically and economically, that gives them their competitive advantage (Picciotto 1991: 4). Correspondingly, states do not inevitably shift towards multinational interests and, if a shift occurs, it will reflect the particular political and economic profile of the individual nation-state. Capitalist country governments have been central actors in shaping the evolution of global capitalism. Thus the issue is not so much about the erosion of function, but rather redefining that role and reordering priorities. It is the state which must manage its insertion into the international economy as it has always done, but now under different conditions of globalization. With the growing internationalization of capital, the role of the state in the process of global accumulation has also been intensified and, in this highly globalized capitalist era has become more complex and contradictory than in the earlier stages of capitalism. The state's task in this period, according to McMichael and Myhre (1991), has been to pursue 'national' policies in an increasingly transnational environment creating a mosaic of variation across space.

The final task of this chapter is to explore the institutional dynamics and the nature of policy-making in this increasingly transnational environment. The empirical focus will be supranational activity in relation to social policy in the EU. It is widely recognized that no other supranational organization has reached a similar degree of integration and regional cooperation (Risse-Kappen 1996). It may also be the case that the regulatory nature of policy-making in the EU will influence the character of broader global regulation. This section will begin by introducing different perceptions on the nature of transnational policy-making. It will then focus on the development of the social dimension of the EU and consider the changing dynamics between social policy, the nation-state and the supranational arena. Deacon *et al.*'s (1997) framework of supranational social policy instruments and provision (redistribution, regulation and provision) will be utilized as a heuristic device to explore the extent and character of supranational social policy.

Intergovernmental policy, multilevel governance or supranational social policy?

There is no one mode of decision-making within the international arena. Neither is it a static relationship between the state and the international arena. The term intergovernmental is used to describe the form of decision-making in many international organizations, for example the ILO. Risse-Kappen (1996: 56) describes **intergovernmentalism** as 'an hierarchical structure of authoritative decision-making enjoying external and internal sovereignty'. Wallace and Wallace (2000) utilize the term 'intensive trans-governmentalism' to refer to a process that goes beyond mere cooperation between governments, and refers instead to more extensive and sustained policy collaboration between nations. They cite Nato and some areas of policy-making in the EU as examples of this particular policy mode.

For Deacon *et al.* (1997) the increasing scope and influence of international organizations have been accompanied by a move towards supranational politics and policies. Supranational governance refers to a framework of rules, institutions and practices at a level above the nation-state whose authority extends beyond just one state. Its authority can override or supersede the sovereign authority of individual states who are constituent members of the organizations involved. The EU and the development of the social dimension provide an opportunity to explore the tensions and difficulties surrounding the integration, coordination and regulation of policies at a supranational level. Wallace and Wallace (2000: 39) refer to the policy process as a 'moving pendulum' between the 'magnetic field of the domestic arena and the magnetic field of the transnational arena'. This moving pendulum is evident when exploring social policy in the EU. There is no clear dividing line between country and European arena and thus the changing dynamics between the community, national and regional levels, and social policy have been particularly significant.

Multilevel governance, social policy and the European Union

The early stages of European integration coincided with increasing affluence for the majority of member state populations, and the rapid expansion of the role of the state in the field of social policy as well as in the economy as forms of Keynesian demand management took hold in various forms in many European countries. According to Tsoukalis (1991) national social policies were linked to establishing nationhood and national political legitimacy and were aimed at the incorporation of the working class into the political and economic systems of nation-states. European integration, he argues, was more about a vision of a European economy big enough to accommodate the scale required for the contemporary technology of mass production.

8679

Thus, the assumption of the European Economic Community (EEC) Treaty signed in 1957 was that welfare would be provided at the national level through the economic growth stemming from the economies achieved through a larger and liberalized market, rather than through the regulatory and distributive capacity of a supranational public policy.

As Denmark, Ireland and the UK joined the EEC in 1973, the broader context of European integration was changing. The integration process was coinciding with stagnating economies and living standards, rising unemployment and, particularly in the 1990s, growing inequality. There was also increasing concern with the 'unevenness' of development within the EU between nations and regions, and with issues of exclusion, social cohesion and a two-speed Europe threatening future integration. Wallace and Wallace (2000) argue that this growing emphasis on regions opened up a new dynamic, and a new policy mode of multilevel governance. This policy mode

> rested on 2 essential points: first that national central governments could no longer monopolize the contacts between the countries and the EU levels of policy making; and secondly, that engagement at the European level created an opportunity to reinforce a phenomenon of regionalization.
>
> (Wallace and Wallace 2000: 31)

By the mid-1980s French President François Mitterand was talking about the development of a social space or *espace social*, a theme that was continued by Jacques Delors when he became President of the Commission in 1985. A range of initiatives emerged in the areas of education and training, health and safety, workers' and women's rights. A whole range of observatories and networks were established to monitor progress in areas such as poverty and homelessness in member states.

The aims and aspirations of the EU in relation to the construction of a 'social dimension' were articulated in Article 2 of the Treaty of the European Union (Maastricht Treaty):

> The Community shall have as its task . . . to promote throughout the Community a harmonious and balanced development of economic activities, sustainable and non-inflationary growth respecting the environment, a high degree of convergence of economic performance, a high level of employment and of social protection, the raising of the standard of living and quality of life, and economic and social cohesion and solidarity among member states (EC 1992).

More recently in the 1994 White Paper *European Social Policy: A Way Forward for the Union*:

> All Member States have reaffirmed their commitment to the social dimension as an indispensable element of building and ever-closer

Union, just as a well-developed social system is both necessary and desirable in each individual Member State. European social policy must serve the interests of the Union as a whole and of all its people, both those in employment and those who are not.

(European Commission 1994: 9)

So to what extent can we identify supranationalized social policy? For Deacon *et al.* (1997) the supranationalization of social policy instruments and provision consists of three elements. The first is *global social regulation*, which is constructed through the mechanisms, instruments and policies to regulate the terms of trade and the operation of firms in the interests of social protection and welfare objectives. Deacon *et al.* (1997: 2) recognize that the mechanisms, instruments and policies at a global level are 'at a primitive stage of development', but refer to the measures introduced by the EU as examples of global social regulation. Indeed, a major element of the European Social Model has been to establish the 'mechanisms and instruments of social regulation' to maintain minimum standards in the workplace through an array of regulations covering health and safety at work, and to promote equal opportunities between men and women. Pierson and Leibfried (1995: 1) argue that the EU does possess 'characteristics of a supranational entity, including extensive bureaucratic competencies, unified judicial control, and significant capacities to develop or modify policies'. However, Leibfried has also stressed the influence of 'negative integration' in which the focus is on 'deconstruction', on removing obstacles for a free market with little interest in tackling the inherent social consequences (Leibfried 1991: 5).

Intervention by the EU in areas of social policy has continued to concern itself with the establishment of a 'level playing field' and preventing 'social dumping'. Social dumping refers to a situation in which dependent groups move to states where social security is more generous. Alternatively, labour intensive industries are attracted to regions where labour is cheap and plentiful and social expenditure levels are low, thus upsetting the balance of competitiveness within the EU. Establishing a level playing field of competitiveness implies that there should be a uniformity in, or in the case of the EU a coordination of, social policy intervention to ensure that those national governments which have introduced more generous provision are not at a competitive disadvantage to those which have not.

Thus, the social policy discourse at the European level has been mainly concerned with improving working conditions and responding to the impact of structural change. The Structural Funds are identified by Deacon *et al.* (1997) as representative of the second element of the supranationalization of social policy in terms of *global social redistribution* involving the transfer of wealth from richer to poorer regions/countries. Pierson and Leibfried (1995) refer to the Common Agricultural Policy (CAP) as an example of redistribution across sectors. The CAP was funded from a collective base, and over the years has accounted for a substantial share of the EU budget (Wallace and Wallace 2000). In the mid-1980s the Structural Funds 'signalled a shift from haphazard distribution of resources (especially from the EU budget) to a more planned redistribution through designed resource transfers' (Wallace and Wallace 2000: 31). However, these strategies of redistribution are more concerned with promoting economic development, competitiveness and social cohesion across the countries of the EU than with ensuring equality and social justice. While the budget for the European Regional Development Fund (ERDF) has increased consistently, the sums involved are not large. Furthermore, the potential enlargement of the EU to include countries of Central and Eastern Europe has raised concern regarding the sustainability and cost of maintaining the structural fund. The intensification of regional imbalances across the European Union will test the commitment of country governments and the institutions of the EU to this form of social redistribution. The current applicants are poor compared to the standards of the existing members. Future applicants to the EU are more likely to be net beneficiaries of EU funds rather than contributors. Their membership could thus be potentially detrimental to the position of Spain, Portugal, Italy and Greece for example who have been recipients of resources from the ERDF and could exacerbate tensions between nations.

For Deacon *et al.* (1997) *global social welfare provision* at a level above that of national governments represents the third element in the supranationalization of social policy instruments and provision. They recognize that this is the least developed aspect of the three. They extend this element to include the notion of the empowerment of citizens through access and recourse to supranational legal authorities such as the European Court of Justice, and the Council of Europe's Court of Human Rights. There has been an extension of power to the European Court of Justice and indeed to the European Commission and the European Parliament. However, it is still the European Council, made up of representatives of the member states, which remains the central decision-making body within the European Union. But even here decision-making is difficult. Until the mid-1980s issues relating to social policy required unanimous support. The Single European Act 1986 and Maastricht extended qualified majority voting but still the context of decision-making is highly political. Leibfried and Pearson (1995) argue that opponents of reform occupy the institutional high ground. Initiating policies is more difficult than sustaining non-decision because the aim is not simply about forging collective policies, but also about individual member states protecting their own interests. Although it is now much more difficult for one member state to block policy initiatives it is still the case that blocking coalitions can stifle moves towards an extended social dimension.

Despite the rhetoric, the notion of EU social policy and the social dimension is vague and the areas of competences of the EU extremely limited. Even in the policy areas for which there are explicit competences – such as education and public health – the power of the EU to act in these areas is limited by the principle of subsidiarity. This principle was reinforced in the most recent White Paper on social policy:

> Social progress can be achieved only through a co-operative partnership between the European Union, the Member States, the social partners and European citizens. The key to this must be a positive and active conception of subsidiarity. This means that the Union shall take action only if, and in so far as, the objectives cannot be sufficiently achieved by or within the Member States themselves and can, therefore, by reason of the scale or effects of the proposed action, be better achieved by the Union. Activities should be selected on the basis of prior appraisal and should yield a Union added-value while achieving maximum cost efficiency.
>
> (European Commission 1994: 11)

Spicker (1991) has suggested that the principle of subsidiarity has been used to limit community activity in a range of areas and that the 'role of the Community must of necessity be minor in relation to that of other providers of welfare' (Spicker 1991: 8). Thus, in the context of a broader renegotiation of the role and powers of the state in an increasingly globalized world, national governments have been keen to retain their remaining power in the sphere of social policy. As Leibfried and Pierson (2000: 270) explain:

> The member governments themselves . . . jealously protect social policy prerogatives. Economic and geopolitical changes since the Second World War have gradually diminished the scope of national sovereignty in a variety of domains. The welfare state remains one of the few key realms of policy competence where national governments still appear to reign supreme.

The tensions between the divergent politics and commitments of the different national leaderships have been a key feature in the progress of the EU and in the development of supranational governance. EU policy is made in the context of an extensive, diverse array of pre-existing, territorially based social policies. Each constituent unit of the EU has its own welfare state. Its own pattern of intervention in the lives of its citizens is already well established. Pre-existing policy structures pose barriers to an expanded social policy competence at the EU level partly because of the sheer diversity of national regimes. Leibfried and Pierson (1995) suggest that the 'social space' for social policy is already occupied. They consider that the development of a 'social dimension' of the European Union has been more

> a saga of high aspirations and modest results, marked by cheap talk proferred in the confident knowledge that the unanimity required for

Council votes would never be reached and the ambitious blueprints would remain unexecuted.

(Leibfried and Pierson 1995: 46)

Member states are well represented in the decision-making institutions of the EU and the centrality of member states to institutional governance is evident.

The EU is increasingly dealing with issues from a wider range of countries. The dynamics of creating economic and monetary union (EMU) and enlargement of the EU will create new challenges for the EU and the development of supranational social policy. Enlargement will involve the inclusion of poorer regions and nations with less developed welfare systems. The inclusion of the rich and valuable members of Austria, Finland and Sweden presented little problem for the EU, though convincing individual country nationals of the benefits of entry has not always been an easy task for national governments. However, the limitations on EU social policy will become even greater as the further enlargement increases the pressure on the EU's already limited redistributive capacity (Hodge and Howe 1999).

The basic requirements for EMU, which seek to establish a convergence and stability of macro-economic conditions across European countries, were established by the Maastricht Treaty and more precisely by the Dublin Stability and Growth Pact in 1996. They include a low budget deficit, relatively low public debt, low long-term interest rates, a stable exchange rate and an inflation rate of not more than 1.5 per cent difference from that of the three most successful EU economies. For many of the 11 countries that have qualified to join EMU, the convergence process has resulted in reductions in social expenditure and the implementation of austerity measures. Mishra (1999) points to the contradictions evident in the development of a supranational social policy measures in relation to social protection. The EU has extended and strengthened the instruments and policies of social regulation for the protection of workers, while at the same time the Maastricht Treaty promotes fiscal austerity and points towards 'the retrenching of social protection in member states' (Mishra 1999: 40) and reinforces the principle of subsidiarity which firmly places responsibility for social welfare with nation-states.

According to Leibfried (1994: 248) the current constitutional position of the EU is one of 'negative joint sovereignty' with member states having 'formally and functionally lost the capacity to act but without the EU at the supranational level gaining its formal authority'. Leibfried sees little possibility for a merger among the distinctive European welfare regimes and suggests that 'the common ground is missing on which a European welfare regime could be built' (Leibfried 1991: 155). What has emerged, according to Marks (1993), is

a complex, multi-layered, decision making process stretching beneath the state as well as above it; instead of a consistent pattern of policy making across policy areas, one finds extremely wide and persistent variations. In short, the European Community seems to be part of a new political (dis)order that is multilayered, constitutionally open-ended, and programmatically diverse.

(Marks 1993: 221)

Within this 'multi-tiered' system (Leibfried and Pierson 1995: 47) the EU's social policy-making apparatus is extremely 'bottom-heavy' – 'from the [weak] center comes a variety of pressures and constraints on social policy development, but little in the way of clear mandates for positive action' (Leibfried and Pierson 1995: 75).

So while the choices available to governments in relation to the shaping of social policy have been restricted this cannot yet be characterized as supra-national social policy (Leibfried and Pierson 2000). Inter-state bargaining, driven by the necessity of maintaining national legitimacy bases, still forms part of the process through which action by the EU is sanctioned, and is an indication of the crucial role the state plays in its interaction with domestic and international policy-making frameworks. Yet it is rather more than intergovernmental policy-making in which the nation-states are seen as primary agents of transformation and integration. It would seem that a dualistic opposition between either the primacy of the state or supranational organizations is somewhat misplaced. The state should be conceptualized as engaged in a complex, multiple and overlapping network of interactions which are embedded in an increasingly transnational society and economy.

Conclusion

The worldwide international economy involves a growing interconnection between national economies characterized by the rapid mobility of capital and the diffusion of manufacturing capabilities around the globe. It also involves the increasing integration of more and more nations and elements of social and cultural life into market relationships. The capitalist system and the welfare state more than ever need to be understood as embedded in global, as well as domestic, processes with the large global enterprises and organizations such as the IMF, the GATT/WTO and the EU contributing to the institutional structures though which ideologies and policies are channelled.

What must be understood is that the articulation of global processes is complex, differentiated and contradictory. Restructuring is not a unified global process. Globalization has benefited many countries, but it has also completely marginalized others, particularly in such of Sub-Saharan Africa and impoverished rural areas of Latin America and Asia. But poverty, social exclusion, and the manifestations of Castells' (1998) 'Fourth World' are increasingly evident in just about every city in the world. Castells (1998) relates these developments to the political demise of the welfare state yet this is not a universal phenomena. While the discourse of neo-liberalism has permeated the policy agenda worldwide, it is the range of competing capitalisms and welfare regimes – German corporatism versus American neo-liberalism for example – still evident which is most striking. And paradoxically, while globalization extends the reach of capitalism, market relations and western culture, it is also reinforcing cultural and political embeddedness and cultural and national specificity as communities adapt global products and practices to meet their own needs.

Globalization has also called into question the position of the sovereignty of nation-states following the internationalization of socio-economic and cultural forms. However, it would seem that, as yet, the international order is still primarily one of politically constructed nation-states, as evidenced by the proliferation of the modern nation-states during the late 1980s and early 1990s as regions have pursued nationhood. However, this is in the context of a reorientation of the state away from an essentially isolated, inward, domestically oriented policy framework of the Keynesian era to a more out-ward looking, interconnected and multilevel framework through which domestic and international concerns are evaluated and negotiated. Despite the assertion by Deacon *et al.* (1997) that the focus of the discipline of social policy should be *supranational* or *global* rather than *comparative,* the discussion here has shown that comparative social policy, incorporating a broader conceptualization of the state and the framework of multilevel governance, is still a valid method of analysis. Cross-national social policy analysis is not only an appropriate strategy, but also a vital one for under-standing the complexity of contemporary social change.

The major contributions of Deacon *et al.* (1997), however, have been to highlight the importance of integrating global politics into cross-national social policy analysis and to develop a framework within which the analysis can be located. Their work has reinforced the argument that it is only through analysis incorporating a number of interrelating levels, macro to micro, than an understanding of the complex processes taking place can be understood and the diversity and differences between nation-states can be highlighted. Thus the following chapters explore the conceptual and ana-lytical challenges involved in this endeavour and consider some of the strat-egies and approaches that may contribute to cross-national social policy analysis.

Note

1 The Gini coefficient measures the extent to which the distribution of income among individuals deviates from perfectly even distribution. The coefficient

ranges from 0 – indicating perfect equality – to 1 – indicating complete inequality (adapted from UNDP 1999: 224).

Further reading

Deacon, B. with Hulse, M. and Stubbs, P. (1997) *Global Social Policy: International Organizations and the Future of Welfare*. London: Sage. This book argues that social policy must now be understood as interacting with the transnational arena and, in particular, international organizations such as the World Bank, the IMF, the UN and the EU. It introduces the idea of the supranationalization or globalization of social policy instruments, policy and provision, and the themes of supranational regulation, redistribution and provision. Through this framework the authors explore the impact of global processes on the welfare state and consider the prospects for the development of a global social policy.

Midgley, J. (1997) *Social Welfare in Global Context*. Thousand Oaks, CA: Sage. This book explores the nature of international social welfare and the global system. It examines global social conditions and the ways in which social welfare is promoted in different parts of the world. The book includes chapters on applied international social welfare and, focusing on social work practice, addresses the concerns of practitioners working in the field.

Mishra, R. (1999) *Globalization and the Welfare State*. Cheltenham: Edward Elgar. This book explores the political and economic aspects of globalization and their impact on the welfare state and systems of social protection. It considers evidence from Sweden, Germany and Japan to show that while neo-liberal ideology exerts the strongest influence on global processes, diverse patterns of integration into the global economy are apparent. The book concludes with proposals for reinforcing the connections between the economic and the social in a globalizing world, through the promotion of social standards and supranational social policy.

Woods, N. (ed.) (1999) *The Political Economy of Globalization*. London: Macmillan. This collection covers many of the core themes of globalization. It considers global finance and investment, regionalism, the role of international organizations and institutions and the extent to which we can talk of a global civil society.

chapter
two

Defining and constructing the research process

Patricia Kennett and Nicola Yeates

Introduction

Cross-national research has a long history across social science disciplines and has increasingly become an important feature of contemporary social policy analysis. As discussed in Chapter 1, there is a more general recognition of the importance of taking a more global perspective in a world in which social, cultural and economic manifestations are imported and exported across national borders. As transnational institutions have proliferated so they have become more proficient in producing large amounts of data on a range of social and economic issues. Organizations such as the EU-Eurostat, UN, ILO and the OECD have contributed to a process which has been referred to as the 'internationalization of analytical categories' (Dogan and Pelassy 1990: 30). In addition, Clasen (1999) points to the development of cross-national research groups and networks which seek to bring together social scientists and facilitate cross-national links and research and funding opportunities.

This chapter, then, is primarily concerned with the *process* of cross-national research. It will begin by introducing various interpretations of comparative, cross-national research. It will go on to consider whether comparative research between countries represents a new or different set of theoretical and methodological challenges from those embedded in the more general process of social scientific enquiry (see also Oyen 1990). The difficulties with and benefits of comparing and interpreting international data will be assessed as will the contribution of the increasing availability of harmonized data. Key factors such as the equivalence and appropriateness of concepts and definitions are discussed and explored empirically through the phenomena of poverty and disadvantage, homelessness, and the labour force.

What is cross-national comparative social research?

The element of comparison forms a key part in any research, whether it takes place in one country or many. It is most often the case that in the process of research social phenomena are studied and compared with other social phenomena. As Oyen (1990) argues:

> no social phenomena can be isolated and studied without comparing them to other social phenomena. Sociologists engage actively in the process of comparative work whenever concepts are chosen, operationalised or fitted into theoretical structures.
>
> (Oyen 1990: 4)

Marsh (1967: 9) is keen to differentiate between intra-societal comparison – 'the analysis of variations within one society' – and inter-societal comparison, which he refers to as the 'systematic and explicit comparison of data from two or more societies or their subsystems' (Marsh 1967: 11). These subsystems might include welfare systems, demography, cultural systems, kinship, polity and bureaucracy, or stratification, for example, depending on the nature of the question to be explored. His explanation for the emphasis on societies is that in most cases 'the *units* being talked about *are* societies, and one should therefore examine more than one unit' (Marsh 1967: 9). Hague *et al.* (1987), in contrast, have suggested that the term 'comparative' can apply to a study incorporating a single country. They argue that a case study has the potential to inform debates which have significance beyond the boundaries of the single country: 'a single case can offer a detailed illustration of a theme of wider interest . . . cases are deliberately chosen, or at least can be written up, as an example of broader phenomena' (Hague *et al.* 1987: 276). They point to the example of focusing on Thailand as a case for exploring the impact and responses of East Asian countries to the financial crisis in the 1990s (Hague *et al.* 1987: 53). However, Rose (1991) refers to this approach as 'extroverted case studies with generic concepts' in that this type of study is *comparable*, rather than explicitly *comparative* in that 'it employs concepts that make it possible to derive generalizations that can be tested elsewhere' (Rose 1991: 454). For Elder (1976) comparative cross-national methodology is 'an approach to knowing social reality through the examination for similarities and differences between data gathered from *more than one nation*' (Elder 1976: 210, emphasis added).

For Przeworski (1987) the key element of comparative research is not comparing but explaining. 'The general purpose of cross-national research is to understand which characteristics of the particular cultures, societies, economies or political systems affect patterns of behaviour within them' (Przeworski 1987: 35). Wilensky and Turner (1987) in attempting to establish the 'state of the art' in comparative social policy set down as one of the criteria that a study had to 'be systematically cross-national covering the same phenomena in two or more countries' (Wilensky and Turner 1987: 382). This view is supported and expanded by Hantrais and Mangen (1996). They argue that

> individuals or teams should be sent out to study particular issues or phenomena in two or more countries with the express intention of comparing their manifestations in different socio-cultural settings, using the same research instruments, either to carry out secondary analysis of national data or to conduct new empirical work.
>
> (Hantrais and Mangen 1996: 1)

They emphasize the necessity for conceptual equivalence and the systematic analysis of phenomena. Only then can a study be classified as cross-national and comparative.

Pickvance (1986), while arguing that all research is comparative, differentiates between comparative studies, comparative research and comparative analysis and asserts that simply because a study involves data from two or more societies does not guarantee that it is comparative. He points to the method which involves 'serial treatment', in that it simply identifies similarities and differences between countries under scrutiny or alternatively where a chapter on each country is provided with no common structure and little explicit comparative analysis (see for example Hallet 1988; Balchin 1996 on housing policy). An alternative style is that adopted by Wall (1996) in her edited collection. Within each country-specific chapter a common framework is maintained. Within this common framework the organization of health care in six countries is explored. Underlying the framework, according to Wall (1996: i) 'is the premise that there are similarities between the countries with respect to the challenges associated with providing health care in the developed world, as well as the differences in the nature of response'. An introductory chapter outlines the common themes and problems to be pursued while the conclusion focuses on explaining the diversity of responses to these issues across countries.

Ginsberg (1992), in his analysis of the social divisions of welfare in Sweden, the Federal Republic of Germany, the USA and Britain, adopts a 'critical structured diversity approach'. Each country-specific chapter is organized around five headings: ideology and welfare expenditure; income maintenance policies and outcomes; 'race' and racial inequalities; women and family policies; the health care system. The focus on the divisions of class, 'race' and gender in his four case studies provides a critical analysis of the ways in which 'a racially- and patriarchally-structured capitalist system' (Ginsberg 1992: 196) has shaped the welfare state in the four countries. While neither the work of Ginsberg (1992) or Wall (1996) could be classified as comparative within the terms discussed above they nevertheless provide in-depth, systematic and theoretically informed international analysis. In particular, Ginsberg's work has emphasized the importance of and the opportunities for adopting a critical approach in cross-national policy analysis.

Equivalence in meanings and concepts

One of the key questions often asked of comparative research between countries is whether it represents a 'new or different set of theoretical, methodological and epistemological challenges' (Oyen 1990: 4) or is it simply an extension of, and therefore subject to, the same problems embedded in the research process involving only one country? According to Marsh (1967: 257), 'the logic of comparative enquiry is much like the logic of social inquiry', with cross-societal comparisons drawing upon and utilizing much the same kinds of data as studies involving only one society. Commentators like Smelser (1976) would argue that comparative enquiry across nations is not an independent form of enquiry and that it offers no methodological challenges unique to itself. Other commentators, however, would argue that there are fundamental differences between comparativists and non-comparativists and would recognize the distinctive characteristics of this type of research.

Oyen (1990) identifies four broad approaches to cross-national comparative research, which she refers to as: *'the purists'* – for whom international comparative research offers no unique challenges, other than considerations involved with multilevel research; *'the ignorants'* – who fail even to consider the possibility of increased complexity involved in cross-boundary comparisons; *'the totalists'* – who, having recognized the problem and complexities involved in this particular type of research, choose the path of compromise and settle for vagueness in relation to concepts and variables influencing the outcome of social phenomenon. The fourth category refers to the *'true comparativists'*. True comparativists incorporate an approach to cross-national research which acknowledges the increased complexity, and difficulties involved with comparative analysis but assert that 'in order to advance our knowledge about cross-national research it is necessary to raise questions about the distinctive characteristics of comparative studies' (Oyen 1990: 5).

While cross-national comparisons enable an analysis of a range of variations to be observed, it is not without risks. The issue of cross-societal equivalence of concepts is prominent in the literature and is clearly a crucial factor in cross-national research given that phenomena or relationships may have different meanings in other societies. In order to compare something across systems it is necessary to have confidence that the components and their properties being compared are the 'same' or indicate something equivalent. As Beals (1954) argues:

Unless initially we use precisely comparative conceptualisations and methodologies, comparative studies are a waste of time, for they will never add up to proof, disproof, or reformulation or anything. Rather we will emerge, not with one set of culture-bound theories and concepts, but with a multitude of culture-bound theories.

(Beals 1954: 308, cited in Marsh 1967: 268)

According to Rose (1991: 447), 'Concepts are necessary as common points of reference for grouping phenomena that are differentiated geographically and often linguistically'. He points out that without concepts, information collected about different countries provides no basis for relating one country to another.

In order to connect empirical materials horizontally across national boundaries, they must also be connected vertically; that is, capable of being related to concepts that are sufficiently abstract to travel across national boundaries.

(Rose 1991: 447)

Appropriateness, then, refers to the methods employed and the conceptualization of issues when undertaking comparative research. As Armer (1973: 50–1) explains, 'appropriateness requires feasibility, significance and acceptability in each foreign culture as a necessary (but not sufficient) condition for insuring validity and successful completion of comparative studies'. Thus, issues of appropriateness and equivalence in the conceptualization of issues are key factors within the research process (May 1997).

Marsh (1967) differentiates between *formal* equivalence and *functional* equivalence of concepts, pointing out that using identical formal procedures when comparing different societies may produce functionally non-equivalent meanings. In order to compare something across countries it is, of course, vital to have confidence that the components and their properties being compared are the 'same' or indicate something equivalent. Pickvance (1986) points to the lack of familiarity one might have with other national contexts which may lead to the omission or misinterpretation of an important feature and have a strong causal influence on the subject of analysis. Iyengar (1993) reinforces this point and is particularly concerned with conceptual rigour in multi-language studies. He argues that linguistic diversity can be a barrier when carrying out both cross-national and single-country studies because of the lack of robust concepts and the difficulties of analysing data in more than one language. He considers linguistic equivalence and measurement equivalence to be vital elements of the cross-national research process. He describes linguistic equivalence as 'validity *within* languages' [emphasis added] but argues that measurement equivalence requires that the linguistic equivalence of concepts 'is operationalised as reliability *across* the languages concerned' [emphasis added] (Iyengar 1993: 174).

What he is emphasizing here is that care must be taken not only to ensure that concepts developed for use in each particular language are up to measuring what they set out to investigate, but also that the range of conceptual frameworks can be integrated and analysed systematically. As discussed earlier, it may well be that concepts when translated and operationalized in a range of national contexts may vary in order to capture the 'language of expressions'. However, 'unless it can be demonstrated that the indices in one particular context are applicable to other contexts, comparison is of little value' (Iyengar 1993: 173). Carey-Wood (1991) has indicated that equivalence in meaning and concepts is not necessarily obtainable by correct translations because of the semantic, cultural and societal differences inherent in words and concepts. Conceptual equivalence, according to Hantrais and Ager (1985), requires intimate knowledge of context and culture, while for Warwick and Osherson (1973: 31), 'linguistic equivalence is inseparable from the theory and concepts guiding the study, the problems chosen, and the research design'. As Hantrais and Mangen (1996) argue, drawing on the work of Lisle (1985)

> language is not simply a medium for conveying concepts, it is part of the conceptual system, reflecting institutions, thought processes, values and ideology, and implying that the approach to a topic and the interpretation of it will differ, according to the language of expression.
>
> (Hantrais and Mangen 1996: 7)

Not only might issues which are held to be important in one national context not be of significance in another, but also values and interpretations of phenomena differ from society to society. It is vital that the researcher does not assume a 'value consensus' across societies, nor 'impose' meaning and interpretations on particular social phenomenon, influencing interpretations about what is legitimate and normal, and therefore what is deviant (May 1997). Lewis (1999) highlights the profound differences in the nature of the debates about lone mothers in Britain and other European countries. In Britain (and the USA) lone mothers have been characterized as welfare dependent, morally feckless and ineffective mothers. Their status, according to Lewis (1999), has evolved from one of 'social problem' to 'social threat'. In other European countries lone mothers have not been singled out as a problem category or demonized by the media, and are also better off in material terms. The reasons for this are complex and varied. Demographic factors, including the larger populations of lone mothers in Britain and the USA, as well as the kinds of lone mothers which predominate in different countries in terms of previous marital status and the age of unmarried mothers, have contributed to the tone of the debate. Lewis (1999) indicates that extramarital birth rates are highest in Scandinavian countries (46.4 per cent in 1990), while England and Wales have a much higher percentage of teenage mothers (33 per cent in 1990) than other European countries, though not as high as in the USA (59.4 per cent). She also highlights the dynamics of class and race in the discourse around lone mothers, pointing out that 'in the United States, unmarried mothers are disproportionately black and on benefit', and in Britain, unlike other European countries 'they are disproportionately poorly educated and unskilled and also on benefit' (Lewis 1999: 185). The welfare dependency of lone mothers in Britain is a product of 'the poverty of their social wage [childcare provision, parental leave, for example] compared to so many of their counterparts in other European countries' (Lewis 1999: 197). While demographics and the characteristics of lone mothers may offer some explanation for the differences in the nature of debates between countries, the key to understanding national differences in policies and the diverse dynamics of integration of lone mothers is the political ideologies within which welfare regimes and family policies have been established and are maintained.

It is vital then that the researcher does not assume a 'value-consensus' across societies and recognizes that concepts and their meanings are dynamic and change over time. May (1997) points to three important elements in the construction of a 'social problem' – culture, history and social power. He argues that power is not evenly distributed between groups. The recognition that a 'problem' exists and the way that it is defined is often a product of 'the relative power that the people who define the social problem have over those who are defined' (May 1997: 47). Thus it becomes not just 'equally valid' as he suggests, but vital to 'examine the process through which a phenomenon became defined as a problem' (May 1997: 47), rather than just accept given definitions. The evolution of debates around poverty and disadvantage, as well as those associated with homelessness, particularly in the EU, offer good opportunities for exploring some of these issues.

Conceptualizing disadvantage

Poverty and social exclusion are the key concepts which have been used to explore disadvantage in society. These are both highly political and contested concepts and have generated substantial debate. For Alcock (1997) the current situation is one in which there exists a series of contested definitions and complex arguments that overlap and at times even contradict one another. Walker and Walker (1997) distinguish between poverty and social exclusion with the former seen as

> a lack of the material resources, especially income, necessary to participate in British society and *social exclusion* as a more comprehensive formulation which refers to the dynamic process of being shut out, fully or partially, from any of the social, economic, political or cultural

systems which determine the social integration of a person in society. Social exclusion may, therefore, be seen as the denial (or non-realisation) of the civil, political and social rights of citizenship.

(Walker and Walker 1997: 8, original emphasis)

Issues of definition have been central to understanding and explaining the causes of poverty as well as the solutions to it. In general the definition of poverty has evolved since the 1930s or so from an absolute to a relative definition. In the early 1900s in Britain the subsistence notion was incorporated into the pioneering work of Joseph Rowntree in York, whose ideas on primary poverty were based on the minimum needed for the maintenance of physical health and physical efficiency. Clearly, the subsistence approach is an absolute concept of poverty and is dominated by the individuals' physiological efficiency. In the 1940s the Beveridge Report (1942) utilized the subsistence idea as the basis for setting new benefit rates:

In considering the minimum income needed by persons of working age for subsistence during interruptions of earnings it is sufficient to take into account food, clothing, fuel, light and household sundries, and rent, though some margin must be allowed for inefficiency in spending.

(Beveridge Report 1942)

In contrast a relative definition of poverty is based on a comparison between the standard of living of 'the poor' and the standard of living of other members of society who are not poor. The introduction of the relative definition in Britain is associated with the work of Peter Townsend (1979):

Individuals, families and groups in the population can be said to be in poverty when they lack the resources to obtain the types of diet, participate in the activities and have the living conditions and amenities which are customary . . . in the societies in which they belong.

(Townsend 1979: 31)

Room (1995) characterizes Townsend's influential contribution to poverty studies as an attempt to break free from the legacy of Rowntree and others but nevertheless concludes that 'with his focus on the resources that individuals need to have at their command, distributional issues are still at the heart of this definition' (Room 1995: 6).

The phenomenon of poverty has proved notoriously controversial and difficult to measure both nationally and internationally, with poverty lines often constructed using a range of methods from food poverty – as in the USA, for example, where the poverty line is based on the least costly budget demonstrated to achieve adequate nutrition with amounts varying according to household size – to the level of the most basic benefits. Calculations can also be based on a percentage of the average standard of living in a society – that is 60 per cent, 50 per cent, 40 per cent. As the percentage rises so the numbers living below or on the margins of the poverty line increases.

International poverty levels set by the World Bank are based on consumption and are outlined in Box 2.1. They allow US$1 per day per person for the least developed countries, US$2 per day per person for Latin America and the Caribbean, US$4 per day for Eastern Europe and the CIS and US$14.40 for comparison between industrial countries.

Box 2.1   The World Bank international poverty lines

US$1 per day per person for the least developed countries
US$2 per day per person for Latin America and the Caribbean
US$4 per day per person for Eastern Europe and the CIS
US$14.40 per day per person for industrial countries

Income-defined poverty lines are problematic in a number of ways. According to the United Nations Centre for Human Settlements (Habitat) (UNCHS 1996: 108), 'Definitions that set a "poverty line" to divide the population into the "poor" and the "non-poor" are often the most inaccurate because they simplify and standardize what is highly complex and varied'. For example, it is often much more expensive for those whose livelihood is in the centre of a major city than for those in rural areas of small towns, yet the very large differences in living costs within nations is not taken into consideration by the World Bank income-defined poverty line. Nor does the calculation highlight intra-household differentials. While a household may appear to be living above the poverty line there may be those within the household who are deprived because of discrimination on the basis of gender or age, in the distribution of resources (UNCHS 1996). According to Townsend (1993) this definition of poverty conforms with an ideology which suggests that the needs of the poor countries are lesser than those of the rich countries. He argues that this definition is unacceptable and leads to misplaced strategies. The UNCHS (1996) report reiterates this view arguing that poverty definitions based solely on 'lack of income' can actually serve to obscure the structural causes and processes that create and perpetuate poverty. The emphasis on poverty alleviation, particularly in developing countries, has tended to focus on economic development and growth as the solution instead of on a more complex and comprehensive set of policy solutions based around redistribution and improved services and facilities as well as economic growth.

More recently the term social exclusion has become widely utilized both in national and international policy arenas and has been described by Byrne (1997: 28) as 'currently the most fashionable term' for describing social divisions in societies. Saraceno (1997: 177) argues that the reconstruction of debates from poverty to social exclusion has involved 'an actual conceptual shift, and a change in perspective; from a static to a dynamic approach, as well as from a distributional to a relational focus'. According to Abrahamson (1997: 148) 'the element that distinguishes social exclusion from poverty and makes it, perhaps, more potent, is . . . the affiliation with the issue of citizenship rights'. So while Room (1991) has defined social exclusion in relation to social rights and the inability of 'citizens' to secure these social rights, for Tricart (1991) social exclusion refers to

> processes and situations by which persons or groups tend to be separated or held at a distance from ordinary social exchange or positions which promote or allow integration or 'insertion' – that is, from participation in institutions or from access to rights, services or resources which imply full membership of society.
>
> (Tricart 1991: 2)

Thus, the term social exclusion is 'a multi-faceted "relational" concept describing a complex set of social processes' (Allen *et al.* 1998: 11). Madanipour *et al.* (1998) refer specifically to social exclusion as a

> multi-dimensional process, in which various forms of exclusion are combined: participation in decision making and political processes, access to employment and material resources, and integration into common cultural processes. When combined they create acute forms of exclusion that find a spatial manifestation in particular neighbourhoods.
>
> (Madanipour *et al.* 1998: 22)

Definitions of social exclusion seek to go beyond measurements based solely on consumption or distribution and to incorporate notions of participation and integration. The term derives from French social policy and became prominent in the discourse of the European Union during the late 1980s. The EU poverty programmes began in the 1970s and by the third programme (1990–4) the use of the term 'social exclusion' had become commonplace. It was accompanied by discussions about developing multidimensional strategies for dealing with disadvantage:

> [Recognizing] that social exclusion is not simply a matter of inadequate [resources], and that combating exclusion also involves access by individuals and families to decent living conditions by means of measures for social integration into the labour market; accordingly request the Member States to implement or promote measures to enable everyone to have access to: education, by acquiring proficiency in basic skills, training, employment, housing, community services, medical care.
>
> (Council Resolution of 29 September 1989)

As Room (1995) points out, the term social exclusion has been included in the Maastricht Treaty, within the objectives of the Structural Funds, and has been linked with the network of observatories established in a number of social policy areas specifically to develop policies to combat social exclusion.

Despite the rhetoric, the policy agenda associated with the concept of social exclusion has been mainly aimed at labour market inclusion through training and education. This approach can be linked to what Veit-Wilson (1998) refers to as the 'weak' version of the discourse where 'solutions lie in altering these excluded people's handicapping characteristics and enhancing their integration into dominant society' (Veit-Wilson 1998: 45). It can also be characterized as 'a discourse deliberately chosen for closure, to exclude other potential discourses in European political debate and to depoliticize poverty *as far as income redistribution was concerned*' (Veit-Wilson 1998: 97, original emphasis, cited in Byrne 1999: 5).

Although the concept of social exclusion has been narrowly defined in the context of the EU, in other arenas it has created an environment and an opportunity for developing more subtle and sophisticated indicators of deprivation on a global scale. In 1990 the United Nations Development Project introduced the human development perspective in order to capture and measure different aspects of basic human development. It uses indicators of deprivation based on health and survival, educational attainment, economic resources, sustainability, human security and ethnicity and gender equality which are then organized into composite indices. Within a single, composite index the human development index (HDI) provides a ranking of countries based on their average achievements. The HDI is accompanied by the gender-related development index (GDI) and the gender empowerment measure (GEM), both introduced in 1995, which attempt to capture the extent of gender inequality not only in basic human development but also in terms of economic and political opportunities and participation. In 1997 the human poverty index (HPI) was introduced. Its aim is to focus not only on poverty of income but also on poverty as a denial of choices and opportunities for living a tolerable life. Box 2.2 outlines the key dimensions of the human development perspective, while Table 2.1 shows the top and bottom five countries in the human development indices.

In 1999 the HDI covered 174 countries with 45 in the high human development category, 94 in the medium human development category and 35 in the low human development category. As Table 2.1 shows, Canada, Norway and the USA rank at the top of the index with Sierra Leone, Niger and Ethiopia at the bottom. As the UNDP (1999: 129) reports, 'wide disparities in human development exist. Canada's HDI value of 0.932 is more than three times Sierra Leone's 0.254. Thus Canada has a shortfall in human development of only about 7 per cent, Sierra Leone one of 75 per cent'. While the HDI reveals that many people across the globe are living longer and healthier lives, in eighteen countries – ten in Africa (of which four are in Sub-Saharan Africa), eight in Eastern Europe and the CIS – life expectancy actually fell (UNDP 1999). Deacon *et al.* (1997) have suggested that the HDI

Box 2.2   Human development perspective

Human development index (HDI)

This is the measure of the average achievements in a country in three basic dimensions of human development – longevity, knowledge and a decent standard of living. The HDI contains three variables – life expectancy at birth, educational attainment (adult literacy rate, combined enrolment ratio) and real per capita income* (in PPP$).**

Gender-related development index (GDI)

Using the same dimensions as the HDI, the focus is on the inequality in achievement between men and women. The GDI is the HDI discounted or adjusted for gender inequality.

Gender empowerment measure (GEM)

This measure is concerned with the extent to which women are able to actively participate in economic and political life. Its focus is on participation and it measures gender inequality in key areas of economic and political participation and decision-making.

Human poverty index (1 and 2)

Using the same dimensions as HDI, the HPI measures deprivation in basic human development. For developing countries HPI-1 focuses on the percentage of people not expected to survive to age 40, the percentage of people who are illiterate, the percentage of underweight children under 5 and the percentage of people without access to safe water and health services. For industrialized countries HPI-2 focuses on the percentage of people not expected to survive to age 60, the percentage of people who are functionally illiterate and the percentage of people living below the income poverty line (50 per cent of median personal disposable income). It is also concerned with deprivation in social inclusion expressed by the numbers experiencing long-term unemployment (12 months or more).

Notes:
 *The GDP per capita of a country converted into US dollars on the basis of the purchasing power parity (PPP) exchange rate.
**Purchasing power parity: the PPP rate gives one dollar the same purchasing power over domestic GDP that the US dollar has over US GDP. PPP can be expressed in other national currencies than the US$. PPP rates allow a standard comparison of real price levels between countries.

Table 2.1 Top and bottom five countries in the human development indices

Index	Top five	Bottom five
HDI	Canada Norway USA Japan Belgium	Burundi Burkina Faso Ethiopia Niger Sierra Leone
GDI	Canada Norway USA Australia Sweden	Guinea-Bissau Burundi Burkina Faso Ethiopia Niger
GEM	Norway Sweden Denmark Canada Germany	Jordan Mauritania Togo Pakistan Niger
HPI-1	Barbados Trinidad and Tobago Uruguay Costa Rica Cuba	Central African Republic Ethiopia Sierra Leone Burkina Faso Niger
HPI-2	Sweden Netherlands Germany Norway Italy	New Zealand Spain UK Ireland USA

Source: UNDP 1999: 128

could be open to the criticism that it simply follows the logic of a 'particularly rationalist paradigm' and that especially in fundamentalist countries some elements of the index are irrelevant and inappropriate. It is therefore nothing more than yet another 'Western liberal construct' (Deacon *et al.* 1997: 30). They conclude, however, that

> there are value choices to be defended about desirable social and political goals . . . pragmatically, for the moment the world, with the significant exception of Islamic fundamentalists states, is (a) moving in the direction of using these criteria to evaluate itself and (b) succeeding gradually in advancing human welfare according to these criteria.
>
> (Deacon *et al.* 1997: 30)

Just as poverty and social exclusion have proved controversial concepts so has homelessness proved to be a fundamentally unstable term. Extensive debates have been generated over the precise definition and the appropriate means of measuring the extent of homelessness. As Marsh and Kennett point out:

> All statistical measures are socially negotiated, but in the case of home-lessness – along with other key political issues like crime and unem-ployment – the fragility of official definitions and measures in particularly stark. Societies with different socio-political traditions are likely to come to very different understandings of the term.
>
> (Marsh and Kennett 1999: 3)

Worldwide, the number of homeless people is somewhere between 100 million and 1 billion, depending on how homelessness is defined. According to the United Nations Centre for Human Settlements:

> The estimate of 100 million would apply to those who have no shelter at all, including those who sleep outside (on pavements, in shop door-ways, in parks or under bridges) or in public buildings (in railway, bus or metro stations) or in night shelters set up to provide homeless people with a bed. The estimate of 1 billion homeless people would also include those in accommodation that is very insecure or temporary, and often poor quality – for instance squatters who have found accommo-dation by illegally occupying someone else's home or land and are under constant threat of eviction, those living in refugee camps whose home has been destroyed and those living in temporary shelters (like the 250,000 pavement dwellers in Bombay). The estimate for the number of homeless people worldwide would exceed 1 billion people if it were to include all people who lack an adequate home with secure tenure . . . and the most basic facilities such as water of adequate quality piped into the home, provision for sanitation and drainage.
>
> (UNCHS 1996: 229)

Within the countries of the EU some 18 million people were considered to be homeless or badly housed. This figure was based on the broad, fourfold classification of homelessness developed by the European Observatory on Homelessness, run by the European Federation of National Organizations Working with the Homeless (FEANTSA). The classification includes (a) rooflessness or sleeping rough, (b) houselessness (living in institutions or short-term accommodation, (c) insecure accommodation and (d) inferior or substandard housing. Despite this broad definition the most commonly used data to emerge from the Observatory is based on research drawn from each member country which is then collated to provide an overall picture. The figure of 1.8 million people shown in Table 2.2 covers only those people who have used public or voluntary services for temporary shelter or who squat or sleep rough. As Avramov (1995) points out, however, it tends to be those countries with relatively good provision for the homeless that come out with

Table 2.2   Estimates of number of persons homeless in Europe

Country	Homeless on an average day	In the course of a year
Austria	6,100	8,400
Belgium	4,000	5,500
Germany	490,700	876,450
Denmark	2,947	4,000
Spain	8,000	11,000
Finland	4,000	5,500
France	250,000	346,000
Greece	5,500	7,700
Ireland	2,667	3,700
Italy	56,000	78,000
Luxembourg	194	200
The Netherlands	7,000	12,000
Portugal	3,000	4,000
Sweden	9,903	14,000
UK	283,000	460,000
	1,133,011	1,836,450

Source: Based on Avramov 1996

the highest number of homeless people. Harvey (1999: 278) suggests that these estimates may be more an indication of 'efficient information-gathering, as much as the size of the problem itself', but nevertheless they provide sufficient evidence to indicate that homelessness is a significant problem in many countries of the European Union.

At a national level, even in countries with 'official' definitions of homelessness like the UK, where local authorities have a duty to respond to those defined as homeless, the legislation excludes many single households, and others considered not to be in 'priority need'. The official definition can be seen as a rationing mechanism, which can be interpreted in a variety of ways by different local authorities. Thus, whether a household is considered to be statutorily homeless depends upon the local discretion applied to interpreting the legal framework as well as 'the political complexion of an authority and the demand for social housing locally' (Marsh and Kennett 1999: 3). This obviously has implications for statistics. Watson (1999) takes the discussion further by arguing that

> how homelessness is understood in each society reflects the ways in which the society is organised and in patriarchal society, these are necessarily gendered . . . If homelessness is defined in terms of men's experiences and practices or men's subjectivities then women's homelessness becomes invisible.

> (Watson 1999: 84, 87)

When considering any estimate of homelessness or poverty then it is important to question how the figures were obtained. This is equally true of the increasing volume of international data which have become available. The next section focuses more specifically on the advantages and difficulties of collating and utilizing international data.

Collecting and interpreting international data

In the process of collating international data the researcher can juxtapose data drawn directly from national statistical sources which are then presented as country-specific tables, presenting statistics on a number of items. The advantage of this type of information for the researcher is that it is 'transparent' in that not only is information relating to each country provided and can thus be manipulated as necessary but also one is aware of the source of the data and the purpose for which they were originally collected. However, there are a number of difficulties in collating data of this kind, particularly in relation to the inconsistency of time-frames, incompatible definitions applied to concepts, the lack of detailed data (or even any data at all).

An alternative or complementary strategy might be to utilize the ever increasing range of harmonized data. International organizations have been particularly active in their role of producing and publishing data on welfare institutions (for example social security, education, health) and the labour market in different countries. A great deal of effort has been put into standardizing official statistics and unifying statistical tools and methods of data presentation. This has given rise to a range of statistical reports, produced on a regular (monthly, annually, biannually) or ad hoc basis. Principal data sources are the European Union (such as Directorate-General for Employment, Industrial Relations and Social Affairs (DGV) of the European Commission and Eurostat), the UN and its associated agencies (ILO, World Health Organization (WHO), UN Educational, Scientific and Cultural Organization (Unesco) and the OECD. Increasingly the data-collecting activities of these institutions are governed by adherence to international guidelines on methodological procedure and standards published by, for example, the UN Statistical Commission. These are aimed at promoting international comparability and consistency of data.

The reasons for the growing proficiency and involvement in data collection stems in part from the role of international institutions. For example, the European Commission has since the 1960s been actively undertaking cross-national studies and collating data on various aspects of the social policies of the member states, while its policy competences have developed mainly since the 1980s. The collation of comparable indicators has been crucial in the development of the European Commission's role as a coordinating and monitoring body of social protection, education, training and health policies. It has played a key role in the gathering and dissemination of European-wide estimates on poverty. Similarly, the OECD acts as a 'repository for vast amounts of data' (Mabbett 1998: 362): its work is oriented towards the production of policy advice for member countries.

The range of comparative data sources now available is quite substantial. While this is a welcome development, it imposes constraints on the research process. This final section examines some of the problems entailed by the increasing involvement of international agencies in data collation. In particular, it looks at the organizations set up to collate such tables, the types of data selected to compile comparative tables, and an illustration of the kinds of problems arising from European-wide surveys and indicators. Given that such data are central to policy-making in that it influences perceptions, interpretations and reactions to an issue, it is necessary to understand the limits as well as the opportunities that such data provide. The collation of statistics can be a fraught exercise for researchers, whether they are involved in the collation of comparable statistics or in the access to and understanding of that data. As with research at a national level, the same principles of critique and deconstruction are necessary elements of comparative social research.

Measuring the workforce: conceptual and definitional problems

Part of critical and feminist social research is about understanding how statistics are (mis)used and identifying how they mitigate against the interests of particular groups. If statistical collation is inherently bound up with the social classification and rank-ordering of the universe, the question arises of who is imposing the order and to what effect? This section examines data on the labour force as a concrete example of the ways in which social indicators commonly provided by international institutions construct the world in a particular light, informing the representation of policy problems and the policy solutions. The final section of this chapter will explore, briefly, the development of standardized data collection systems, and consider the contribution of harmonized data to cross-national social policy research.

Governments aim regularly to collect information on the size and composition of the labour force to monitor changes and trends and to inform the direction and context of policy. One method is the use of 'labour force surveys', which are 'designed to obtain information on employment and related issues' (CEC 1990). These data are obtained through personal interviews with members of a sample of households undertaken once every second year. Labour force surveys are thus distinct from censuses of the population, which collect information once every ten years about the entire population, not only about employment but also about a broader range of issues (for example household structure, housing, transport and education). Due to the fact that labour force surveys are designed to collate data specifically on labour force and employment issues, and that they are produced more frequently and at a lower cost than censuses, they are regarded as a more useful tool for the purpose of monitoring changes in the labour force.

Labour force surveys are undertaken by both national and EU (Eurostat) statistical institutions. The EU survey, known as the European Community Labour Force Survey (ELFS), aims to produce comparable information on a range of indicators for all member states. These data are collated by compiling the results of the 12 (at the last survey) member states' labour force surveys, which contain 50 variables specifically developed for the ELFS, to produce an EU-wide database. In other words, the EU survey is more the sum of the national surveys rather than a survey undertaken in addition to or alongside national surveys. While this approach avoids duplication, it is not evident that the codification of the features of a country's labour force produced by national statistical institutions will be the same as that which is used by Eurostat. This is despite the fact that both use the same survey collected from the same households, and a 'harmonization' process is carried out via a working party consisting of representatives of member states who attempt to agree the questions, the definitions of key concepts and common coding practices. This emphasizes the general point that social researchers need to be vigilant when using and interpreting survey results for two quite different conclusions can be drawn. However, it also draws our attention to the 'non-symmetry' of national studies and EU studies of national systems!

There are three main reasons why national surveys differ from the EU surveys' results. First, Eurostat's results include persons who are residents of 'private' households, and exclude those who live in 'non-private' households (for example hostels, hotels, hospitals) and homeless people. In national surveys, persons in non-private households make up 2–3 per cent of the population. Second, age limits may differ between national and EU surveys. Thus, until 1991 Eurostat's labour force survey included 14 year olds as this is the school leaving age in some member states, while national surveys will take the school leaving age in their own jurisdiction (15 in Ireland, 16 in the UK). Third, and most significantly, perhaps, is that Eurostat and national statistical institutions adopt different concepts of economic activity – the *ILO definition* and *principal economic status* (PES), respectively. While these concepts overlap on many respects, they diverge on others, notably the measurement of economic activity.

These differences in measurement can lead to divergences in official measures of the labour force. In the case of Ireland, an additional 36,000 women and 17,000 men are defined as economically active using the ILO definition compared with the PES method (Table 2.3).

Some of this difference between PES and ILO measures of economic

Table 2.3 Economically active men and women in Ireland: PES and ILO measures (thousands)

	PES	ILO
Men	935.0	918.2
Women	540.2	576.2
Total	1475.2	1494.4

Source: Labour Force Survey 1996 (Central Statistics Office 1997)

activity for women can be explained by women's description of their 'usual situation with regard to employment' as being on 'home duties'. This category comprises large proportions of women who are not currently in employment and who are ready to take up work, but who have not registered as unemployed, do not describe themselves as such, and are not actively seeking employment. These women comprise the 'hidden' labour reserve. They are mainly married women who work occasionally, on a part-time, short-term or casual basis, doing seasonal work on a day-to-day basis when the opportunity presents itself. While they do not appear as economically active using the PES measure, they are classed as economically active using the ILO measure if they have undertaken even one hour's work in the week prior to the survey.

This example highlights the point that official statistics are gendered in that they do not adequately capture types of work undertaken on an informal or irregular basis and therefore distort women's relationship to the labour market and to employment. The problem is both an economic and a political one. Thus, for example, if women who described themselves as being on 'home duties' registered as unemployed, women's unemployment would swell by over half a million and would raise women's unemployment rate from about 9 per cent to 56 per cent (1996 figures).

Harmonized data: help or hindrance?

The EU is said to offer a unique opportunity to create and develop systems of equivalence through harmonized data. The European Community Labour Force Survey discussed above is an example of this. In addition, the Statistical Office of the European Union (Eurostat) in Luxembourg is developing and operating a standardized system of data collection, notably in the field of poverty. Other harmonized data include the European Community Household Panel Survey (ECHP). This survey is based on a sample of some 60,000 households in EU countries and covers the circumstances of the same people over several consecutive years. It covers a wide range of social topics using a harmonized questionnaire. A recent report published by Eurostat on poverty and income distribution in the EU (not including Sweden and Finland) drew on the second wave of the ECHP and showed that the 'poorest' 10 per cent of the population received only 2.6 per cent of total income while the top 10 per cent enjoyed a quarter (24.0 per cent), with the largest inequality in income distribution in Portugal, and the greatest equality in Denmark and the Netherlands (Eurostat 1998).

An alternative source of data is the Luxembourg Income Study (LIS). The project began in 1983 and its main objective has been to create a database containing social and economic data collected in household income and expenditure surveys from different countries and to create a resource for analysing income distribution cross-nationally. It contains information for around 25 OECD countries. However, even with harmonized data the quality of the statistics depends on the quality of national data collation systems and on the cooperation of national statistical institutions with international statistical bodies. As Atkinson *et al.* (1995: 25) recognized, 'the value of this study [LIS] depends crucially on the quality of the underlying survey data'. Data collected may not be entirely comparable for a number of reasons: the use of different kinds of sources for obtaining data and the differential valuations of statistical aggregates (for example national income, wages, salaries, industrial output) (United Nations 1994), or because of problems of measuring self-employment income, property income and some social assistance benefits across national boundaries (Atkinson *et al.* 1995: 25). Although attempts are made to standardize data before collection, this is not always possible, reducing comparability. Thus, the LIS survey authors (Atkinson *et al.* 1995) conclude that, while every effort was made to improve comparability of income distribution estimates, they emphasize three points, which are worth citing in full:

1 Full comparability is impossible and differences will always remain between data for different countries or in the interpretation of data in the social and economic contexts of different countries [p. 38] . . . Comparability is a matter of degree; achieving an acceptably high level is the only reasonable goal [p. 26];

2 Adopting a common set of definitions means that estimates for any one country may be less satisfactory if that country were isolated, since in a comparative study one is compelled to use the most common practice rather than the optimum in each case; and

3 Standardising on a common approach does not necessarily imply comparability: the same definitions may be applied in two countries but with different consequences (e.g. the choice of equivalence scale may affect the relative extent of low incomes in two countries, because one has a higher proportion of large households) [p. 38].

(Atkinson *et al.* 1995)

Mabbett and Bolderson (1999) provide a detailed discussion on the LIS and suggest that the database has not made as great a contribution to policy analysis as originally expected. While the database has been utilized in a number of studies (Mitchell 1991; Castles and Mitchell 1992; Bradshaw *et al.* 1993) its emphasis and narrow focus on 'cash-income' has limited its usefulness because of the lack of detailed policy and background information, vital for carrying out cross-national analysis.

While there can be little doubt that the amount and quality of standardized data have improved dramatically, according to Glover (1996) the harmonization of data can never be more than partially successful. For Glover the process tends to blur the distinction between each country and render invisible the details behind each national classification, and the differences between social institutions and social policies from one country to another. Desrosieres (1996: 18) identifies two conflicting dimensions that are apparent in comparisons of modern statistical systems and asserts that the 'universalisation of techniques has to be set against the specificity of national traditions'. He sees an inherent contradiction faced by statistical agencies in having to combine two distinct forms of social legitimacy: science, which is universal, and the state, which differs from one country to another. Desrosieres (1996) argues that the history and current status of comparisons of national statistical systems can be interpreted as the outcome of tensions between these two opposing poles and the distinctive ways in which individual countries have managed the relationship between them. As Glover (1996: 35) argues, 'Harmonised data will always be at the level of the lowest common denominator, providing less rather than more detail, distilling information rather than amplifying it'.

Conclusion

Social policy, social welfare or social security cannot be regarded as carrying any universal connotation; different terms, with underlying conceptual and administrative differences, prevail in different countries. It is vital then to regard any international data as a first source of data, to be carefully and critically interpreted and qualified by more in-depth statistical and empirical work. Because social institutions and social policies differ so much from one country to another, researchers need to be as knowledgeable as possible about the construction and the history of national classifications. While harmonized data overcomes some of the difficulties of using juxtaposed national data sets, there is the danger that this depth is taken away through the harmonization process. National data sets are produced within particular epistemological and institutional contexts which vary from country to country. In other words, data collection is embedded within social processes and, as discussed in Chapter 3, theoretical assumptions about the way the world works. In some ways it is the understanding of these processes and frameworks which is the essence of cross-national social policy analysis.

Further reading

Clasen, J. (ed.) (1999) *Comparative Social Policy: Concepts, Theories and Methods*. Oxford: Blackwell. This book begins by considering some broader themes relevant to cross-national research. These include trends and developments in welfare states, and theories and methods in comparative social policy. The book then adopts a comparative focus on substantive themes and areas of policy. The chapters range from housing health and social assistance to lone motherhood and migrants' access to social security benefits in the EU.

Hantrais, L. and Mangen, S. (eds) (1996) *Cross-National Research Methods in the Social Sciences*. London: Pinter. This collection focuses on the process of cross-national comparative research. The book is organized into four themes: quantitative methods, qualitative methods, approaches adopted for accessing comparable information; and the evaluation of cross-national analysis. Each section covers similar themes including labour markets, ageing and family policy, social exclusion and social security, all in the context of the EU.

Hill, M. (1996) *Social Policy: A Comparative Analysis*. London: Prentice Hall. This book is concerned with issues and concepts in cross-national social policy analysis as well as explanations for the development of particular patterns of policy in different countries. The book has a chapter-by-chapter overview of a range of policy areas including social care, health, education, housing, employment and environmental policy. Examples are drawn from a wide range of developed countries.

Theory and analysis in cross-national social policy research

Introduction

Theory gives direction and meaning to just about everything we do, whether we are aware of it or not. Theories are generalizations about what exists in the world around us and how the different components fit together. Combined with robust and appropriate concepts they help us to produce ordered, systematic observations of social phenomena. As Stoker (1995) puts it, social theory

> helps us to see the wood for the trees. Good theories select out certain factors as the most important or relevant if one is interested in providing an explanation of an event. Without such a sifting process no effective observation can take place. The observer would be buried under a pile of detail and be unable to weigh the influence of different factors in explaining an event. Theories are of value precisely because they structure all observations.
>
> (Stoker 1995: 16–17)

Different theories highlight different aspects of social reality. Each brings into view different dimensions of the effects and consequences of particular events and policies. Early work on the growth of welfare states, for example, emphasized the growing convergence in social policy development among all the nations of the older industrialized world. This approach was compatible with what Kerr referred to as the 'logic of industrialism' (Kerr *et al.* 1964). Social policy was seen as a natural outcome of a 'modern' or 'developed' society with the level of expenditure indicating the extent of welfare development. More recently there has been a greater interest in cultural and institutional differences, and the gradual inclusion of qualitative evidence which has called into question the correlation between social expenditure, patterns of welfare and convergence. There has been a recognition of diversity, a greater interest in the context, the processes and the outcomes of social policies in different countries (Esping-Andersen 1990) and their impact on different groups (Ginsberg 1992; Sainsbury 1994).

This chapter will explore some of the more influential perspectives which have sought to explain the dynamics of the development of social welfare and which have provided the analytical frameworks and conceptual tools through which social phenomena have been articulated and understood. Each perspective begins its analysis from a particular assumption that determines the kind of question that they ask, how they ask it and the answers they find. These different perspectives demonstrate how there is no one social reality. Interpretations of social phenomena are formed through specific epistomological and philosophical constructions and traditions which vary over time and space.

Industrialization and modernization

Explanations for the development of welfare states and growth of policies are varied and have traditionally drawn heavily on sociological and political thinking. Central to much of the earlier work on interpreting welfare state effort was the impact of industrialization and modernization and the normative assumption that the welfare state is a force for good, a symbol of progress. The coming of the welfare state was seen to be a product of the 'logic of industrialism'. Industrialization brought about rapid urbanization, the dislocation of the extended family and increasing social problems such as poverty and disease. As family and kinship networks were broken down the institutions of the welfare state, with the increased resources generated by industrialization, took on many of the functions formerly filled by family units.

For structural functionalists, such as the classical Durkheim (1964) to the more modern functionalists, such as Parsons (1964) and Smelser (1964), the welfare state is understood as a response to structural changes, as the division of labour weakens old associations and increases the opportunities for industrialization. This individualization and differentiation involves a loosening of ascriptive bonds. The centralization of social life can be seen as a response to the need to regulate the new exchange processes, as public bureaucracies take over many of the functions formerly filled by smaller social units. For Durkheim, the contemporary welfare state represents a partial answer to the anomie and alienation experienced by individuals following industrialization, with the institutions of welfare performing a broadly problem-solving and integrative function. As Pierson (1991: 14) explains, 'the origins of the welfare state were seen to lie in secular changes associated with the broad processes of industrialisation' such as economic growth, the creation of a landless working class, the division of labour, the rise of cyclical employment and the increasing need to reproduce a reliable, healthy and literate workforce (Pierson 1991). Thus, the massive changes in the social and industrial character of capitalist societies in the nineteenth century transformed the context for state action, generating new and pressing demands for state involvement.

The modernization approach has been characterized as a 'politicized' version (Pierson 1991) of the industrialization thesis. Like the industrialization thesis it is shaped by a progressive-evolutionary logic which suggests that all traditional societies are moving towards a desirable modern type. However, unlike the industrialization thesis it emphasizes the role of mass democracy as well as economic growth in the development of the welfare state. The modern world, of which the welfare state is part, is associated with two revolutionary changes, the industrial revolution and the political revolution with the widespread introduction of the franchise. As Flora and Heidenheimer (1981) argue, the welfare state is

> a general phenomenon of modernization . . . a product of the increasing differentiation and the growing size of societies on the one hand and of processes of social and political mobilization on the other . . . the historical constellation in which the European welfare state emerged [was one of] growing mass democracies and expanding capitalist economies within a system of sovereign nation states.
>
> (Flora and Heidenheimer 1981: 8, 23, 22)

So the coming of the welfare state is one aspect of a more widespread process of modernization (progress). It is associated historically with the extension of political citizenship and particularly the rapid expansion of suffrage and the consequent development of mass political parties at the turn of the century. The analysis is further developed along Weberian lines and argues that with the development of the welfare state a new system of domination is established consisting of 'distributing elites', 'service bureaucracies' and 'social clientele'.

These approaches can be linked to the merging of a dominant theoretical perspective of the day with the development of a new economic instrument, the calculation of GNP and GDP (see Box 3.1). Modernization was captured in the evolutionary perspective of Rostow (1960) in his *Stages of Economic Growth*. According to Rostow:

> It is possible to identify all societies, in their economic dimension, as lying within one of five categories: the traditional society, the preconditions for take-off, the take-off, the drive to maturity, and the age of high mass consumption.
>
> (Rostow 1960: 5)

The key to development through these various stages was increased production which in turn, it was argued, would lead to increased well-being. A measure of the average material living standard of a nation's people was to be calculated on the basis of the GNP per capita. The economic context in most developed countries following the Second World War was one of boom and growth, full employment and low inflation. The economic success of OECD countries during the post-war years gave credence to maintaining and perpetuating the modernization perspective and GNP/GDP as a measure of a nation's well-being.

The emphasis on the impact of economic development as an indicator of welfare state effort was clearly articulated in the work of a number of commentators in the 1960s and 1970s (Cutright 1965; Rimlinger 1971; Wilensky 1975; Hage and Hannemann 1977). These studies relied heavily on the analysis of social security spending as a fraction of GNP or GDP as a measure of social welfare effort. Wilensky (1975) attempted to develop a causal model to explain the relationship between economic level, the age of a welfare system, and spending. He compared social security spending as a proportion of GNP in 64 states for 1966. He showed that welfare effort (social security/GNP) varies by economic level. However, he did concede that this relationship is, to some extent, mediated by demographic and bureaucratic outcomes. In other words, the proportion of elderly people in the population and the age of the system influence welfare state development. According to Wilensky (1975):

Over the long pull, economic level is the root cause of welfare state development, but its effects are felt chiefly through demographic changes of the past century and the momentum of the programmes themselves, once established. With modernization, birth rates declined and the proportion of aged was thereby increased. This increased importance of the aged, coupled with the declining economic values of children, in turn exerted pressure for welfare spending. Once the programmes were established they matured, everywhere moving toward

---

Box 3.1: Definition of gross domestic product (GDP) and gross national product (GNP)

Gross domestic product (GDP) measures the size of the economy. It is an output measure of goods and services produced for final use by an economy.

Gross national product (GNP) comprises the total domestic and foreign output claimed by residents of a country in one year. Thus, GNP is a measure of national income, and GNP per capita is a measure of the average income of each member of the population, including what they may earn or receive from abroad.

convergence and higher benefits. Social security begins as a natural accompaniment of economic growth and its demographic outcome; it is hastened by the interplay of political elite perceptions, mass pressures, and welfare bureaucracies.

(Wilensky 1975: 47)

His overall conclusion was that economic level, that is GNP per head of population, overwhelms regime type as a predictor of social security effort over the long term. In other words, for Wilensky (1975), it is factors such as different levels of economic development, mediated by demographics and bureaucratic factors, which are crucial in explaining differences in social security spending, rather than particular welfare ideologies or the political profile (totalitarianism, authoritarianism or liberal democracy) of a country. Industrial and economic (and to a lesser extent demographic and organizational) pressures dictate which provisions will be available and push welfare provision in both capitalist and socialist countries in a similar direction. Despite their different starting points, both systems will move towards each other and eventually complete their development with a mixture of private market provisions and state supported services. Thus this approach incorporates two key notions, first, that the welfare state was a desirable and indispensable part of the structure of industrial societies, and second, that economic growth (industrialization) was *the* key to the development of welfare. Wilensky (1975) (along with Cutright 1965; Pryor 1968 to name but a few) adopts a structural functionalist view and supports the thesis of convergence, which suggests that particular stages of economic growth and industrialization encourage convergent welfare state forms despite differences in political ideology.

Concern regarding the limitations of this approach focused primarily on its emphasis on broad aggregate data analysis used in many of the studies mentioned above. It was increasingly recognized that this emphasis might actually obscure diversity in that broad sectoral headings such as 'Health' or 'Education' conceal important variations such as conditions of eligibility, benefit levels, duration of benefits, for example (Dierkes *et al.* 1987). Alber's (1981) study adopted a similar approach to Wilensky but focused on the sub-aggregate unemployment insurance programmes of 13 Western European democracies. Alber's investigation showed that the post-war period was characterized by a general pattern of social expenditure growth throughout Western European democracies. Not only did social spending consistently increase its share in GDP, but also the pace of this accelerated over time.

Alber (1981) identified average expenditure for 1949 at 9 per cent of GDP. During the 1950s all countries increased their shares of social spending in GDP, but modestly – the mean Western European ratio was around 11 per cent. During the 1960s the speed of growth doubled with the average social expenditure ratio rising by 4.4 per cent. By the 1970s social outlays averaged 15.8 per cent of GDP and increased to 22.4 per cent of GDP by 1977. After 1975 the pace began to slow, but Alber (1981) nevertheless felt that there were sufficient data to characterize a *general* pattern of social expenditure growth throughout the Western European democracies. However, he was keen to emphasize that though there were common tendencies they were accompanied by important national variations. He claims that Western European welfare states did not become more similar during the phase of general expansion and there was no trend towards convergence. On the contrary, the trend was towards decreasing homogeneity, as shown in Table 3.1.

The increasing homogeneity of social expenditure levels was accompanied by distinct patterns of welfare state development which significantly changed the ranking of high and low spending countries over time (see Table 3.1). By 1977 the rank occupied by each country bore little resemblance to its relative postion in 1950, leading Alber (1981) to conclude that there was no evidence of a 'catch-up' phenomenon, a central tenet of modernization theory or any indication of a convergence in welfare regimes.

Politics, ideology and the welfare state

The emphasis on ideology, power relations and political forces as elements central to understanding the growth and the social relations of the welfare state across nations emerges in a number of perspectives. For Flora and Heidenheimer (1981), it was the rise of mass democracy in Europe that favoured the development of welfare states because political elites had to confront a more organized working class and compete for votes. For Castles (1982, 1998; see also Esping-Andersen and Korpi 1984), however, it is not just the rise of mass democracy but the character of institutional frameworks through which political demands and interests are expressed which influences the development of the welfare state. According to Castles (1998)

Table 3.1 Social security expenditure in Western Europe 1950–77*

	AU	*BE*	*DE*	*FI*	*FR*	*GE*	*IR*	*IT*	*NE*	*NO*	*SW*	*SZ*	*UK*
1950	3	2	7	11	4	1	9	6	10	13	8	12	5
1960	3	1	6.5	12	4	2	10	5	6.5	11	8.5	13	8.5
1970	3	4	6	11	9	5	12	7	1	8	2	13	10
1977	8	4	5	10	3	6	12	7	2	9	1	13	11

Note: Rank-order of social expenditure ratios in 1950, 1960, 1970 and 1977
Source: Alber 1983: 161

the notion that ideologies and institutions may have a major influence on policy outcomes challenges modernization thinking fundamentally by implying that the modern expansion of the role of the state may owe much to factors other than socio-economic transformation.

(Castles 1998: 65)

The growth of the welfare state can be seen as the by-product of the changing power relations in western countries where labour unions and left parties have increasingly gained influence in the policy-making arena. Castles (1982) argues that high levels of welfare effort can be associated with the dominance of left-wing political parties, and low levels of welfare-state effort can be associated with party systems that include a dominant and cohesive right-wing party. Castles (1998: 27) concedes that 'in order to make sense of post war policy development, it is vital to understand changes across all the dimensions; economic and social as well as ideological and institutional'. He nevertheless feels that it is political institutions and political ideologies which are key factors in shaping policy outcomes.

Explanations for the development of welfare policies and the welfare state from a Marxist perspective developed during the 1970s as a critique of how capitalism as an economic system functions and the role of the welfare state in the reproduction of capitalist social relations. As George and Wilding (1994) explain, central to Marxist analysis is the idea that the capitalist mode of production is both exploitative and conflict ridden. It is exploitative because the means of production are owned by a small minority, the bourgeoisie, who try to maximize for themselves the profit generated by the production system. It is conflict ridden because the workforce attempts to improve its wages and working conditions. Class conflict and exploitation are thus the inevitable result of the private ownership of the means of production which is the essential feature of a capitalist economic system.

For many Marxists the term 'welfare capitalism' is preferable to the term 'welfare state' (for example Ginsberg 1979; Gough 1979). The term 'welfare state' presents an image of the caring face of capitalism, and thus distorts the real function of the welfare state (George and Wilding 1994). The welfare state is not about egalitarianism or redistribution, but is a form of capitalism. As Ginsberg (1979: 2) argues 'it remains part of the capitalist state which is fundamentally concerned with the maintenance and reproduction of capitalist social relations'. In order to facilitate the maximization of production and private profit the capitalist system is in constant need of 'support, regulation and protection' if it is to survive and thrive (George and Wilding 1994: 104). And in relation to social policy and social welfare Miliband (1977: 91) argues that:

The intervention of the state is always and necessarily partisan: as a class state it always intervenes for the purpose of maintaining the existing system of domination even where it intervenes to mitigate the harshness of that system of domination.

Miliband (1969: 109–10) also describes the extension of the social services at the end of the Second World War as 'part of the "ransom" the working class has been able to extract from their rulers in the course of a hundred years'.

Traditional Marxist explanations stressed the idea of 'the needs of capital' when analysing the nature of the state and state intervention. While this theme has remained important in later work, the analysis has been extended to incorporate 'class struggle'. This dual approach was exemplified in the work of Gough for whom there are

> two factors of importance in explaining the growth of the welfare state. The degree of class conflict and, *especially*, the strength and form of working class struggle, and the ability of the capitalist state to formulate and implement policies to secure the long-term reproduction of capitalist social relations.
>
> (Gough 1979: 64)

As George and Wilding (1994) argue this class conflict model of the growth of welfare is action based, in that it involves actors in the development of the welfare state and does not see welfare as an automatic response to the needs of capital or as performing specific functions purely to satisfy the needs of capital. Neo-Marxists view the welfare state as a contradictory formation. Gough (1979: 11) asks if the welfare state is an 'agency of repression, or a system for enlarging human needs and mitigating the rigours of the free market economy? Aid to capital accumulation and profits or a "social wage" to be defended? Capitalist fraud or working class victory?'. In the British context Ginsberg (1979) explored these themes in his analysis of two areas of social policy housing and social security. He argued that housing policy is directed towards regulating the consumption of a vital commodity for the reproduction of the labour force – and only secondarily as an attempt at providing secure and adequate accommodation for the working class. In a similar vein he states that the social security system is concerned with reproducing a reserve army of labour, the patriarchal family and the disciplining of the labour force. Only secondarily does it function as a means of mitigating poverty or providing 'income maintenance'. Levels of social security benefit may act to keep down the price of labour (wages) by establishing an official subsistence minimum which is well below the existing value of labour power (in other words below the standard of living achieved by the working class at a particular point in history). It also maintains work incentive and commodifies the individual through pressure to sell labour power. (The notion of commodification and decommodification has more recently been utilized by Esping-Andersen (1990) in his comparative work on welfare regimes, discussed later in this chapter.) The social security system also acts as a form of discipline and restraint by imposing stringent conditions on access to benefits that are not directly related to need.

According to Ginsberg (1979), one of the predominant concerns of the social security system throughout history has been in relation to women. He argues that 'the social security system not only reflects but strengthens the subordinate position of women' (Ginsberg 1979: 79). Social security policy has sustained the position of women, particularly married women, as low-paid, casual wageworkers, and as a unique stratum of the reserve army of labour. This has been encouraged through the lack of support in maternity provision, and the inappropriate nature of the contribution principle of social security, in that it does not accommodate for women's intermittent employment history. The social security system has sought to perpetuate the dependence of women on men and to discourage the break-up of marriage by rendering single motherhood distinctly less eligible and attractive. He argues that 'the great majority of women have been excluded from any *independent* rights of citizenship to social security simply because they have married and have been assumed to be dependent on their husbands' income' (Ginsberg 1979: 80). Ginsberg (1979) argues that patriarchal social relations have been shaped and adapted to the requirements of advanced capitalism, and the patriarchal family remains one of its bedrock institutions. The patriarchal family is of fundamental economic, political and ideological importance to the capitalist mode of production. More recent work by Ginsberg (1992) (discussed briefly in Chapter 2) has extended this critical approach to include ethnicity, a greater range of policy areas, and a number of different countries.

Neo-Marxist's analysis of the dysfunctions as well as the functions of large-scale state intervention to capital accumulation have been most influentially articulated in O'Connor's (1973) work *The Fiscal Crisis of the State*. There are two main strands to his work. O'Connor's first point is that 'the capitalist state must try to fulfil two basic and often contradictory functions – *accumulation and legitimation*' (O'Connor 1973: 6). Not only must the state provide services which improve the profitability of private capital, it must also strengthen the acceptability of and support for the capitalist system. As George and Wilding (1994) explain the state is unable to ignore either of these functions.

> If it neglects its accumulation function then profitability and economic growth suffer; if it ignores its legitimation function then it will ultimately have to resort to coercive measures and this will undermine its public image and its legitimacy.
>
> (George and Wilding 1994: 115)

O'Connor's second point relates to the fiscal crisis of the state. For O'Connor (1993) state expenditure has had a twofold function, that of accummulation and legitimation. State revenue is divided between social capital (which is expenditure required for profitable private 'accumulation' such as state-financed industrial parks and services which lower the reproduction costs of labour) and social expenses (which is expenditure to maintain social harmony and fulfil the state's 'legitimation' function such as the welfare state). O'Connor (1993) argues that it is these dual functions which inevitably lead to crisis. The growth of state expenditure is indispensable to the expansion of private industry. Thus, the result is the steady growth of social capital over time. The state must also seek to maintain its legitimacy by meeting the demands of those who suffer the 'costs' of economic growth. This requires a larger volume of social expenses. Thus, the greater the growth of social capital, the greater the growth of the private and productive sector – which in turn leads to greater state expenditure on the social expenses of production.

For O'Connor (1993) the growth of the state sector is indispensable to the expansion of private industry. However, though the state has socialized or appropriated more and more of capital's costs – the profits of capital are appropriated privately. This creates a gap between the socialization of costs and the private appropriation of profits – between state expenditure and state revenues. The result is a tendency for state expenditure to increase more rapidly than the means of financing them. More and more is financed through tax revenues, with a greater reluctance on the part of the public to pay new taxes or higher rates of tax. The fiscal crisis occurs as a result of, on the one hand, public demand for more and better government services, and on the other, the unwillingness of the public to pay the necessary taxes. Reference to the 'fiscal crisis' of the welfare state has become commonplace in social policy literature, and has been extremely influential in political and ideological debates regarding the role of the state in the provision of welfare.

More recent analysis from a neo-Marxist perspective has emerged in the work of the regulation school (Aglietta 1979; Lipietz 1984a, 1985; Boyer 1986), which originated in France in the 1970s. Regulation theory has subsequently developed both internationally and across disciplines (Lipietz 1985, 1986; Jessop 1989; Overbeek 1990). While it is now inappropriate to refer to one unified 'regulation theory', it is still the case that through the various strands of the approach the substantive concerns remain those derived from general Marxist traditions of 'historical materialism, interest in the political economy of capitalism and the anatomy of bourgeois society' (Jessop 1990: 154). The original emphasis of regulation theory was to theorize economic change and to challenge orthodox economic theory based on general equilibrium and growth. It also sought to overcome criticisms that the approach was functionalist and overemphasized the role of the economy, as well as reject the notion proposed by Adam Smith of the 'invisible hand' of the market. It is an approach which seeks to avoid the criticism of 'techno-economic determinism' (Elam 1990: 23) by 'breaking down the compartmentalization of economics and politics and linking them in a dynamic integrated framework' (Elam 1990: 23). For Lipietz (1987) the work of regulationists, at a general level, can be understood as a triple effort: to show that capitalist reproduction 'doesn't run by itself'; to show why, for vast periods of time, it is pursued 'however' (despite the conflictual nature of capitalist social relations); to show why, at the end of a certain time, a crisis erupts.

The starting point for regulation theorists is that the organization of late twentieth century capital has experienced a period of transition. The theory provides a framework for understanding the complex processes underway. Within regulation theory each capitalist development of society can be associated with different regimes of accumulation representing a particular pattern of production and consumption, and a corresponding mode of social and political regulation. The concept of Fordism has been used by regulation theorists to describe the development of the post-war political economy which in most western industrial economies linked mass production and mass consumption through an 'ensemble of productive, institutional, social and political relations and practices that, in combination, regulate the accumulation process' (Schoenberger 1989: 101). The *regime of accumulation* is concerned with the macro-economic structure and fulfilling the basic requirements of expanded reproduction. Yet production is interdependent with the activities of distribution, exchange and consumption and is shaped by a set of broader institutional and organizational arrangements of society, including the welfare state, referred to by regulation theorists as the mode of regulation. The *mode of regulation* forms the

> totality of institutional forms, networks and norms (explicit or implicit) which together secure the compatibility of typical modes of conduct in the context of an accumulation regime, corresponding as much to the changing balance of social relations and to their more conflictual properties.
>
> (Lipietz 1985: 121, cited in Jessop 1989: 262)

For Jessop (1990) it also refers to the pattern of integration and social cohesion in a society. The stabilization of a regime of accumulation with a mode of regulation ensures a successful period of capitalist development. Just as there is nothing inherent within capitalism to create this necessary correspondence so there is no linear logic as to the form of the particular configuration within a specific phase of capitalist development. Nor does the particular model of regulation simply fulfil a functional role in facilitating the stabilization and perpetuation of a particular accumulation regime. It is conflict between classes and political groups, the strategies of organized social movements, and political processes unfolding within the state which influences the emergence of a specific type of regulation. Which one succeeds depends on the economic success of different models and on the influence of coalitions and the actions of the state. As Peck and Tickell (1991: 22) assert, it is precisely 'because the mode of social regulation is not determined functionally by the accumulation system this search for a regulatory "fix" is one susceptible to political processes and struggles'. 'New' configurations are, to some extent, shaped by the needs of capital, but other groups in society and their struggles also shape state policy. Florida and Jonas (1991: 352) state that 'central to the process of institution building are mutually reinforcing patterns of adjustment between the economy, society and the state'. The relevance of this argument becomes particularly apparent when analysing different countries, where each not only has its own particular mode of growth (Lash and Bagguley 1988) emerging from its specific political and industrial profile, but also its own mode of insertion into the international economic system (Jessop 1989). Jessop (1989) highlights developments in Britain and the former West Germany to show that the nature of Fordism in both societies was very different, while Lipietz (1984b) has focused on the global political economy and, in particular, developing countries.

The regulationist approach has been criticized by a number of commentators (Pollert 1988; Sayer 1989; Williams 1989; Brenner and Glick 1991). However, what is important, according to Jessop (1988), is whether the research agenda suggested by regulation theory offers an opportunity for theoretical and political advancement (see also Harvey 1989). Although the language of regulation theory is complex, it is argued that the research agenda offered by the approach

> provides a clear commitment to concrete analysis of concrete conjunctures through a rich and complex range of economic and political concepts directly related to the nature of capitalism exploitation and domination.
>
> (Jessop 1988: 162)

Thus it is regulation theory's conceptual framework and empirically verifiable focus on the relationship between various elements of a particular mode of development and on the causal processes which generate the stabilization from these relationships which are seen to be the perspective's strengths and innovations.

Shift in theory and analysis

The contested theme of transition has permeated academic debates in recent years. In different ways the notions of transition and transformation have been central not only to regulation theory (mentioned above) but also to the increasingly influential perspective of **postmodernism**. These approaches are mostly presented as dualistic opposites, the former generally associated with a political economy approach, the latter emerging from the poststructuralism of the 1960s and 1970s. However, a diverse range of meanings have been applied to postmodernism and postmodernity, terms which according to Carter (1998: 20) have 'become both contested and congested and now conflate a wide range of insights and arguments'. A fundamental distinction has been made by Williams, between postmodernity 'as a condition' on the one hand, and 'as a particular shift in theory and analysis' on the other (Williams 1992: 204–5). Both aspects are relevant to social policy analysis.

The first of these distinctions – postmodernity as a 'condition' – is generally associated with a political economy approach and is articulated through the frameworks of post-Fordism and postindustrialism (discussed in more detail in Chapter 1), for example. The emphasis is on the economic, political, social and cultural shifts which have occurred across societies. The changing context of social policy is explored focusing on transformations in the global economy, the structure of employment, combined with the reorientation of the welfare state. The certainties of the past are said to have 'melted into air' – nation, class, workplace, community and family. An era characterized by risk, insecurity and uncertainty for the majority of the population, not just the poor, has emerged. Increasingly, the social relations of everyday life have come to be associated with complexity and uncertainty, independence and individualism (Beck 1992; Giddens 1992). This approach is exemplified in the work of Harvey (1989) and Jameson (1984) for whom postmodernism represents the cultural logic of the third great stage of capitalism.

The interpretations of postmodernism mentioned above, according to Gibbins (1998), have their foundations in structuralism rather than poststructuralism. In other words 'postmodernism is understood as the cultural and ideological (including academic) epiphenomenon of late capitalist modifications' (Gibbins 1998: 38). In contrast, interpretations of postmodernism as 'a paradigm shift' – the second distinction referred to by Williams above – are usually embedded within the work of poststructuralists such as Derrida (1970), Lyotard (1979) and Foucault (1980). The emergence of postmodernism and poststructuralism during the 1970s and 1980s brought about a fundamental reappraisal of the assumptions embedded in social science research. This approach challenges the rationality, essentialism and universalism of policy discourses and practices through which the welfare state was established and has been maintained. Postmodernism encourages the examination of knowledge through the 'deconstruction' (Derrida 1970) of the universalizing dialogue, reasoning and 'truths' emerging from the Enlightenment. For Foucault (1972) it is language or narratives that construct the social world. He utilizes the notion of a 'discursive regime' in which processes, procedures and apparatus construct truth, knowledge and belief within a power/knowledge nexus. Discursive regimes incorporate some form of social constraint which varies in content over time and includes such phenomena as the valorization of some statement forms over others, and the devaluation of others, the institutional licensing of some persons as authorized to offer authoritative knowledge claims and the exclusion of others, and the proliferation of discourses oriented to objects of enquiry which become targets for the application of social policy. Thus, the discursive frame of social policy, which has been constructed through the narratives of professionals and experts and based on the rationale of meeting universal human need, is an indication of the power/knowledge/discourse of modernity. It is the experts and professionals who are responsible 'for a misplaced universalism incapable of meeting the diverse and different needs of people' (Deacon and Mann 1999: 419). It is a universalism which usually refers to the experiences of the white, able-bodied, heterosexual worker and which is unable to capture the 'particular' experiences and social needs of diverse ethnic, cultural, sexual and gender interests.

Postmodernism has called into question 'the adequacy and legitimacy of theoretical and analytical traditions in the social sciences' and has contributed to

> a rejection of the major tenants associated with Enlightenment theories and philosophical traditions; those which envisioned a universal subject (the working class, the rational actor), an essential human nature (species being, self interest), a global human destiny or collective social goal. It involves a rejection of Marxism, liberalism and scientific modes of thought in which human history is claimed to represent a unilinear development.
>
> (O'Brien and Penna 1998: 206, 105–6)

Postmodernists are particularly dismissive then, of the project of modernity, formulated in the eighteenth century by the philosophers of the Enlightenment and derived from their efforts to develop objective science and universal law. Particularly with the onset of the Industrial Revolution, modern societies were characterized by the efforts systematically to control and transform their physical environment. For Lyotard (1984), the use of the term 'modern' is

> to designate any science that legitimates itself with reference to a discourse . . . making an explicit appeal to some grand narrative, such as the dialectic of the spirit, the hermeneutics of meaning, the emancipation of the rational or working subject or the creation of wealth.
>
> (Lyotard 1984: xxiii)

He rejects the application of meta-narratives. Lyotard (1984: 37) argues that 'the grand-narrative has lost its credibility' and instead there has been an atomization of the social into small-scale, local narratives. The modernist ideas of technological progress and economic growth, so central to the development discourse considered in more detail in Chapter 4, and to explanations for the growth of the welfare state in Western Europe discussed earlier, have been rejected and replaced by a belief in the plurality of 'power-discourse' (Foucault 1984). Foucault argues that power is not something that is acquired or seized, but is something that circulates: 'power is everywhere, not because it embraces everything but because it comes from everywhere' (Foucault 1984: 93). Large-scale, comprehensive and integrated solutions have been devalued and instead there is an emphasis on 'micro-politics' and micro-relations, 'the point where power reaches into the very grain of the individuals' (Foucault 1984: 93).

The literature on postmodernism and poststructuralism is diverse and nuanced (see Penna and O'Brien 1996 for an overview). Some of the key concerns of postmodernists can be summarized as the deconstruction of knowledge, non-essentialism and anti-reductionism. The emphasis on diversity, difference and contingency and the notion of spatial and temporal variation challenge many of the assumptions on which the theoretical and epistemological traditions of social policy have been built. However, for some commentators it is these very challenges which should be treated with caution for, as Bauman (1992: ix) argues, 'Postmodernity . . . does not seek to substitute one truth for another . . . It braces itself for a life without truths, standards and ideals'. Taylor-Gooby (1994) is concerned that the influence of postmodernism on social policy

> may cloak developments of considerable importance. Trends towards increasing inequality in living standards, the privatisation of state welfare services, the strict regulation of the lives of some of the poorest groups may fail to attract the appropriate attention if the key themes of policy are seen as difference, diversity and choice.
>
> (Taylor-Gooby 1994: 403)

For postmodernists, however, the concept of difference has the potential to illuminate and emancipate. An individual's horizon of experiences is not fixed by a single collectivity or categorical framework (Calhoun 1995) thus rendering invalid attempts to find 'universally valid solutions to universally experienced problems' (Thompson and Hoggett 1996: 23). The influence of postmodernism and poststructuralism has been to encourage a greater appreciation of agency, a recognition of the diversity in the 'lived experiences' of individuals, and a reflexivity in policy and research. A resurgence of the phenomenological tradition in cross-national social research is apparent in an emerging literature which focuses on particularity, private lives and biography (Bertaux 1981, 1984; Chamberlayne *et al.* 2000). It is an approach which is concerned with the 'recognition of contingency, of the spaces within which individuals create meaning and devise strategies for their lives' (Rustin 2000: 47). But it is also concerned with historicity and the reciprocal synthesis which governs the interaction between an individual and a social system. As Gershuny (1998: 35) argues, 'People's actions are both constrained and enabled by social structures'. Individuals make choices but ultimately the choice is between opportunities offered within a structured context (Franklin 1989). And at any point in time social policy is part of this 'structured context', part of the constantly shifting structural milieux in which individuals pursue strategies and through which life-course trajectories are established.

Recognizing difference and diversity

In cross-national social policy research, the emphasis has moved from ranking countries according to their welfare effort to a recognition that there are different types of welfare states, that formal social policies are only one element in the arrangements of welfare, and that social policy is not just about ameliorating the impact of social inequality or about altruism. The welfare state itself contributes to social division. For example it perpetuates the reproduction of oppressive patriarchal and racialized social relations. The biographical method discussed earlier provides the opportunity to incorporate a qualitative, multilevel analysis into cross-national research. The work of Esping-Andersen (1990) has also proved to be a catalyst for a more differentiated and multicausal approach to cross-national research (see Abrahamson 1999 for a comprehensive review) at a meso, institutional level. With the demise of the centralized planned economies and the bureaucratic state collectivist system of welfare which characterized the former Soviet Union and other countries of Eastern Europe, the transition to market economies and democracy has provided Deacon *et al.* (1992) with the opportunity to utilize Esping-Andersen's model to explore the 'diverse ways in which the new governments of Eastern Europe and the former Soviet Union are approaching the development of a new social policy' (Deacon *et al.* 1992: 1). Goodin *et al.* (1999) draw upon socio-economic panel studies across three countries (the USA, Germany and the Netherlands) to investigate what 'life is *really like* for individuals and families' (Goodin *et al.* 1999: 7, original emphasis) across welfare regimes and over time. More fundamentally, Esping-Andersen's work has provoked substantial comment regarding the gendered and ethnocentric assumptions permeating definitions and theories in cross-national research. These contributions to cross-national social policy analysis will be explored later in this chapter. First, the key elements of Esping-Andersen's work will be outlined and the contributions and limitations of his approach considered.

In *The Three Worlds of Welfare Capitalism* Esping-Andersen (1990) developed the notion of welfare regimes which he applied to 18 OECD countries. He utilized the concept to grasp the diverse nature of the delivery of welfare provision, and the diverse nature of welfare institutions across countries. His approach provides an alternative to an emphasis on expenditure levels which he claims actually obscures an understanding of difference and cultural and institutional diversity. Instead, his analysis into the transformations and diversity of outcomes in the nature of the welfare state focuses on the notion of *welfare regimes*. He investigates the degree to which social rights permit people to exist independently of the labour market by eroding the commodity status of labour in capitalist society. He also interprets the welfare state as a system of social stratification in its own right and views the welfare state as 'an articulation of distributional conflicts' (Esping-Andersen 1985: 224).

For Esping-Andersen traditional analyses of the welfare state centring on, for example, levels of public expenditure are inadequate given that 'historical conflicts have centred around the institutional arrangements of social policy' (Esping-Andersen 1990: 224). It has been the demands of the working class which have influenced the shape of the welfare state as has the women's movement whose agenda has included attempts to alter the institutional arrangements and the social relations of the welfare state. Huge expenditure is not an indication of redistributive effects and, in addition, fails to indicate the basic institutional differences in how social policy is applied – 'measures such as spending easily obscure the presence of distinctly different welfare state regimes' (Esping-Andersen 1990: 225). For Esping-Andersen, then, the benefit of his approach is that is offers an alternative means of analysing the welfare state in its broadest sense.

This broader approach to conceptualizing the welfare state is evident in the earlier work of Titmuss (1968, 1974). Titmuss offered one of the first distinctions in welfare, differentiating between the residual welfare model, the industrial achievement-performance model and the institutional redistributive model (outlined in Box 3.2). Esping-Andersen (1990) develops this typology further by arguing that

> Contemporary advanced nations cluster not only in terms of how their traditional social welfare policies are constructed but also in terms of how these influence employment and general social structure. The talk of a 'regime' is to denote the fact that in the relation between state and economy a complex of legal and organizational features are systematically interwoven.
>
> (Esping-Andersen 1990: 2)

Thus Esping-Andersen does not just concentrate on formal social policies but links them to employment and to patterns of inequality thus embedding welfare in its social context. He measures the accessibility, coverage and redistributive impact of benefit systems, and develops performance indices for pensions, sickness and unemployment benefits on the basis of the balance between public and private pensions, the degree of universal access to benefits, and the extent of differential benefits for different social groups.

Box 3.2   Models of welfare

Residual welfare model

'based on the premise that there are two "natural" (or socially given) channels through which an individual's needs are properly met; the private market and the family. Only when these break down should social welfare institutions come into play and then only temporarily'.

Industrial achievement-performance model

'incorporates a significant role for social welfare institutions as adjuncts of the economy. It holds that social needs should be met on the basis of merit, work performance and productivity'.

Institutional redistributive model

'sees social welfare as a major integrated institution in society, providing universalist services outside the market on the principle of need'.

Sources: Titmuss 1968, 1974: 30–1

Esping-Andersen (1990) suggests that social rights entail a decommodification of the status of individuals in relation to the market and thus an erosion of the commodity status of labour in capitalist society. He refers to these processes of decommodification as 'the degree to which individuals, or families, can uphold a socially acceptable standard of living independently of market participation' (Esping-Andersen 1990: 37). Greater decommodification exists if living standards are guaranteed regardless of previous employment record, needs test or financial contribution. He constructs a rank-order scale of decommodification by which social security benefits exempt workers from offering their labour power as a commodity and identifies three distinct clusters. These correspond and are linked to Esping-Andersen's emphasis on classifying countries into three different regime types – conservative, liberal, or social democratic, which are explored below. Germany, the USA and Sweden are discussed as the concrete ideal types of his three worlds of welfare capitalism and, taking account of both economic development and political power, exhibit strong elements each of the particular regime.

Welfare state typologies

The *conservative regime*, incorporating nations such as Germany, Italy, Austria and France, reflects a strongly corporatist tradition, heavily influenced by the Church. The principle of subsidiarity serves to emphasize that the state will intervene only when the family's capacity to service its members is exhausted, thus echoing the doctrine of the Church and its strong commitment to the preservation of traditional familyhood in a regime type in which women are discouraged from working. The dominant feature of this regime is the state's emphasis on the preservation of status differentials, and consequently the insitutionalization of rights attached to class and status rather than citizenship. There is little commitment to redistribution as the maintanance of status differentials is paramount.

In Germany the old age pension, first introduced as a statutory social insurance scheme in 1889 under Bismarck, represents a substitute for wages, indexed to wage inflation with payments firmly based on contribution records and the contributor's former earnings. There is no universal, noncontributory statutory pension. The social security system has been characterized as a system which is 'status-maintaining' rather than 'opportunity creating'. The benefit system divides the registered unemployed into several groups of different status and, therefore, different income. *Arbeitslosengeld*, for the short-term unemployed with a full contribution record, is calculated as a percentage of the recipient's previous, net, take-home pay; it is the most generous benefit available for a limited period. *Arbeitslosenhilfe* is a means-tested insurance benefit and offers a slightly lower percentage of former pay, while means-tested social assistance (*Sozialhilfe*) offers a flat-rate benefit level far below the other schemes. Benefit levels and eligibility rules are prescribed by federal law, but within these legislative guidelines the local social welfare offices have considerable freedom to award benefits according to the individual circumstances. The local assistance scheme is administered by the local authorities who provide the majority of the finance, with the balance coming from the *Länder* (apart from the city states of Bremen and Hamburg). These benefits are subject to particularly harsh assessment of need, are financially meagre and are associated with social stigma, thus severely curtailing the redistribution and decommodification effect.

It is those employees who have 'earned' benefits, together with the dependent members of their families, who have access to them. Thus it is the male breadwinner who has been assumed to spend his life in full-time employment and who achieved the necessary entitlement for full pension and unemployment rights. Built-in assumptions around the gendered division of labour ensures that a woman's entitlements are derived from her institutional status within the family as wife and mother. Thus, the social divisions found in the labour market, of class, gender and race, are replicated within the social security system. As Ginsberg (1992: 76) has commented, 'benefits are strictly earnings – and contribution – related in accordance with the social market philosophy which reinforces material and status inequality'.

Though the German model comprises compulsory state social insurance with fairly generous entitlements, the extent of decommodification is probably not substantial since the eligibility criteria and benefit rules are almost totally dependent on contributions and thus participation in work and employment. As Esping-Andersen highlights:

> it is not the mere presence of a social right, but the corresponding rules and conditions which dictate the extent to which welfare programmes offer genuine alternatives to market dependence.
>
> (Esping-Andersen 1990: 22)

The USA, Canada, Australia and Britain are classified within the *liberal model* of welfare which

> minimizes decommodification-effects, effectively contains the realm of social rights, and erects an order of stratification that is a blend of a relative equality of poverty among state-welfare recipients, market-differentiated welfare among the majorities, and a class-political dualism between the two.
>
> (Esping-Andersen 1990: 27)

Within this regime type means-tested assistance, limited universal transfers or social insurance schemes predominate.

In the USA, the dramatic growth of the welfare state during the 'Great Society' era of the 1960s substantially extended the state's involvement in most areas of welfare. It was built on the systems of Aid to Families with Dependent Children (AFDC), Medicaid, Food Stamps and unemployment insurance. As Ginsberg (1992: 100) points out, the ideological framework for the development of the welfare state in the USA has been 'formed out of a pragmatic and flexible combination of voluntarism and liberalism', which is, in part, a result of the vacuum created by the relative absence and lack of influence of social democracy and socialism in the USA (discussed a little later in this chapter). Voluntarism refers to the emphasis on the responsibility of the individual and the patriarchal family, for their own welfare, with the support of private agencies, charities, churches, employers and unions where necessary. The goal of public welfare intervention should be to restore the individual and the family to self-sufficiency and should deter dependence on public support. The Reagan administration reasserted these central elements and initiated a series of cuts in welfare expenditure and introduced stringent regulation to limit coverage. However, by the mid-1990s there were 14.2 million people receiving AFDC, representing one in seven US children (*The Economist*, 5 March 1994: 21–4). President Clinton's response was to propose a two-year lifetime limit on case support beyond which recipients would have to find employment, or be offered work in publicly subsidized jobs at minimum wage. Unlike workfare, which has become so prevalent, the programme does not simply impose sanctions or reduce AFDC, but 'after two years there are no more AFDC cheques – only pay cheques. If you do not work, you get nothing' (*The Economist*, 5 March 1994: 24).

Castles and Mitchell (1992), however, have criticized the inclusion of Australia within the liberal regime. They have suggested that Australia belongs to a radical 'Fourth World of Welfare Capitalism' in which the emphasis, particularly from the political left, has been on achieving equality in pre-tax, pre-transfer income rather than through welfare rights. In this radical 'Fourth World', 'the welfare goals of poverty amelioration and income equality are pursued through redistributive instruments rather than by high expenditure levels' (Castles and Mitchell 1990: 16). The Australian system of welfare is discussed in more detail in Chapter 5.

The third and smallest cluster of nations is represented by the *social democratic regime* type, including the Scandinavian countries. According to Esping-Andersen (1990), for countries within this regime type, the social democratic goal has been to promote a welfare state based on 'equality of the highest standards, not an equality of minimal needs as was pursued elsewhere' (Esping-Andersen 1990: 27). This regime type is characterized by universalistic programmes offering high decommodification potential. There is no role for the market, with the costs of caring for children and elderly people, for example, socialized through state provision. Esping-Andersen (1990: 28) considers the fusion between welfare and work as the most salient feature of this regime type. The costs of maintaining a 'solidaristic, universalistic, and de-commodifying welfare system' mean that revenue income must be maximized and social problems, particularly unemployment, kept to a mimimum. Thus this regime is 'at once genuinely committed to a full-employment guarantee, and entirely dependent on its attainment' (Esping-Andersen 1990: 28).

Leibfried (1991) has sought to extend Esping-Andersen's analysis and, utilizing the concept of poverty regimes, identifies four ideal types – *Scandinavian*, *Bismarck*, *Anglo-Saxon* and *Latin Rim*. The Scandinavian welfare states (essentially the Swedish model) are characterized by universalism and the promotion of full employment, with the welfare state as '*the employer of first resort*' (Leibfried 1991: 140), particularly for women. Entry into or non-exit from the labour market is subsidized by and facilitated through the welfare state. In the 'universalist work-centred' Scandinavian countries the primary focus of the welfare state and the institutionalization of social citizenship has not been via income redistribution and income transfer strategies, but on the right to work and participate in the labour market.

Germany and Austria are incorporated within the Bismarck model which is associated with an institutional welfare state, a commitment to (male) full employment and based on the 'male citizenship model'. Bismarck countries rely on a strategy of 'paying off' social problems by subsidizing exit or non-entry from the labour market by substituting a right to social security for a right to work. Thus, in contrast to the Scandinavian model 'the welfare state is not the employer but the *compensator of first resort'* (Leibfried 1991: 140, original emphasis).

The Anglo-Saxon model is characterized by a selective approach to social policy with entry into the labour market facilitated more by coercion than by subsidization or training policy as in the Bismarck model. English-speaking countries such as the USA, New Zealand and Australia epitomize the 'residual welfare model' (Anglo-Saxon countries). Like Esping-Andersen (1990), Leibfried confidently conflates the British and US experiences

> Putting the US and the UK into one league, treating them in effect as if they were 'one country' makes more sense today as the effects of Thatcherism on the welfare state becomes visible. As long as 'freedom from want' and Beveridge-style social reform was prominent in England the divergence from the US was rather pronounced.
>
> (Leibfried 1991: 19)

While there has certainly been an erosion of the institutional structure established during the post-war era the similarities between Britain and the USA have seemed to emerge around generalities and rhetoric and do not really take account of the concrete reality as it has emerged in the two countries. As indicated earlier, the philosophies and rhetoric of Thatcher and Reagan were a dominant theme of the 1980s in both countries. However, the backdrop against which each was cultivated and the specific condition of crisis and transformation which have emerged have been very different. Esping-Andersen (1990) succinctly characterized the post-war British experience and outlines the inheritance of the Conservative government in the 1980s:

> the Labour Party's breakthrough in Britain is evidenced by the fact that Britain scored in the top decommodification group in the 1950s: the universalist social citizenship of the Beveridge model that was launched after the war placed Britain as the highest scoring nation internationally. The system was certainly not undone by the 1980s but it failed to progress further.
>
> (Esping-Andersen 1990: 54)

The transatlantic experience has been somewhat different. In the USA the expansion of entitlement welfare programmes in the 1930s and 1960s was, as Fox Piven and Cloward (1984) argue, brought about by pressure from popular pressure movements. However, the American experience could not be characterized by the mobilization and incorporation of the working class in relation to the implementation of welfare state policies, in contrast to the European experience. For Florida and Jonas (1991), while the New Deal moved the USA closer in the direction of 'social democracy', this course was radically altered by the 1950s as the power of the state was brought to bear against the labour movement as Communists and Socialists were eventually purged from trade unions. McCarthyism and the repressive legislation embodied in the Taft-Hartley Act 1947 and the McCarran Act 1950 served to stifle 'working class expressions of solidarity' (Florida and Jonas 1991: 360). Though southern households, and displaced and recently urbanized black households in the North, had precipitated an explosion of political and social unrest during 1966 and 1967, the response in the shape of the 'Great Society' did little to tackle the structural roots of income poverty and unemployment. According to Katznelson:

> American Keynesianism has been conservative, choosing to deal exclusively with questions of demand and distribution. Peak association corporatism linking business, labour and government is virtually unknown. There is no national capacity to plan. Employment policy is a pastiche of ameliorative programmes incapable of making a dent in structural and cyclical unemployment.
>
> (Katznelson 1986: 308, cited in King 1989: 243)

Though government strategies throughout the 1980s were aimed at weakening trade unions and societal support for the institutions of the welfare state, particularly in Britain, the welfare state has always relied on a complex mixture of cross-class alliances (Taylor-Gooby 1988) and will continue to do so. Clearly a fundamental restructuring of the welfare state has taken place, but to conflate the evolution of the British welfare state with that of the USA fails to uncover the complexity and diversity of the developments that have taken place. At any particular point a welfare regime will be the residue of successive layers of restructuring. Thus, once the institutions of a particular regime are established they have considerable durability. The welfare state, through its role as employer and service provider has created substantial and powerful interests committed to its maintenance. Leibfried (1991) himself includes numerous caveats in his analysis, which would seem to indicate that the case of Britain represents the limits of regime typology which seems to have difficulty in maintaining an historical context crucial to understanding contemporary welfare state forms.

Leibfried's fourth social policy regime includes the southern countries of Western Europe (Spain, Greece, Portugal and to a lesser extent southern Italy and France). He claims that these countries 'seem to constitute a welfare state regime of their own' (Leibfried 1991: 141). The 'Latin Rim' countries, in which agricultural and subsistence economies predominate, are characterized as having rudimentary welfare states, stressing residualism and forced entry into the labour market. It is a regime type which can be seen as 'a rudimentary welfare regime combining both liberal and corporatist elements . . . but lacking a full employment tradition and de facto stressing residualisation and forced "entry" into the market' (Leibfried 1993: 141). Leibfried's (1993) analysis represents one of the first to include the countries of Southern Europe, many of which have been largely ignored in cross-national social policy research (though see Ferrera 1996). However, his suggestion that the development in these countries of a 'normal welfare system' seems likely – referring to the system that exists in Northern Europe and Germany – has encountered criticism. Marinakou (1998) is critical of Leibfried's approach, which is based on the assumption that the economies and welfare systems of Southern Europe will 'catch up' with those in Western Europe. The emphasis on modernization and convergence is inadequate for capturing the 'internal idiosyncracies of the social formations in Southern Europe' (Marinakou 1998: 235). Its inability to capture and appreciate both the politically and economically distinctive traits of the region is an indication, to some extent, of the ethnocentrism that permeates cross-national social policy research. The following section will consider the influence of the 'western paradigm' in cross-national research. It will review the contribution of a number of commentators who have sought to overcome the gendered and ethnocentric assumptions which permeate the concepts and framework of welfare state typologies.

The gendered and ethnocentric construction of social welfare

Both Esping-Andersen's (1990) and Leibfried's (1991) accounts provide fertile ground for investigating and developing an understanding of the complexity of the dynamics of welfare state development across nations. Esping-Andersen (1990) makes important links between the welfare state and the labour market as well as the relationship between the state and the family under different regimes, but the assumptions of women's dependence built into the benefits system and the differing impact and meaning of decommodification for women are not discussed.

Although feminist researchers have been successful in bringing gender in from the periphery to the centre of social policy and welfare state analysis (Wilson 1977; Ungerson 1985; Pascall 1986; Williams 1989; Lewis 1992), cross-national research has, until recently, been gender blind. As Sainsbury (1996: 35) argues, 'the key mainstream conceptions and assumptions are gendered in the sense that they are primarily rooted in the experiences of men'. Dominelli's (1991) cross-national study, based on an antiracist, feminist perspective, is probably the first and only one of its kind. She explores the differences and similarities in women's experiences of the welfare state, and 'the racism enshrined in welfare provision' across six countries with varied economic and political systems. Langan and Ostner (1991) have sought to highlight the significant differences in the consequences of different welfare regimes for women and, in essence, to combine gender research with the work of Esping-Andersen (1990) and Leibfried (1991). They assert that not only do the differing proportions in which the household, the market, the state, the firm and the Church provide have important implications for women, but also whether the focus of welfare is on transfers or services, individuals or households. The Scandinavian (socialist) model treats women equally as individual wage earners. The model emphasizes services rather than monetary transfers. However, the maintenance of full employment has become reliant on the welfare state as a major employer, particularly of women. According to Langan and Ostner (1991: 135), 'what appears as a highly egalitarian society turns out to be a highly segregated one: men work in private industry, women work in public services'. They characterize this model as 'a universalisation of female social service economy'.

The Bismarckian (conservative) model is referred to as 'a gendered status maintenance model', in that it seeks to uphold and reproduce various existing social divisions, including those between men and women, thus 'supporting the male "normal worker" and the female "normal wife"' (Langan and Ostner 1991: 138). The state provides money transfers rather than services and emphasizes the role of the 'traditional family' as the primary provider of welfare services. In Germany the welfare system has not offered women the alternative employment avenues that has been the case in other countries, and policies have clearly been aimed at encouraging working mothers to remain at home.

The Anglo-Saxon (liberal) model is based on equality of the marketplace in which individuals are free to sell their labour with little recognition of status as parent. Langan and Ostner (1991) highlight the 'availability for work' rules governing eligibility for benefit which treat women as though, like men, they have no special responsibilities for childcare and other domestic tasks. In stark contrast the private realm of the family is subsumed as dependent on the male citizen, provided for through the male family wage or residual benefits. In Britain a variety of policies such as community care initiatives and the reduction or complete removal of benefits to the under-25s have created an arena of enforced dependency with women, particularly working class women, forced to remain in the private sphere as primary carers, with meagre state support or participate in the labour market often on a part-time and unprotected basis.

For Langan and Ostner (1991: 130) 'different social groups and, crucially, different gender categories, have different relationships with the processes of commodification'. They emphasize that men and women are 'gendered commodities' with different experiences of the labour market resulting from their different relationship to family life. Thus, in Germany for example, where policy is still primarily oriented towards the married couple and the dominant objective is to encourage mothers to stay at home, women's experience of decommodification within the family is not liberating but subordinating and dependence-creating. As Borchost (1994: 28) has argued, 'it is crucial for the position of women, whether they are entitled to benefits as individuals or whether rights are tied to families, of which men are usually the head'. O'Connor (1993) has suggested that the experiences of women could be better understood if the concept of decommodification was supplemented by the concept of personal autonomy or insulation from dependence. This would cover both personal dependence on family members and/or public dependence on state agencies. Lister (1994) suggests that the notion of 'defamilialization' would be more appropriate. This is 'the degree to which individual adults can uphold a socially acceptable standard of living, independently of family relationships, either through paid work or social security provision' (Lister 1994: 37, cited in Sainsbury 1996: 39). This concept would provide a more appropriate framework for evaluating social rights for women than decommodification, utilized by Esping-Andersen (1990).

While debates surrounding the adequacies of the conceptual and theoretical frameworks for analysing the social relations of welfare and their implications and interactions with women across countries are playing a vital role in the development of cross-national research, the same cannot be said in relation to race and the ethnocentric orientation within cross-national research. Walker and Wong (1996) argue that the way in which welfare and the welfare state have been socially constructed reflects the dominance of a 'western paradigm' permeating definitions and theory in 'ethnocentric western social research' (Walker and Wong 1996: 67). The classification of welfare state regimes has tended to focus on advanced capitalist parliamentary democracies which are members of the OECD:

> Welfare states have been constructed as a capitalist-democratic project: they are commonly referred to as 'welfare capitalist states' or 'welfare capitalism'. Those societies without either one or both of the supposed core institutions – a capitalist economy and a western parliamentary democracy – are effectively excluded from what is an exclusive club of mainly OECD members that are labeled, both popularly and scientifically, 'welfare states'.
>
> (Walker and Wong 1996: 69)

This bias, according to Walker and Wong (1996) has resulted in cross-national analysis neglecting large sections of the globe, including not only developing countries, but also many of the countries of the Asian Pacific area considered to be capitalist societies and 'highly developed' such as Singapore and Hong Kong. (When the article was written Hong Kong had been under British colonial administration since 1841, with only limited democracy introduced since 1985. In 1997 Hong Kong became a Special Administrative Region of the People's Republic of China and under the principle of 'one country two systems' retains a high degree of autonomy.) This latter group have tended not to be considered as welfare states 'even though many of their welfare institutions resemble those found in the western welfare state club' (Walker and Wong 1996: 68).

Underlying the definition and classification of the western paradigm of welfare state regimes are two fundamental principles: first, institutional, in that the welfare states are regarded as inextricably linked to capitalism and democracy, and second, functional or utilitarian, wherein the welfare states are defined in terms of the aims and extent of state intervention. Walker and Wong (1996) suggest that the dominance of these principles in cross-national analysis can be linked to the way that the development of the welfare state has been conceptualized in western analysis. The earlier part of this chapter explored explanations where the emphasis was on the growth of state activity in social policy as an adjunct to the market economy, and as a response to mass democracy. Thus, Walker and Wong (1996) argue that

> the advent of state welfare programs in western non parliamentary systems . . . makes the dominant conceptualization of the welfare state . . . look more like the straightforward rationalization of an existing phenomenon by western analysts, rather than a convincing explanation of the political economy of state welfare.
>
> (Walker and Wong 1996: 72)

In other words, social systems that do not 'fit the model' being developed have simply been excluded. The fact that welfare-state programmes have evolved in non-capitalist societies, and in societies lacking parliamentary democracy calls into question fundamental conceptions of the development of the welfare state. The emphasis on 'welfare state' as a democratic-capitalist project, and the narrow focus on one single institution – the state and its role in social policy – has not only failed to capture the different sources of welfare in both western and eastern societies, but also perpetuated the development of 'narrow western ethnocentric paradigms' (Walker and Wong 1996: 75). What is needed is 'a rethinking of both the ideological and intellectual constructions of welfare state regimes' (Walker and Wong 1996: 70) in order to enable comparative research to capture the diversity of welfare provision across societies.

More recently there has been a growing interest in the countries of East Asia, in particular Japan and the newly industrialized countries of South Korea, Taiwan, Singapore and Hong Kong. This has been accompanied by the emergence of an expanding body of literature which seeks to explore, explain and categorize East Asian welfare systems (for example see C. Jones 1993; Goodman and Peng 1996; Kwon 1997; Goodman *et al.* 1998; Gough 2000; Holliday (forthcoming)).

The welfare states of the tiger economies of South-East Asia have been described by Catherine Jones as:

> Conservative corporatism without (Western-style) worker participation; subsidiarity without the church; solidarity without equality; laissez-faire without libertarianism; an alternative expression for this

might be 'household economy' welfare states – run in the style of a would-be traditional, Confucian, extended family.

(C. Jones 1993: 214)

Kwon (1998: 27) would argue, however, that although 'The East Asian experience is distinctive, differing decisively from the Euro-American models current in social policy discourse', the evidence suggests that the welfare arrangements between countries are diverse and the similarities insufficient to support an all encompassing 'East Asian Welfare Model' (see C. Jones 1990, 1993; Goodman and Peng 1996; Kwon 1997).

Within Esping-Andersen's (1997) analytical framework, Japan is cautiously classified as a hybrid welfare regime. Like Castles and Mitchell (1992), Peng (2000) questions the appropriateness of the key concepts utilized by Esping-Andersen (1990). She argues that the parameters of Esping-Andersen's typology – decommodification and stratification – 'are not the most revealing questions to ask in the case of Japan' (Peng 2000: 91). She considers that there are two important (and interrelated) factors in analysing the Japanese system of welfare. First, the nature of individual–family and of individual–labour market relations, thus she stresses the need to highlight the role of the family and the labour market in providing welfare and contributing to decommodification. The second important factor is the purpose of welfare. According to Peng (2000), within the regime approach the assumption is that

> progressive social welfare development will be underlined by greater citizenship rights particularly in terms of being decommodified. It therefore assumes that the ideal welfare state will liberate the individual from market dependence.
>
> (Peng 2000: 93)

She asserts, however, that this assumption runs counter to the experience of Japan. The most important welfare function in post-war Japan has been to ensure (male) employment security and to achieve a basic level of economic security for the family by establishing the right of the individual to be employed. This has, to an extent, protected some citizens from the vagaries of the market. The relationship between the role of the family, the labour market, the welfare system and citizenship are discussed in Chapter 5.

Conclusion

The aim of this chapter has been to elaborate the relationship between theoretical assumptions, the ways in which the development of the welfare state is depicted and the concepts and research tools which are used. As O'Brien and Penna (1998: 3) argue, 'there is no such thing as atheoretical research and no such thing as pure, empirically based policy'. There are a range of approaches to understanding the development of the welfare state. Each has its own starting point and particular areas of concern which will impact on how the research is carried out, the types of data that are utilized, the issues to be explored and how the findings are interpreted. It is not really a case of choosing one case or perspective over another. It is more about being aware of the theoretical and epistemological assumptions embedded in the research context. Theoretical perspectives are historically embedded and should therefore be understood within their specific temporal contexts. Calhoun (1995: 36) suggests that past theories should be approached not just as 'exemplars, partial successes or sources of decontextualized insights, but as works bounded by or based on different histories from our own'. Different theoretical perspectives do not seek to offer 'truths' but rather offer the potential for extending the range of possible alternatives in the hope of providing a more enlightening explanation for the phenomena being studied. Calhoun (1995: 36), drawing on the work of Taylor (1989), refers to this process as 'epistemic gain'. Thus, the development of theoretical perspectives is not an abstract process, nor does it occur in isolation. As Chapter 4 will show in relation to cross-national social research and developing countries, it is a process which is located in history, in different intellectual traditions as well as in the contemporary social world.

Further reading

Abrahamson, P. (1999) The welfare modelling business, *Social Policy and Administration*, 33(4): 394–415. This article explores the substantial increase in the use of welfare state typologies in cross-national comparative analysis. It provides a summary of Esping-Andersen's (1990) typology and debates that have emerged from it. It then considers the adequacy of the parameters of the typology in terms of its focus on social insurance provision and the simultaneous neglect of the personal social services, as well as the family and networks in the analysis.

Pierson, C. (1998) in *Beyond the Welfare State? The New Political Economy of Welfare*, 2nd edn. Cambridge: Polity. This book introduces the major theoretical approaches to the welfare state and various interpretations of the 'crisis of the welfare state'. The book concludes by considering the extent to which we are moving to social and political arrangements that are 'beyond the welfare state', and the challenges this may present for traditional social democracy.

Sainsbury, D. (1996) *Gender, Equality and Welfare States*. Cambridge: Cambridge University Press. This book draws on a feminist perspective to consider the implications of different welfare states for women, as compared to men. It focuses on the USA, the UK, Sweden and the Netherlands to highlight the similarities and differences between countries. It then goes on to identify and reconceptualize the key dimensions of welfare state variations specifically in relation to their impact on women.

Walker, A. and Wong, C-K. (1996) Reconstructing the western construction of the welfare state, *International Journal of Health Services*, 26(1): 67–92. This article discusses the adequacy of the conceptual and theoretical frameworks utilized in cross-national analysis. It argues that western ethnocentrism has contributed to the way in which the welfare state has been constructed. The emphasis on 'welfare state' as a democratic-capitalist project is an example of the ethnocentrism that has resulted in large sections of the globe being excluded from cross-national research.

chapter

four

Development, social welfare and cross-national analysis

Patricia Kennett and Ben Oakley

Introduction

Comparative cross-national analysis between developing countries and those of the industrialized west is unusual. Development research has emerged as a distinct subject, with its own literature, theories and method. This is partly attributable to the conceptual distinctions which have been used to categorize and differentiate areas of the globe, such as First/Third World, Developed/Developing, North/South, Low-income/High-income, which has tended to encourage a separation or a 'false segregation' (Walker and Wong 1996) of countries for comparative analysis. It is also an indication of what MacPherson and Midgley (1987: 5) refer to as 'the parochialism of many social policy researchers in industrial countries such as Britain and the United States who have often regarded their own societies as a macrocosm for social policy analysis'. The lack of a clear identity for social policy in many developing countries and, in most cases, its subordination to economic policy has also inhibited the expansion of cross-national research across categories. In developing countries it is the broader term 'social development' (Midgley 1997) which is generally used in relation to social policy, indicating the direct link between social policy and economic development policies and programmes. This chapter will explore the various interpretations that have been applied to 'social development', their implications for social policy and the relevance of the approach in promoting human welfare across all societies. First, it is necessary to establish how the general development of '**Third World**' countries has been theorized and conceptualized.

This chapter does not provide extensive or finite coverage of theoretical explorations in development thinking. Instead it will consider the relationship between theory construction, the research process and the policy implications.

Thus it will draw on and critique the most influential perspectives. More recent dissatisfaction with the universal explanatory models which have been applied to development thinking has led to a re-evaluation of theory, analysis and research strategies in the countries of the South. The final section of this chapter will consider these recent innovations and their potential to contribute to the reconstruction of the cross-national research paradigm and the expansion of cross-national comparative research between developed and less developed countries (LDCs).

Development as a discourse

There is general agreement that the discourse around development and the notion of the 'Third World' was formulated in the 1940s and 1950s. It was used to describe and define the emerging independent states freed from colonial rule after the Second World War. The discourse emerged against a backdrop of the bipolar, Cold War conflict between the west and the former Soviet Union and their rivalry in attempting to secure the allegiance of the newly independent states. At least until the late 1960s it was thought appropriate to consider developing countries as a similar and homogenous grouping about which it was possible to make generalized statements.

While the notion of the Third World has never been a particularly valid one, there were some common themes and interests between the countries of the region which served to reinforce this characterization. The majority of the countries of the Third World had, in varying forms, been subject to colonial rule. The legacy of colonialism created similar social, political and economic pressures for newly independent states. As McGrew (1992) argues:

> from the 1950s through to the late 1970s, common economic problems, the desire to stand outside the East–West conflict, and the commitment to restructuring the global economic system provided the political motivation for these newly independent states to operate collectively as a block in the international arena.
>
> (McGrew 1992: 256)

The international system established after the Second World War (IMF, World Bank, UN, GATT and later the OECD), as discussed in the Introduction, was dominated by the USA and Britain and disproportionately represented the interests of the industrialized, developed countries. However, a Third World bloc was established within the global system – Group of 77 (G77 now represents over 120 states) – which brought together the majority of Third World states as a voting bloc within the UN system. The G77 has functioned as a counterbalance to the influence of the western industrial states within the UN and other global institutions and, according to McGrew (1992: 257), was successful in redirecting 'the global political agenda away from East–West issues to the needs of the newly independent states' at least until the 1980s. However, this challenge to the dominance of the west failed to result in any real or sustained economic and social gains for the people of the Third World. By the 1980s the fragile Third World coalition had begun to fragment as conflicts of interest between countries began to take centre stage. Religious conflict, political revolutions and differential development (for example between the newly industrialized countries and the countries of Sub-Saharan Africa) contributed to the demise of what McGrew (1992: 259) refers to as 'Third-World-ism'. This process was accelerated throughout the 1980s with the widespread acceptance of monetarist and free market ideologies, discussed later in this chapter.

The development discourse was premised on the role of modernization. Key elements in the process of modernization were urbanization and industrialization, which in turn were linked with capital investment and economic growth. Capital investment in the countries of the Third World, imperative for economic growth and development and unavailable in the individual countries, was to come from the countries of the developed world. The plethora of international organizations established during this period were to play a key role in establishing the framework, structures and procedures through which this would take place. Rist (1997) argues that:

> Whereas the world of colonization had been seen mainly as a political space to encompass ever larger empires, the 'development age' was the period when economic space spread everywhere, with the raising of GNP as the number one imperative.
>
> (Rist 1997: 79)

This quote from Rist (1997) highlights the economic emphasis of the development discourse. It is an indication of the influence of the dominant theoretical perspective of the day, encapsulated in the evolutionary perspective of Rostow (1960), and a new economic instrument – the calculation of gross national product. The economic success of most OECD countries following the Second World War gave credence to the idea of replicating and perpetuating the systems within western industrial countries to developing countries. As Toye (1987) argues:

> The process of development consisted . . . of moving from traditional society, which was taken as the polar opposite of the modern type, through a series of stages of development derived essentially from the history of Europe, North America and Japan – to modernity, that is, approximately the United States of the 1950s.
>
> (Toye 1987: 11, cited in Hewitt 1992: 224)

This was the age of Enlightenment and rationality and it was the forces of modernization that were seen as the most appropriate for eradicating the 'traditional' society. According to Rist (1997):

> The seductiveness of modernization theory has been explained in two ways. For the countries of the North, it justified the continuation of existing policies that emphasized domestic growth and foreign aid as ways of countering communist designs. For the countries of the South, it entrusted the promise of a better future to the new ruling classes that were accumulating tokens of Westernization as they lined their own pockets.
>
> (Rist 1997: 109)

According to Escobar (1997), partriarchy and ethnocentrism permeated the development discourse and were influential in the shape that development took. The development discourse was ethnocentric in the sense that it was not just economies that had to be 'modernized' but also indigenous populations. This meant adopting the values 'embodied in the ideal of the [white] cultivated European' (Escobar 1997: 89–90). Rooted in Enlightenment thought, the development enterprise was premised on the correlation between modernization and development. The process was seen as a linear process, in which nations or peoples moved from underdevelopment, which was equated with 'traditional' institutions, to full societies, that is modern/rational/industrialized societies based on the Northern model. The rationale for this progression was provided by colonial (and later neo-colonial) discourses which compared 'backward, primitive' Third World peoples and cultures unfavourably with the 'progressive' North. As Parpart and Marchand (1995) argue:

> Much of the discourse and practice of development has exaggerated Western knowledge claims, dismissed and silenced knowledge from the South and perpetuated dependence on the Northern experience.
>
> (Parpart and Marchand 1995: 12)

Women were initially seen as an impediment to development, if they were considered at all. Perceptions of Third World women were as 'tradition-bound beings, either unable or unwilling to enter the modern world'. This representation fitted 'neatly into Western and neo-colonial gender stereotypes, and provided a rationale for ignoring women during the first two development decades (1950s and 1960s)' (Parpart and Marchand 1995: 13). Development programmes rendered women invisible as producers and perpetuated their subordination (Escobar 1997). Western experts undervalued the knowledge of women and failed to appreciate the complex strategies and informal networks put in place by women for economic survival.

There was growing awareness in the 1970s that many development projects, rather than improving the lives of Third World women, had deprived them of economic opportunities and status. There was also a general recognition that the non-formal arrangements for promoting the well-being of individuals, families and communities should be not only recognized and respected, but also supported and reinvigorated. These changes in perception, combined with the emergence of a range of alternative theoretical explanations discussed in the next section, have served to weaken the dominant position of the modernization paradigm in the development discourse.

Theorizing development and the Third World

Dependency theory was introduced as an alternative explanation for the continuing subordinate position of developing countries and originated from a range of sources including Latin America (Cardoso and Faletto 1979; Frank 1967, 1978). It questioned the dualistic model of the 'traditional' and the 'modern' incorporated into modernization theory and argued that obstacles to development were not to be found in the internal socio-cultural characteristics of 'traditional' societies but are actually external to the underdeveloped countries. The approach incorporated two dimensions, political and economic, and emphasized that underdevelopment was not just about low productivity but was a historical condition brought about by the legacy of colonialism. Dependency theory was critical of the structures of western industrial capitalism within and through which Third World economies had become enmeshed in such a way as to create and maintain underdevelopment and exploitation. These linkages, and the one-way transfer of resources from the Third World periphery to the western capitalist core, were maintained and reinforced through 'agents of capitalism' which include multinational corporations, international banks, and intergovernmental agencies such as the IMF and the World Bank, as well as local elites (Midgley 1997).

For Frank (1967, 1978) the prospect for Latin American countries within a world capitalist system could only be continuing and inevitable underdevelopment. Cardoso and Faletto (1979) however, preferred the term 'dependent development' and rejected the inevitability of the underdevelopment of Latin American countries as predicted by Frank (1967, 1978). Rather, through a process of 'delinking' the countries of the South could break away from the exploitative relationship with western industrial nations.

The various interpretations of dependency were strongly critical of the Eurocentric modernization theory and did promote a new way of looking at and understanding development theory. It provided an alternative intellectual perspective and acted as a catalyst in the development of theory. It recognized development and underdevelopment as interrelated processes.

However, dependency theories came under sustained attack, particularly through the 1980s and 1990s. The earlier criticisms were directed at the predictive elements of dependency – short of a socialist revolution and the overthrow of the world capitalist system there was very little to offer in the way of future development for the developing countries. In addition, the newly industrialized countries of South-East Asia (for example South Korea, Hong Kong, Taiwan), where significant economic and social development had occurred, proved difficult to explain using the notion of dependent development. Wallerstein's (1974, 1979) 'world systems theory', a version of dependency developed in the mid-1970s, refined the theory to incorporate such changes. For Wallerstein, the world economy is constituted through one capitalist world system, consisting of countries falling into the core (the industrialized countries), the semi-periphery (the NICs) 'which act as a buffer between the core and the periphery' (Schuurman 1993: 8) and the periphery (agricultural export countries). Wallerstein saw little prospect for Third World countries to 'delink' from the global system. However, the fluidity of global capital provides country governments with the opportunity of influencing capital flows. Thus, a peripheral country can move from the periphery to the semi-periphery and then to the core. World systems theory emphasized that

> the origin of development and underdevelopment is found in the incorporation of countries within the world system. Underdevelopment occurs because countries are subject to a trade regime and produce for a world market that is characterized by unequal trade.
>
> (Schuurman 1993: 9)

But this is not a static relationship, with the circumstances of the NICs of East Asia indicating that the opportunities of the global economy can be grasped by astute governments.

So while dependency theories, perhaps because they had grown out of, and as a reaction to, the weaknesses of modernization explanations for development, tended to overemphasize the 'external' factors limiting development such as colonialism, neo-colonialism and the resulting economic dependency, world systems theory has been criticized for its unidimensional perspective as well as its level of abstraction. Where modernization theorists had emphasized 'internal' variables and cultural attributes, for example the absence of the work ethic in a developing country, dependency theorists were keen to avoid this 'mistake', which many had viewed as a subtle form of racism. The result has been a polarity that only emphasizes the weaknesses of both. For where modernization theorists could correctly be accused of having largely ignored the huge impact of colonialism from 'outside', dependency theorists did not attach enough significance to the impact of 'internal' factors inhibiting development, such as ethnicity, gender or corruption. This dissatisfaction with theories of development contributed to a 'theoretical vacuum' (Schuurman 1993) in the 1980s. It coincided with the recognition that one of the major elements of development in the Third World was its diversity rather than its homogeneity, that the gap between the rich and poor countries had not decreased and that the development strategies of the previous decades were increasingly ineffective. The next section will briefly explore the strategies and policies pursued during the colonial and postcolonial era and under the auspices of the modernization paradigm. It will consider their influence on the development of both formal and non-formal welfare in developing countries. It will also examine the implications of structural adjustment programmes of the 1980s in an era in which the ideological and policy context of development were transformed.

Development and social welfare

The patterns of welfare across the South vary depending on each country's distinctive historical pathway. However, a major force in the recent history of developing countries has been the impact of colonialism and colonial rule, through which the first limited social services were introduced. The nature and extent of colonial rule varied from country to country but wherever it was imposed it transformed societies, economies and institutions (MacPherson and Midgley 1987). Pre-existing traditions were almost universally viewed as 'obstacles to progress' by missionaries and colonialists. African societies, for example, were viewed as 'in a most elementary state of civilization, far below that of Europeans in the evolutionary ladder' (Osei-Hwedie and Bar-on 1999: 90).

Focusing on the African experience Osei-Hwedie and Bar-on (1999) have identified three distinct periods in the development of welfare – the colonial period, the first decades of independence and the more recent era of macro-economic structural adjustment. For MacPherson and Midgley (1987) the imperatives behind the colonial administration's interests in developing welfare came from two sources: first, the need to ensure economic activity for the ultimate benefit of the European capitalist system, rather than the colonial regimes – the emphasis was on minimum provision of infrastructure and social services to meet this end – and second, the 'civilizing mission', which legitimized the destruction of pre-existing cultures and social arrangements. Religious education, for example, served to 'improve the moral and social character of Africans' (Osei-Hwedie and Bar-on 1999: 90).

So for the colonial government administrations, the expansion of formal social policy was largely determined by the imperatives of economic expansion, the exploitation of the resources of the colonies (Aina 1999) and the maintenance of social order. As Fadayomi (1991) argues:

economic growth was superseded only by economic exploitation, while the minimal degree of social development that existed had resulted entirely from colonial provision of the basic social services and physical infrastructure necessary to facilitate the exploitation of natural resources. In other words, social development was merely incidental for the development of the metropolitan economy.

(Fadayomi 1991: 137)

Formal education, health and social services were the main elements of provision, and were concerned with producing a healthy, efficient and trained workforce. Missionaries and voluntary agencies played a key role particularly in providing education as part of the civilizing mission and 'for the production of people to service both the colonial administration and its economy' (Aina 1999: 75). Services and provision were generally staffed with 'specialists/experts' from the North, whose values permeated provision and welfare institutions. Provision was minimal, residual and discriminatory, generally benefiting the expatriate communities and those members of the local community who were considered beneficial to the colonial mission, thus reflecting 'the concerns of the rulers rather than the needs of the ruled' (Boyden 1990: 180).

At independence the national governments inherited from their colonial rulers societies that were rapidly urbanizing and which had experienced economic and social dislocation. Pre-existing communities, and thus the traditional networks of welfare, had been eroded and yet the social service infrastructure inherited from the colonial administration was generally 'close to nil and inherently residual' (Osei-Hwedie and Bar-on 1999: 90). While no two countries experienced the same pattern of change there were aspects of the legacy of colonialism which were common across Africa, particularly in relation to the state, the economy and the social structure. The emphasis on export production during the colonial period exposed post-colonial African states to fluctuations in international commodity prices and increased their dependency on external markets. Though a period of stability during the early years of independence contributed to economic growth and increasing affluence, an additional strategy was to look to internal markets and establish domestic industries to supply markets previously served by imports. This process is referred to as import substitution industrialization.

The colonial state throughout most of Africa had been authoritarian (allowing little or no popular participation in decision-making), bureaucratic and elitist (Potter 1992). Existing bureaucracies were firmly entrenched and difficult to dismantle. Colonial societies experienced extreme inequalities with a small privileged elite gaining access to education, housing and health services. This was a group socialized into the values and orientations of the colonial government, and were generally the local people who replaced the colonial administration in policy-making positions. In addition, the colonial state had played a major role in shaping the economy in order to maximize accumulation for the European colonial powers. While some countries (Kenya for example) chose to utilize the colonial links and follow the capitalist path to development, in many countries across Africa early postcolonial rule was accompanied by the widespread acceptance of a socialist philosophy and the extensive state ownership of national resources and the means of production. Diamond *et al.* (1988) argue that

> both for its resonance with socialist and developmentalist ideologies and for its obvious utility in consolidating power and accumulating personal wealth, the legacy of statism was eagerly seized upon and rapidly enlarged by the emergent African political class after independence.
>
> (Diamond *et al.* 1988: 7–8, cited in Potter 1992: 219)

Social policy initiatives played an important role in legitimizing postcolonial governments, with major social programmes in education, housing, urban planning, health, and price subsidies and controls. As Osei-Hwedie and Bar-on (1999) point out, the emphasis was on social development, rather than social assistance and income transfer schemes. The reliance on subsistence-level agriculture in Africa meant that 'a very small sector of the population had income to be transferred to others, and even fewer could contribute to building national social insurance systems' (Osei-Hwedie and Bar-on 1999: 95). In other developing countries the nature of income support programmes has varied between provident funds and social insurance schemes (Midgley 1997). In parts of Asia and the Caribbean, for example, the British colonial government introduced provident funds for those in regular wage employment. These are compulsory savings programmes through which workers accumulate contributions, to be paid out when the worker retires. In contrast, in the French colonies the emphasis was on social insurance.

By the beginning of the 1970s, while growth, increasing affluence, and an improvement in the living conditions of most of Africa's people did occur at least in some developing countries, it became apparent that the strategies of the reconstruction period were unsustainable. The overemphasis on import-substitution policies had undermined agricultural production and export markets. Excessive subsidies into the industrial infrastructure, large bureaucracies and armies were all a drain on the public purse. As Osei-Hwedie and Bar-on (1999) explain, the solution was to print money and raise loans from abroad, thus increasing Africa's indebtedness. Political instability, drought, a drop in the price of primary commodities, defaults on loans, and corruption were circumstances with the potential to deepen the crisis. The result was a drastic reduction in public sector provision (schools, hospitals, and so on) which could no longer be maintained, and in expenditure, with devastating consequences for the majority of people in Africa.

Most countries of the South experienced a decline in economic growth rates, high inflation levels and an increasing debt burden during the 1980s compared to the 1970s. Oil prices doubled in 1979–80 and interest rates rose steeply (from an average level of 6.6 per cent in 1976 to 17.5 per cent in 1981). For non-OPEC (Organization of Petroleum-Exporting Countries) developing countries external debt increased from US$130 billion in 1973 to US$612 billion in 1982 representing almost a fivefold increase (Weiss 1991: 150). This period is often referred to as the 'lost decade' in terms of economic performance, a general decline in infrastructure and services, and an increasing proportion of national revenues devoted to debt servicing. The debt crisis and economic decline became the key issues across the region and according to Aina (1999: 79) were 'the outcomes of the combined effect of the initial colonial structure of African economies, the failure of the post-colonial regimes to correct these effects, and the pressures of economic globalization'. The response from the IMF and the World Bank was the formulation of a set of policies known as economic stabilization or structural adjustment programmes, which were greatly to influence social policy and the lives of many people in the South.

The New Right, structural adjustment and developing countries

The World Bank and IMF-sponsored structural adjustment programmes embarked upon in the early 1980s were *originally* intended as a short-term set of economic conditions designed to alleviate the worst effects of the heavy debt burden that had mushroomed through the 1970s. In 1982 Mexico announced that it could no longer service debt payments. As the threat of default shook the international financial community, the IMF and the World Bank were to play key roles in ensuring its survival. Through the imposition of policy packages focusing on austerity measures and the rescheduling of loans, debtor nations were encouraged to continue servicing loans. Such was the 'success' of these measures that by 1984, the deficit had begun to decline in some developing countries, thus ensuring the interests of the creditors. For the debtor nations, however, 'the effect of these policy measures was to put the economies of the debtor countries into reverse gear, sending them reeling in a downward spiral towards economic depression' (Adams 1993: 154).

For many countries of the South external debt is still a major burden. The total debt of developing countries in 1997 was almost US$2.2 trillion, with 41 countries (33 of them in Africa) classified as heavily indebted poor countries (HIPCs). The external debt of the HIPCs has tripled since 1980, two-thirds of which represents arrears unpaid or earlier debt (UNDP 1999). The servicing of external debt exceeds expenditure on health and education in nine HIPCs. According to the *Human Development Report*, 'Tanzania's debt service payments are nine times what it spends on primary health care and four times what it spends on primary education' (UNDP 1999: 106); it also points out that the nature of the debt has changed from private to 'official and multilateral debt' (UNDP 1999: 107). While more than half of external debt was owed to private creditors in 1980, by 1997 the figure was only one-fifth. The vast majority of debt is now owed to multilateral organizations such as the IMF and the World Bank. In recent years international debt relief and debt 'forgiveness' schemes have been implemented for the world's poorest countries. G7 countries have agreed to increase the value of their contributions towards debt relief, with some agreeing to write off debt owed to them providing the countries meet certain conditions. However, funding delays, intergovernmental wrangling and the inability of many developing countries to meet the criteria on which they are deemed eligible for debt relief has meant that the strategy has had only a slight impact. The Debt Initiative for heavily indebted poor countries has been described as 'roundabout, untransparent and utterly limited' (*The Times* 2000). In addition, the focus of this initiative is on bilateral debt when the majority of debt is owed to international bodies such as the IMF as mentioned about. Multilateral debts have been subject to only partial cancellation. However, Jubilee 2000, a coalition campaigning for debt relief, estimate that once the relief had been awarded, the debt relief of the poorest countries will be reduced by an average of 40 per cent (*The Times* 2000). While failing to fulfil the hype and promise of earlier claims of the eradication of Third World indebtedness, it is at least a recognition of the devastating effects of escalating debt, caused in part by the strategies of the international institutions and discussed in the next section.

Where the World Bank had previously lent to projects in developing countries, a new style of lending had emerged in the 1980s. New loans were conditional on policy changes proposed by the World Bank (initially, following agreement with the IMF) on a series of macro-economic reforms, called 'stabilization' policies) and agreed by the recipient country. Indeed, some 30 African countries 'abandoned their experiments with socialism – usually after a sharp arm-twist by foreign creditors – in favour of the free market creed preached by the World Bank and the IMF' (*The Economist*, 5 March 1994: 21). Many of the poorer HIPCs needed loans urgently to repay existing loan interest, which in turn might avert a more serious economic disaster. The package of measures required for IMF stabilization typically included deregulation, cuts in public expenditure and bureaucracy, export-led economic growth, devaluation of the currency to boost exports, the elimination of subsidies for food staples and the removal of protection for local crops in order to reduce labour costs and encourage foreign investment (Landau 1993). The measures incorporated the notion of 'short-term suffering for long-term gain'.

This new economic orthodoxy reflected a shift in the thinking of the more influential subscribers to the World Bank and IMF in the early 1980s, with a belief that the problems of development were primarily ones of economic (mis)management, inefficiency and state corruption. Improvements in social welfare, it was believed, could only flow from improved economic performance. With the political support of the leaders of major capitalist countries – Reagan in the USA, Chancellor Kohl in Germany and Thatcher in the UK for example – a New Right ideology for understanding and relating to developing countries emerged. Underlying this New Right agenda was a belief that the free market was the only way to solve economic problems, coupled with a mistrust of the developing country state as corrupt and inefficient. Conditions were attached to aid designed to deal with perceived inefficiencies, including privatization of state-run organizations, liberalization of the economy, export-led growth to balance the budget of indebted developing countries and retrenching of the public sector (including state social welfare provision). The mistrust of the developing country state further manifest itself by a commitment to channel more aid through NGOs (though the overall amount of aid by OECD countries was to fall steadily from the 1980s).

The increasing globalization of the world's economy as well as the impact of the Cold War have also been crucial elements in the shaping of relations between developed and developing countries. In the pre-Cold War past it had been possible to use friendliness to western capitalist countries as a means to maintain or increase development assistance, or to play the threat of defecting loyalties to the 'East' or 'West' as leverage. Many developing countries now find it increasingly difficult to attract development funding without satisfying conditions laid down by developed countries and the international financial institutions (IFIs) like the World Bank and the IMF. In addition, they are often competing for funds with those countries now described as 'in transition', mainly in Eastern Europe and the former Soviet Union. The effects of economic globalization on developing countries have contributed to increasing differentiation in the Third World, with high-growth middle-income economies in the Far East and extremely poor countries with negative growth in Africa representing extreme cases in the differentiation process. For the poorer countries, like many within the Sub-Saharan African region and parts of South Asia, entire countries are being marginalized. That is to say, some of these countries are lagging behind so far, not only in economic growth rates, but also in infrastructural developments and technologies such as communications (vital for modern markets), that they may never be able to catch up with the rest of the developed world. The inability of these countries to attract foreign direct investment increases their dependence on aid at a time when net official development assistance (ODA) has fallen from US$60 billion to US$50 million, with assistance to the least developed countries falling from US$17 billion to US$14 billion between 1995 and 1997 (UNDP 1999).

By the late 1980s, growing criticism of the social effects of structural adjustment programmes persuaded the IFIs to reconsider what had become almost a blueprint for indebted developing countries. At the micro-level, the human costs of the SAPs have meant increased hardship for the poorest and most vulnerable members of society. An influential study by the United Nations Children's Fund (Unicef), along with much other criticism, highlighted the negative social impacts of SAPs (Cornia and Jolly 1987). Although the IFIs have responded to some of these criticisms, SAPs remain controversial as a means to promote development. It is difficult to assess the social impact of these programmes or to assert whether indebted countries would have performed better without SAPs, or with another model, since such arguments are purely hypothetical (Mosley *et al.* 1995). Osei-Hwedie and Bar-on (1999) point to the reliance on undisaggregated data and a lack of detailed, reliable information and comprehensive household surveys. It is also a matter of interpretation in that it is difficult to distinguish the effects of SAPs compared to other events. What is clear, however, is that it is areas such as education and health which have experienced the greatest deterioration in provision and the widespread introduction of user fees, and which have had the greatest impact on the well-being of women and children. It is also the case that in Sub-Saharan Africa, per capita incomes were lower at the end of the 1990s than they were in 1970 (UNDP 1999). As Table 4.1 shows, for many countries in Sub-Saharan Africa (as well as those economically weaker South Asian countries), economic performance shows little sign of improvement from earlier decades. Where social welfare indicators indicate improvements, these statistics need to be put into perspective: population increases mean that although a larger proportion of people enjoy improved social conditions, the overall numbers of people adversely affected continues to increase.

Table 4.1   Selected economic and social indicators from some Sub-Saharan African countries which have undergone SAPs during the 1990s, with a UK comparison

	GNP per capita, 1998 (US$)	*% average annual growth rate, 1997–8*	*Under-fives mortality rate (per thousand)*		*Public expenditure on health % of GDP 1990–7*
			1980	*1997*	
Kenya	330	−0.9	115	112	1.9
Burundi	140	−2.3	193	200	1.0
Tanzania	210	0.6	176	136	1.1
Nigeria	300	−1.7	196	122	0.2
UK	21,400	1.9	75	80	5.7

Source: World Bank 1999

Significant changes in the global economic system, greater familiarity and exposure to the development experience and the negative impact of development strategies, and a recognition of the increasing differentiation between developing countries have all contributed to an almost universal acceptance of the need to reassess the theoretical, epistemological and policy contexts of the development paradigm. The next section will explore the dynamics of 'post-impasse' thinking and some of the theoretical and methodological approaches emerging from these debates.

Reviewing the research paradigm

Given the weaknesses of the 'grand' theories discussed earlier in this chapter, the 1980s and 1990s have seen what has been described in the literature as an 'impasse' in theorizing about development (see for example, Shuurman 1993). Increasingly, the concerns of the late twentieth century have highlighted the inadequacy of these earlier paradigms. Both modernization and dependency failed to incorporate important variables such as gender, governance, or environmental issues. No new 'grand' theory has sprung up to replace earlier ones. What we now see is less reactive (in the sense of refuting earlier theorizing), but more fragmented. The emerging literatures are now more concerned with broadening perspectives, rather than creating paradigms. To illustrate, perspectives on sustainable development discussed in the next section, or on gender issues and their impact on development, have widened our understanding of the impact of these factors on development, but have not yet been incorporated into an overarching, universalist theory.

An influential element of the new research agenda is the massive literature on 'sustainable development'. Links between environment and development came to the fore on the international stage at the Stockholm Conference in 1972, recognizing the separate problems of environmental degradation and poverty. The Brundtland Commission, reporting in 1987, recognized that it was not possible to tackle the effects of environmental degradation without addressing the causes of poverty that often induced it – known as the 'pollution of poverty' thesis (WCED 1987). In 1992, another UN conference at Rio de Janeiro (the 'Earth Summit') attempted to make 'sustainable development' possible. Just as with the concept of 'development', 'sustainable development' is an essentially contested concept, with no universally accepted definition. The term is commonly used in the literature without reference to content and critics have argued that this renders the term almost meaningless (Redclift 1987). A widely quoted definition emerged from the Brundtland Commission Report (WCED 1987): 'development that meets the needs of the present without compromising the ability of future generations to meet their own needs'. However, this definition is, as Bartelmus

(1994) points out, too vague to be useful: 'It gives no indication of the time horizon ("future generations"), the scope and substance of human needs, nor of the role of environment (not even mentioned in the definition) in development' (Bartelmus 1994: 69). Sustainable development, then, is a general descriptive term used by a variety of disciplines and interests, usually (though not always) highlighting links between environment and development, though from a plethora of conceptual foundations. For example, where some 'greener' ecologists might take as a precondition a no-growth economy, sustainable development, for the World Bank by contrast, would be funded by economic growth. As Schuurman (1993) argues:

> the 'green' notion of sustainable development could be incorporated without effort into both the 'blue' development model (neo-liberal) and the 'red' development model (socialist, and these days social democratic) . . . one can therefore hardly speak of an *alternative* development model.
>
> (Schuurman 1993: 22)

Environmental issues have been a neglected part of social theorizing and social research, but this is changing and a new environmental activism is evident in many developing countries, though with an agenda that is not always synchronous with that of western countries. High on the western countries' agenda will be such concerns as global warming, pollution, ozone depletion in the stratosphere and biodiversity loss, where developing countries' concerns will cluster around the more directly felt issues of land degradation, soil erosion and salination, deforestation and desertification. These latter have a direct impact on rural livelihoods and well-being. One problem of a mismatch of environmental agenda results in misunderstanding of the nature of what may be a regional or global problem. An example of this is the way a western organization concerned with saving endangered elephants from extinction in Africa (preserving biodiversity) have to address the different agenda of Africans, who may view the animal as a pest which regularly destroys the crops their lives depend on. It would matter less to such a person that the animal was the last in Africa, if the more immediate demands of family survival are threatened. Innovative ways to combine environmental and social issues are the subject of renewed academic and practitioner interest.

At the national level, political considerations also become important in achieving the commitment to development and environmental improvements. Many indigenous environmental NGOs have sprung up and grown in response to deteriorating environment and social conditions. Box 4.1 shows how one environmental movement, the Green Belt Movement (GBM) in Kenya, which started life as a single issue environmental NGO, has become more involved in national campaigning on a variety of issues from gender awareness to promoting democratic change.

Box 4.1 The Green Belt Movement in Kenya

The Green Belt Movement (GBM) was started in 1977 by Professor Wangari Maathai (Kenya's first woman PhD and university professor) as a grassrooots environmental NGO. The NGO initially targeted women to plant tree seedlings as a response to desertification, initially with free tree seedlings donated by the Kenyan government. As it developed, the GBM introduced a broader development ethic that sought to impact on the lives of rural women in more fundamental ways than tree planting, through education and empowerment.

The GBM's philosophy critiques the marginal position of women and the poor in general in Kenya. This expansive philosophy is condensed into the simple and practical activity of tree planting. As Maathai states: 'When we plant trees in Kenya we know that we will eventually have our hands on politics, on economics, on culture, on all aspects that either destroy or create a sustainable environment' in Ndegwa 1996: 94).

From the mid-1980s, Maathai and the GBM became more outspoken, challenging the state on a range of environmental, social and political issues. The distance from the state has grown, yet despite state repression of GBM the movement continues to be one of the largest and most prominent NGOs in Kenya. Maathai herself has suffered personally from this repression: most recently she was beaten while watering tree seedlings planted in an area of indigenous forest near the capital (Karura forest) that had been cleared and was believed to have been sold to friends of the ruling party. The GBM continues to campaign and to plant its trees. Wangari Maathai stood as a presidential candidate at the 1997 elections and although unsuccessful, helped to foster the idea that women may legitimately stand for high office.

Research into indigenous environmental organizations like the GBM has demonstrated that holistic approaches to development, like this 'sustainable development' approach, coupled with participatory and empowerment education, may be important in mobilizing support within developing countries for the kinds of social, political and economic change needed. How these organizations interact with the state, with their members and with organizations outside their country of origin offers a rich comparative research agenda in the twenty-first century.

Another important strand of 'post-impasse' thinking has been the growth of interest in the historiography of developing countries. The present and future development of any country is conditioned by its unique history. Where earlier theorizing tended to categorize and group developing countries in various ways (e.g. LDCs or NICs), scrutiny of a country's individual history not only can assist in understanding the development constraints and opportunities, but also may offer up more fruitful comparative research.

The colonial histories of African countries, for example, may differ significantly depending on whether they were administered by British, French or Portuguese colonists. Ethnic, gender and environmental histories are also offering fruitful insights. In Kenya, a recent study of a semi-arid region, Machakos, discovered that population growth in the area had actually improved environmental conditions (Tiffen 1994). This was due to a variety of factors, including the geographical proximity to a large urban centre and possibilities for alternative sources of income to complement farming activities. Also revealing was the limited impact of central government policies over time. These and similar studies have revealed the complexity of development interactions, overturning general assumptions about development (in this case that increased population levels equals environmental degradation), but opening up more holistic lines of enquiry.

These developments have been accompanied by a shift from disciplinary perspectives, more common in the past, to a more interdisciplinary conceptualization of development. In order to be able to understand the complexities of development, a number of disciplinary perspectives are essential, including politics, economic, environmental science, sociology, anthropology and history. There has also been a move to adopt more innovative, appropriate and inclusionary research strategies. The emphasis here has been on techniques such as participatory research appraisal (PRA), the use of facilitators, and recognizing the power relations between vulnerable groups and the agencies who seek to assist them. PRA is a research technique practised by a range of organizations and institutions, from small-scale projects to World Bank participatory poverty assessments (World Bank 1999). PRA and its related techniques such as participatory action research (PAR) and participatory learning and action (PLA) are the most documented. PRA can be described as a

> family of approaches, methods and behaviours, that enable people to express and analyse the realities of their lives and conditions, to plan themselves what action to take, and to monitor and evaluate the results.
> (Institute for Development Studies (IDS) 1996)

PRA developed from the earlier rapid rural appraisal (RRA), which was essentially participatory data collection. However, with RRA the analysis was conducted by outside agencies. RRA was still extractive and did not give people access and control over the findings of their research. PRA and related techniques, by contrast, are designed as a process to empower local people by increasing their insight into the causes of their poverty and giving them the means to do something about it. PRA methods have developed as an eclectic collection, but usually involve highly active processes and visual methods such as group discussions and analysis, mapping (both social and physical) simple flow diagrams, time-lines and calendars. These methods, although at first used most extensively in farming systems research, have now been transferred to other areas such as resource management, anti-poverty programmes, housing schemes, literacy and education programmes as well as credit and cooperative ventures. PRA is now used in over 100 countries (by both governments and NGOs) with networks existing in 30 countries.

Why are the participatory approaches and related techniques useful? There are a number of reasons to explain why they are seen by many who use them as offering a voice for marginalized people and communities. The first reason is that the whole concept of the role of the development worker is altered. With participatory techniques, the development worker is a facilitator or enactor, but not a director or manager. Facilitation is a process and begins by giving people the necessary skills to act on their own behalf. These can range from skills such as confidence-building to literacy or bookkeeping. Within PAR, conscientization is seen as a primary aim, giving the poor the confidence to be able to research, plan and implement their own projects. Participatory approaches emphasize a process of development and crucial to this is the involvement of people in researching their own situation. People have been shown, unsurprisingly, to have extensive knowledge of their environment. Chambers (1993) gives extensive evidence that the knowledge of local farmers is often far greater and more detailed than that of outside technical experts. Furthermore, the process of participatory research can bring about new insights and understandings of different issued for both the people involved and for development and workers.

In Morocco, for example, PRA has shown that women's development problems differ not only from men's but also between women depending on access to services, infrastructure and social background (IDS 1996). In Rajasthan, India, a small NGO was able to facilitate tribal women to have the confidence and skills to negotiate a higher price for the 'tendu' leaves they sell to contractors (Mathur 1995). Another example is the experience of the Grameen Bank in Bangladesh. This organization, which is both a bank and a poverty-alleviation organization, set up small-scale rural credit schemes (with loans averaging about US$60–70), allowing them enough credit to invest in small businesses. Borrowers are organized into groups of five who are responsible for weekly (rather than annual) repayments and weekly savings into a group and an emergency fund. An integral poverty-alleviation centre and a programme to empower communities ensure its success. Where banks had been unwilling to lend small amounts to poor people in the past because of high administration costs and high default records on repayments, this system overcame these obstacles in an innovative and effective way. Valuing the capacities of people through empowering them is a dominant value of Grameen Bank practice and a key ingredient for its success. This model has also proved to have had a wider applicability than rural credit in Bangladesh; as Holcombe (1995: 170) points out, 'As a specific model, Grameen is being applied in the developing world, and in North America and Europe'. The Grameen Bank experience was used recently to set up small-scale credit for marginalized groups in Los Angeles, following major riots in the city.

The literature on PRA is replete with examples of similar successes and it does seem that those involved in this style of research have a far greater voice in their development than when traditional research methods are used. Participation is important at the research phase of a project to ensure participation at later stages. From carrying out research themselves, the people involved 'own' their information. They can analyse it and use it themselves, which differs significantly from 'traditional' research where the information was extracted and used by outside agencies. This is a crucial form of empowerment, as people are put on an equal footing with development agencies and researchers.

A wide literature has emerged around the themes of participation and empowerment, ranging from anthropological insights into farming systems to debates on the impact of globalization on indigenous communities (see for example Chambers 1993; Scoones and Thompson 1994). Much of this literature refers to practical techniques and issues. One of the main themes emerging from these studies, however, indicates that there is little firm evidence that development practitioners have achieved widespread success in attaining goals of empowerment or participation. In addition there is also the possibility that in pursuing a broader and more holistic approach to development, wider theorizing may be submerged under the mass of emerging research. As Leys (1996) aptly puts it,

> There is . . . a discourse of 'complexity' in which everything is dissolved into its details, and the possibility of abstracting and trying to act on the main elements and forces at work in the world is obscured (if not actually denied); and for all its shortcomings the great merit of development theory has always consisted in being committed to the idea that we can and should try to change the world, not just contemplate it – which means, in practice, being willing to abstract from the detail, to identify structures and causal relationships and to propose ways of modifying them.
>
> (Leys 1996: 196)

For Booth (1994: 14) there is the danger then that 'post-impasse' thinking is merely 'glorified empiricism', in contrast to the over-generalized and one-dimensional theorizing of the 1960s and 1970s. He sees the challenge ahead as the endeavour to reconcile indigenous and local research, which captures the lived experience of development as well as the realities of different social worlds, with macro-dynamics. This will facilitate historically grounded comparison which is not constrained by abstract theoretical constructs, but which is informed by consistent, systematic and multilevel frameworks and analysis. It is only then that the cross-national research paradigm will be able to capture the diversity of processes and the range of players involved in social development.

Non-governmental organizations and the state

The third sector now has a far more significant role in promoting social development and providing social services than ever before, particularly since the virtual collapse of welfare systems in many developing countries. As Hulme (1994) points out, this emphasis on the use of the third sector has been consistent with both New Right aid policies of governments in, for example, the USA and the UK as well as the 'alternative' aid policies of the donor countries of Scandinavia and the Netherlands. The strategy has been bolstered by the rhetoric of decentralization, local participation, self-help and partnerships and reinforced by western government and multilateral donors as an alternative to funding so-called corrupt and inefficient developing country governments.

NGOs in general have become a major influence on the direction of change and the research agenda. There is a bewildering array of organizations that could be included under the broad rubric of NGO. The OECD, for example, suggests that NGOs may include:

> profit-making organisations, foundations, educational institutions, churches and other religious groups and missions, medical organisations and hospitals, unions and professional organisations, co-operative and cultural groups, as well as voluntary agencies.
>
> (OECD 1988: 14)

While in many developing countries the role of the state has been reduced (UNDP 1999), there has been a concomitant increase in NGO activity, particularly in the field of social welfare provision, with these organizations seen as conduits of development assistance, particularly during the 1980s and 1990s. Indeed, the growth of NGOs, particularly from the 1980s, has been remarkable. Development NGOs registered in OECD countries grew from 1600 in 1980 to 2960 in 1993, with total spending rising from US$2.8 billion to US$5.7 billion in the same period (Smillie and Helmich 1993). In developing countries the growth in numbers of NGOs is even more staggering, particularly since the late 1980s. In Tunisia, for example, from 1988 to 1991 the number of NGOs rose from 1886 to 5186 (Marzouk 1997). International NGOs have flourished too, from approximately 200 in the 1960s to 28,900 in 1993 (Commission on Global Governance 1995).

A major force shaping the third sector in terms of scale and composition is the changing relationship between official donor agencies and the third sector (Hulme 1994). As well as the growth in numbers of NGOs, the size of many of these organizations is also increasing: 'the Bangladesh Rural Advancement Committee now has more than 12,000 staff and has plans to work with over three million people' (Hulme and Edwards 1997: 4). According to World Bank estimates, donor funding (both bilateral and multilateral) to NGOs has increased from about 1.5 per cent of total income for development in the 1970s to around 30 per cent in the mid-1990s (Overseas Development Institute (ODI) 1995: 1). There is, however, considerable variations between bilateral donors (country to country lending) as to how much funding NGOs in particular countries will receive: in Austria, around 10 per cent of NGO income is from official sources, in Sweden the figure is a massive 85 per cent (Hulme and Edwards 1997: 7). What is clear from the above is that NGOs are a growing and significant force in development. The surge in funding they receive from governments and multilateral donors (lending from institutions with multiple-country subscribers, like the World Bank or UN organizations) has implications for the label 'non-governmental'.

These changes, with the concomitant danger that 'he who pays the piper may call the tune' have blurred the boundaries between what is truly *non-governmental* and what is not.[1] For those southern governments who resent the diversion of funds to NGOs where previously the state had controlled most donor monies, restriction and/or control of NGOs operating within their national boundaries are not uncommon. National registers of NGOs and issues of licences to those NGOs the government approves of, has offered the possibility for governments to assert some control over NGO activities. However, it can also be the case that 'the state . . . merely acts as a passive recipient . . . Driven by poverty and want . . . [it] cannot afford to challenge the NGOs lest the assistance is taken away to another country' (Mwansa 1995: 72–3, cited in Osei-Hwedie and Bar-on 1999: 110) – even when the interests of the providers do not coincide with those of the national government.

Alternatively, some southern governments set up their own NGOs and compete for official donor funding with other NGOs – what have been called 'governmental non-governmental organizations' (GONGOs). Quasi-autonomous non-governmental organizations (QUANGOs) and donor non-governmental organizations (DONGOs) give similar problems. What seems to be relevant for inclusion as an NGO in these cases is the status of having a self-governing structure (which at times needs to be flexibly interpreted to allow inclusion as an NGO), rather than as strictly non-governmental.

Tvedt (1998) argues that, as donor governments increase lending to NGOs, a kind of 'isophomorphism' occurs where NGOs increasingly resemble the values and organizational structure of donors. 'By adapting to the donor states' requirements regarding aid profile, professionalism, and reporting systems, organizations [i.e. NGOs] have been reshaped in the ways they operate and conceive of themselves' (Tvedt 1998: 214). Certainly, donors and NGOs share similar discourse, 'donor-speak' is increasingly also 'NGO-speak', in which there is a common rhetoric about what is 'good development' and what is 'not good development'. There is a hegemonic discourse, where previously NGOs were more valued for their independence from, or opposition to, the state. Hulme (1994) also argues that increased dependence on external resources dramatically affects the activities of NGOs, given official donors' general preference for project activities such as small loans and income-generation schemes. Thus, the activities of NGOs are 'projectized', 'while in proportional terms mobilization, conscientization, the development of local leaders and advocacy become less significant' (Hulme 1994: 266). Assessment of NGO performance is difficult to generalize about, because of the absence of a large body of reliable evidence from which to make such judgements. What is usually released by NGOs themselves comes closer to propaganda than rigorous assessment. The evidence that is available (Fowler 1985; Bebbington and Thiele 1993; Wellard and Copestake 1993; Vivian 1994) increasingly questions claims that NGOs are 'closer to the poor' or are more cost-effective providers of services. Although there are examples of NGOs that are more cost-effective at providing services, other evidence contradicts this (for example Tendler 1989), and there is no general case that can be made for NGO cost-effectiveness. Even when lower costs are achieved, it usually fails to reach the poorest of the poor (Farrington and Bebbington 1993; Hulme and Mosley 1996).

Bebbington (1997: 118) argues for a rethinking of NGO roles in the face of the very limited impact they have had. Those more hostile claim that 'the social processes that these organisations generate are reactionary in content, elitist in terms of the interests they represent, and insensitive to the real interests of the poor and the dispossessed' (Fernando and Heston 1997). Salamon (1994: 34) points to the NGO phenomenon as equalling the significance of the nation-state in the nineteenth century. Whichever is the more accurate, NGOs are firmly on the agenda for social research not only in relation to developing countries but also those within the OECD where there has also been a growth in the role and influence of NGOs.

Conclusion

The effectiveness of traditional development thinking has provoked intense debate. Greater experience of development outcomes has highlighted that there is nothing 'inevitable' about the direction of development and thus no single explanation or strategy for achieving development goals. There is growing awareness of the complexity and multifaceted nature of development, as well as the diversity of experience throughout the countries of the

South. The Eurocentric paradigm of modernization constructed and perpetuated the discourse and policy orientation of development by dictating
which questions were to be asked, the types of methods to be used, as well
as the theoretical frameworks to be employed. However, far from closing
the gap between rich and poor countries, the gap has widened. The inability of this approach to effect sustainable forms of development, and the
continuing and in some cases, deepening levels of poverty and human
suffering have opened up the opportunity for alternative strategies. Social
policy, historically seen as subordinate to the key goal of economic growth,
is beginning to emerge as a distinct sphere through which to improve the
well-being of individuals and communities and improve human and social
capital. Though influenced by the neo-liberal preoccupations of efficiency,
privatization, targeting and residualism, it is an indication of the broadening of the development paradigm. It is now not only about economic
growth and poverty alleviation but also about educational and health
reform as well as empowerment, participation and sustainability. The
rhetoric has not yet become a reality, with many of the primary needs of the
people in the countries of the South going unmet. Polarization in the distribution of wealth and the growth of poverty and social exclusion is evident
in most countries around the world, both developed and developing. Chapter 5 considers the dynamics of inclusion and exclusion in Australia, Britain
and Japan. These dynamics are complex and overlap with the social division of class, gender and ethnicity. Thus, the interpretation of social
development as a multidimensional strategy towards human development
incorporating skill enhancement, participation by individuals and communities, as well as the equitable distribution of resources and opportunities is becoming increasingly relevant for promoting the well-being of
people not only in the South, but also in other parts of the world. In the
context of the apparent failure of Eurocentric paradigms to solve the problems in western capitalist societies and Eastern and Central Europe the
recommendation from Wignaraja (1999) that we should look for an
alternative intellectual framework emanating from within the countries of
the South seems highly appropriate.

Note

1 There is some controversy among NGOs themselves about the extent of donor
   influence on NGOs as a result of higher proportions of their funding being derived
   from governments. The older, more established NGOs, like Oxfam in the UK, are
   suspicious of the proliferation of 'new' NGOs, their competitors for funding,
   arguing that such organizations may act more opportunistically than those NGOs
   with more clearly defined long-term developmental goals. For a full discussion of
   the impact of official aid on NGOs see Edwards and Hulme (1995).

Further reading

MacPherson, S. and Midgley, J. (1987) *Comparative Social Policy and the Third World*. Brighton: Wheatsheaf. This book sets out to critique conventional cross-national comparative research which focuses on welfare institutions in industrial countries. It focuses on countries of the 'Third World' and the themes of need and deprivation and welfare institutions and attempts to extend the breadth of comparative analysis. It considers the theoretical and conceptual implications of linking the North and South into an integrated global framework.

Morales-Gomez, D. (ed.) (1999) *Transnational Social Policies: The New Development Challenges of Globalization*. London: Earthscan. This useful collection examines theoretical and practical issues relating to developing countries, as well as the domestic and global challenges facing the countries of the South. Comparative chapters cover West and Central Africa, Sub-Saharan Africa, South-East Asia and the Americas. The book concludes by considering the critical role of social policy in establishing a 'new development paradigm', and the institutional framework through which the process can take place.

Rahnema, M. with Bawtree, B. (eds) (1977) *The Post-Development Reader*. London: Zed Books. This reader brings together a range of issues associated with the countries of the South and the development paradigm. It covers the theoretical, ideological, institutional and practical dimensions of development. A number of chapters focus on the potential for a 'post-development' age, and suggest alternative perspectives and paradigms to bring about change.

chapter

five

Ethnicity, gender and the boundaries of citizenship: Australia, Britain and Japan

Introduction

The 1980 and 1990s have seen issues of ethnicity and gender gaining a more prominent place in social research, something that has yet to be achieved in cross-national analysis. This chapter introduces the theme of citizenship as a dynamic analytical tool for undertaking critical, cross-national analysis. The focus of this chapter will be Australia, Britain and Japan. Citizenship is fundamentally concerned with the articulation of relations between people and the institutional arrangements in a society and, in this analysis, the influence of the social relations of gender, ethnicity and class. This chapter will demonstrate how boundaries of social rights are constructed within specific discourses which legitimize the exclusion of, for example, women and ethnic minorities from full citizen status, and which reinforce divisions between the deserving and the undeserving poor.

Key elements of this discussion include not only who should be considered a citizen of a particular society and thus have particular entitlements and who should not, but also the nature of and the balance between rights and obligations. It emphasizes the dynamic nature of the concept of 'citizenship' and the social contract and shows how the meaning of the terms shifts over time and across national boundaries. Australia, Britain and Japan have experienced diverse historical pathways in the development of social policy, with their specific webs of welfare emerging in different cultural, political and ideological contexts. Thus, they provide the opportunity for highlighting aspects of 'differentiated citizenship' in cross-national perspective.

The citizenship theme

The notion of citizenship stretches back to the ancient Greeks but has re-emerged more recently in relation to the expansion of welfare provision in industrial societies immediately after the Second World War, and now in relation to concern about the reorientation of the state, a renegotiation of the social contract and new sets of supranational influences impacting on the role of the state and the nature of citizenship. The term citizenship, in its original Greek formulation, was principally an issue of political rights and participatory democracy, though even then women and slaves were excluded as they were not considered full citizens. More recently Hill (1994: 9) has observed that 'Citizenship is both a status, derived from membership of a collectivity . . . and a system of rights and obligations'. As Dahrendorf (1996) points out:

> Citizenship describes the rights and obligations associated with membership in a social unit and notably with nationality. It is therefore common to all members, though the question of who can be a member and who cannot is part of the turbulent history of citizenship.
> (Dahrendorf 1996: 31)

So one is a citizen of a collectivity, which has most commonly been viewed as the nation-state. With the rise of modernity, the creation of the nation-state and the establishment of the modern social contract in place of feudal bonds 'the ancient idea of citizenship' (Dahrendorf 1996: 30) became generalized.

There is no overarching model of citizenship. It is subject to various political interpretations and social forces which change over time and from country to country. As mentioned above, the concept has a long history but is most commonly associated with the work of T.H. Marshall (1950) for whom citizenship is based upon rights and entitlements. His central theme was that the rights of citizenship involve national constitutional rights such as civil and political rights, as well as embracing social rights, each of which is closely associated with social and political institutions as indicated in Table 5.1.

The hallmark of advanced industrial democracies is the eventual institutionalization of all three types of rights and, in particular, social citizenship. For Marshall, the citizenship rights that accrue to members of a political community integrate previously unintegrated segments of the population and serve to mitigate some of the inequalities of class, thus altering the pattern of social inequality. Marshall discusses 'class fusion' which he refers to as the 'general enrichment of the concrete substance of civilised life, a general reduction of risk and insecurity, and equalisation between the more or less fortunate at all levels' (Marshall 1950: 6). This leads 'towards a fuller measure of equality, an enrichment of the stuff of which the status is made

Table 5.1 Elements of citizenship

Element of citizenship	Introduction of rights	Characteristics of rights and associated institutions
Civil rights	Eighteenth century	'The civil element is composed of the rights necessary for individual freedom – liberty of the person, freedom of speech, thought and faith, the right to own property and to conclude valid contracts, and the right to justice.' Civil and criminal courts of justice.
Political rights	Nineteenth century	'By the political element I mean the right to participate in an exercise of political power, as a member of a body invested with political authority or as an elector of such a body.' Parliament and local elective bodies.
Social rights	Twentieth century	'By the social element I mean the whole range from the right to a modicum of economic welfare and security to the right to share to the full in the social heritage and to live the life of a civilised being according to the standards prevailing in the society.' Educational system and social services.

Source: Marshall 1950: 74

and an increase in the number of those on whom the status is bestowed' (Marshall 1950: 29). Marshall's thesis has been criticized for its evolutionary and Anglocentric nature (Giddens 1982; Mann 1987). The sequential development of citizenship rights outlined by Marshall (1950) might well reflect the English experience, but 'is misleading when applied to other countries' (Rees 1996: 14). It is also said to place too much emphasis on class. As Marsh (1998) points out, general accounts of citizenship often render other social divisions in society, such as gender and ethnicity, invisible. Pedersen (1993) argues that

> Marshall . . . developed a theory of 'social citizenship' that claimed to be universal but was constructed in such a way as to be applicable only to men. Women were not defined by Marshall as 'dependent' – they disappeared from the picture entirely – and with their going the manifold ways in which the welfare state addressed family and dependency relations vanished as well.
>
> (Pedersen 1993: 6)

Marshall (1950) also fails to recognize the contingency, flexibility and fragility of the social contract between the state and the individual and that the attainment of citizenship rights and the opportunity to exercise such rights is a process of constant struggle and negotiation. The progression from civil to political and social rights is not the smooth, inevitable process that Marshall suggests, but has always been dependent on political struggles between social movements, groups and classes. Retrogression and the erosion of the rights of particular groups are an ever-present possibility. Giddens (1982: 171) in particular is keen to stress that 'each of these three sets of citizenship rights . . . had to be fought for, over a long span of historical time'. And for Smith (1989), it is precisely these conflictual elements which make the citizenship framework a

> comprehensive vehicle through which to explore systematic discrepancies between the obligations required of, and the rights extended to members of a nation-state. Enduring variations in the availability of these rights, or in the opportunities to exercise them effectively, can thus be conceptualised as forces shaping or structuring society.
>
> (Smith 1989: 148)

Citizenship configurations are not only the outcome of class struggle but, according to Williams (1994), also involve the interplay of the relations of other forms of social power such as racism and patriarchy, and are equally significant in the reproduction of 'race' and gender-related inequalities. While welfare systems reflect the cultural, economic and political specificities of individual nation-states they are also, to varying degrees, a product of the 'interrelation between capitalism, patriarchy and imperialism' (Williams 1994: 61). Marshall (1950) was interested in the integrative implications of citizenship rights. More recent interpretations have focused on the contingent and differentiated nature of the citizenship framework and have been concerned with the content of and the balance between rights and obligations. Access to citizenship rights, the ability of individuals to exercise those rights and the nature of rights have been shown to vary both within nations and between nations and also to change over time.

Welfare and citizenship

The concepts of citizenship and social rights are encapsulated within the institutions and ideology of the welfare state. Britain, Australia and Japan represent variants of post-war social policy, each with its own particular 'web of welfare' as outlined below. The following discussion on the formulation of social rights will attempt to capture the different historical legacies, the varying ideologies and thus the contingency, flexibility and fragility of the social contract between the state and the individual in Britain, Australia and Japan.

In both Britain and Australia following the Second World War, the ethos of egalitarianism prevailed and the trends were towards decreasing social inequality. This was an era in which 'the concept of citizenship was given an invigorated meaning' (Tomlinson 1996: 4). The British context was that on an ideological commitment to social planning and to the welfare state. The post-war welfare consensus emphasized an explicit commitment to state intervention through universal access to direct public provision of welfare benefits. It accepted an extended role for the state in economic and social policy and implicitly guaranteed social rights of citizenship for the whole population. In reality the welfare citizenship of women, black people and the poor was not secured. As Ginsberg (1992: 141) comments, 'the whole notion of welfare citizenship at the heart of the post-war consensus was ideological in the sense that it carried nationalist overtones and implied the exclusion of certain people from the benefits of citizenship'. Nevertheless, the post-war expansion in welfare enormously extended the range of state support for the individual.

In Australia the strong emphasis on citizenship and equality translated into equality to participate in the labour market and receive a living wage, at least for the organized, white, male population. The Harvester Judgment of 1907 ensured that a 'fair and reasonable wage must be based on need . . . The minimum wage should be that amount that would allow a worker to live as a human being in a civilized community and to keep himself and his family in frugal comfort' (Macintyre 1985: 55). Distinctions were made between male and female employment categories, and the ensuing wage discrimination was not legislated against until 1972 (Levi and Singleton 1991). Levi and Singleton (1991: 12) characterize the early period of Australian welfare history (1890–1910) as a 'beacon of progressive and innovative policies' with, for example, the introduction of the Invalid and Old Age Pensions Act 1909. As the Australian welfare system expanded to include compensation for various circumstances in life, such as unemployment and lone parenthood, the assurance was of only minimum income security through an extensive range of flat-rate, means-tested and targeted pensions and benefits. The emphasis was on minimum support for the needy rather than universal or earnings-related support. The main focus of state intervention has been wage regulation in and social protection through the labour market, resulting in the distinctive pattern of social policy outcomes labelled the 'wage earners' welfare state' (Castles 1988), reflecting the role of the labour movement in the shaping of social rights. It has been the notion of the 'industrial citizenship' (right to strike, form trade unions, and so on) which has been paramount within the conceptualization of the 'wage earners' welfare state' and promoted individualism and limited direct state provision. According to Jayasuriya (1991: 32), industrial citizenship emphasized 'the industrial activity of men, rather than advocating political citizenship for men and women alike'. The maintenance of this system involved three main pillars which Castles (1988) has referred to as a policy strategy of 'domestic defence'.

The first was a system of compulsory conciliation and arbitration of industrial disputes with the aim of 'simultaneously achieving a social policy minimum (a "fair wage" sufficient to support a breadwinner and a family) and of adjusting wage levels to take account of fluctuations caused by dependence on a highly unstable commodity market' (Castles 1993: 8). The second was a series of tariff and import controls which were used to protect domestic manufacturing from overseas competition, and the third involved the regulation of migration to control labour supply and exclude low-wage labour, minimize unemployment and protect wage levels negotiated through arbitration. Michael Jones (1996: 10) refers to the uniqueness of the Australian approach to social welfare as, more accurately, 'a planned attempt to create a white society based on high wages in an economy sheltered from overseas competition'. The policy of 'domestic defence' was the inclusionary policy mechanism through which the government and an organized working class could attempt to ensure and maintain the social rights of the employed citizen (white and male) and which justified the principles of residualism and selectivism in the development of social policy which sought 'to encourage even the moderately affluent to provide for their own welfare in retirement and during troubled times in their lives' (M. Jones 1996: 10).

In Japan, the immediate post-war experience was of Allied Occupation until 1952 (mainly by the USA), poverty and hunger. It was also a period of high unemployment and popular unrest orchestrated by the political Left and the then influential trade union movement. Reconstruction and recovery began with the eradication of 'the ultra-nationalism of the wartime period' and the introduction of the 'concepts of democracy, liberalism and citizenship' by the Occupation government (Goodman 1998: 143). Constitutional reform granted Japanese citizens 'a minimum standard of healthy civilized life' on an equal basis, and legally abolished the pre-war family system of the *ie* (discussed in more detail later in the chapter). Article 14, Para. 1 of the 1947 Constitution stipulates that 'All of the people are equal under the law and there shall be no discrimination in political, economic or social relations because of race, creed, sex, social status and family origin.' Although comprehensively changing the legal position of women, even the most liberal constitution in the world has had only limited impact on the lives of women in Japan (see Mackie 1988).

By the 1950s and early 1960s 'epoch-making steps towards a welfare state were taken in Japan' (Takahashi 1997: 83) as economic reconstruction and recovery were overtaken by economic growth. These steps included the reform and extension of the complex social insurance schemes for health care and pensions to cover the whole population not just those in privileged sections of the labour market. Takahashi (1997) points out, however:

> Despite their universalistic principle and appearance, the pension and medical care systems kept selective features to some degree. [Nevertheless] this reform meant a remarkable step forward escaping from the pre-war style of division of citizens according to different social and occupational status.
>
> (Takahashi 1997: 84)

This was the beginning of a period in which the development of social security schemes and the extension of citizenship were seen to complement and enhance the possibilities for modernization and sustained economic growth, vital in Japan's efforts to catch up with the west. By 1973 Japan had entered the 'beginning of welfare' era with the introduction of free medical care for elderly people, child allowance and a reassessment of the general level of benefits. The oil crisis of 1974, however, precipitated the curtailment of Japan's economic growth and led to recession, austerity and pressure for a reconsideration of welfare.

Key features of the Japanese social and welfare structure include the family system, which still remains strong, and the labour market structure. The family system has been relied upon to provide many of the benefits provided by the state in other industrial countries and a legal framework supports the notion of familial obligation and responsibility within the public welfare system (see Peng 2000). This process has been reinforced by the complex relations of the *ie* family system, despite its abolition after the Second World War. These elements are interwoven into the fabric of the Japanese system of welfare and will be discussed later in this chapter. In relation to the labour market, enterprise based full employment has relied on a highly regulated, 'closed' economy, with non-tariff barriers severely restricting foreign competition (Mishra 1999). Japanese employment practices can be characterized by the broadly accepted system of indefinite (career long) employment, pay scales pegged to seniority and length of service, and enterprise unions. These elements are common practice in most major corporations but have been adopted to a considerable degree in smaller firms as well.

Traditionally larger companies have guaranteed lifetime employment and have themselves provided social benefits such as housing and health care and have filled the gap left by the state. As Catherine Jones (1993) argues:

It is for occupational social security cover that Japan stands out. Pensions, health insurance, unemployment protection, even help with home purchase: for those in mainstream employment, especially with a major corporation, quality of career very much spills over into quality of social entitlements.

(C. Jones 1993: 212)

In addition to age, gender and qualification, household structure and family life cycle of the worker also play an important role in determining salary (Peng 2000). Peng (2000) points to the paradox that while Japanese workers are highly dependent on the labour market,

the notion of family income, along with Japanese companies' commitment to lifetime employment and automatic seniority system can, ironically, imply a relatively high decommodifying condition for male workers and their families as well.

(Peng 2000: 93)

However, there are substantial differences in salaries, benefits and conditions between types and size of companies and the nature of an individual's connection to the labour market. The large companies employ only a minority of the Japanese workforce, with the bulk of the labour force employed in small or medium-size enterprises. According to Sugimoto (1997) it is the small and medium-sized enterprises (companies which employ more than 300 persons or whose capital does not exceed a particular sum) which are the mainstay of the Japanese economy. Nationally, large corporations with 300 or more workers employ less than one-eighth of the labour force in the private sector. In Tokyo, 99 per cent of Tokyo's enterprises are medium and small-sized establishments, and they employ 72 per cent of all the workers in the city. The Tokyo Metropolitan Government (1997: 119) recognizes that 'the level of working conditions and welfare of the workers of these medium and small enterprises is considerably lower in comparison with that of workers in large enterprises' and sets itself the 'fundamental goal to improve working conditions'. The Japanese labour market also includes a system of subcontracting and more casual forms of employment, such as day labouring, for those at the bottom end of the labour market. Peng (2000) argues that the major achievement of the post-war Japanese welfare state has been the establishment of the individual's right to be employed and to employment security, exemplified in the system of lifetime employment. However, in times of recession, while larger enterprises can fulfil the commitments of the employment practices mentioned earlier, the flexibility is absorbed by the day labourers and contract workers who bear the brunt of the impact of market fluctuation. These workers, often from minority groups, are invisible in the dominant image of the model Japanese citizen – the middle class salaryman, a white-collar male company employee in the private sector. According to Sugimoto (1997):

He embodies all the stereotypical images associated with the Japanese corporate employee: loyalty to his company, subservience to the hierarchical order of his enterprise, devotion to this work, and a long and industrious working life, and job security in his career.

(Sugimoto 1997: 37)

It is also the case that this notion of the model citizen and the labour practices which support it are premised on a quite specific model of family life and gender division of labour in Japanese society.

Linking citizenship and gender

In all three countries dimensions of inequality have been created based around patriarchy and racism. Though women have made substantial gains in relation to both civil and political rights, an investigation of their social rights and status as citizens reveals, according to Pateman (1989: 35), 'the patriarchal character of ostensibly universal categories'. Women are incorporated as members of the family, a private sphere that is essential to, but separate to and opposite from, the public sphere of civil society and the state, which are historically male constructs. The white male worker represents 'the individual', 'the citizen' in the public sphere, and is legitimized in the private sphere as the 'breadwinner'. A range of policies construct women as wives, mothers and carers in the private (domestic) sphere, regulating their social role and reinforcing their dependency. The form and specific historical source of patriarchy shifts over time and place and, according to Pateman (1989), has evolved from the 'father' to the 'husband', with the state and the economy particularly significant as the site of patriarchy during the post-war years. This in turn is influenced by the social relations established between the state and the individual which vary across national boundaries and over time. To understand the position of women one must analyse the significance of the discourse and legitimation for different patterns of participation, choice and citizenship.

Gender figures heavily in the extent to which men and women are assigned the same or different rights. Social rights to welfare resources reflect and reconstruct relations between men and women through the linkage between welfare resources and the social structures of family and dependency. Japanese society since the Meiji era (1868–1912) has been centred on the family and the place of women within the family in a complex relationship called the *ie*. Traditionally, women were subsumed into the hierarchical ranks of the family on the basis of their relationships to male kin – father, husband, eldest son or eldest brother. This familial ideology, established in the Meiji era, has provided a structure and basis for the Japanese social structure reinforced by the notion of the 'traditional' and 'unique' Japanese family system. According to Mackie (1988: 59), it has been used as 'an "ideological construct" . . . to justify women's relegation to the domestic sphere'.

The Meiji era was a period of modernization and transformation in Japan. As the feudal state of the Tokugawa regime disintegrated, Japan became a constitutional monarchy. Institutions of the Meiji state were concerned with maintaining the pivotal position of the emperor as the ruler and ensuring that the people would be loyal to the ruler as the embodiment of their 'general will' (Eisenstadt 1996). Within the Constitution of 1890, rights and duties were considered subject to the power of the emperor and included 'a number of laws which relegated women ideologically – if not in fact – to the domestic sphere in the patriarchal family based on the principle of primogeniture' (Mackie 1988: 54). Thus, as Mackie (1988) points out, the democratic rights of the people, particularly women, were severely curtailed.

Meiji ideology emphasized 'traditional' values and virtues, with the imagery and symbolism of the emperor himself referring to the restoration of an ancient imperial system. In addition, the Meiji state utilized neo-Confucian principles and, to a lesser extent Buddhism, to support a collective ideology and national ethos. Confucianism was originally introduced into Japan in the seventh century and emerged as an important element in both the Tokugawa and Meiji regimes. Neither Buddhism nor Confucianism were influential enough to 'transform the basic premises of Japanese social organization . . . nor create . . . distinctly new modes of social organisation' (Eisenstadt 1996: 225). However, there can be no doubt that reformulated Confucian themes such as hierarchy, harmony, discipline and loyalty were selected and incorporated into the national discourses with the aim of creating a national ethos, and reinforcing the basic premises of the existing social and political order. As Eisenstadt (1996) explains:

> in Meiji Japan the symbols and symbolic constructs promulgated by the bearers of the official ideology, whether in the constitution, the civil code, or the rescript on education – and their appropriation and reconstruction of tradition, which included the use of existing religious settings . . . continuously emphasised the sanctity of an ostensibly older primordial-sacral hierarchical order, even if these 'traditional' themes were actually entirely new constructs.
>
> (Eisenstadt 1996: 48)

The family and kinship networks were constructed as central elements in promoting traditional values and virtues, with the system itself reflecting the relationship between the emperor and the nation, with the patriarchal head holding virtually absolute power over the household members (Sugimoto 1997). Despite substantial reform and the extension of citizenship rights in the post-war period, remnants of the patriarchal system still permeate the

Japanese institutional and social structure. The authority relations of the *ie* were seen as representative of those which should exist in all aspects of Japanese society – male dominance and filial obedience. As mentioned earlier, the lifetime employment system is based on a quite specific model of family and gender divisions of labour. Male workers are expected to become responsible breadwinners and to be called upon for sustained and loyal participation in the workplace. Domestic and familial responsibilities are the domain of women, which was actually institutionalized and supported by governments in a series of policies labelled the 'protection of motherhood'. The Labour Standards Law 1947 severely restricted the work that women could do outside the home. However, in recent years the number of women in the labour force has increased quite substantially. The number of employed women increased by 7.7 million or 57 per cent, between 1980 and 1997, compared with 6.4 million, or 24.5 per cent, for men. In 1997, women accounted for 39.5 per cent of all workers. The revised Equal Employment Opportunity Law came into effect on 1 April 1999, prohibiting gender discrimination in hiring, placement and promotion. In addition, the Revised Labour Standards Law took effect, lifting restrictions on women working overtime and late at night. Despite the implementation of the Family-Care Leave Law in 1995 only 60.8 per cent of companies had actually made provision for childcare leave by 1996 (Foreign Press Centre 1999). As Ichibangase (1992: 87) points out, it is still the case that a woman in Japan 'leaves her working place twice – for bearing children and for looking after her aged relations' (cited in Takahashi 1997: 110).

In post-war Britain, the importance of women's role as wives and mothers in ensuring the continuation of the British race was enshrined within the Beveridgian settlement in which women were treated as dependants of the male breadwinner. Policy supported and was directed towards the patriarchal family, particularly in areas such as housing and social security entitlements. The 'married women's option' exemplified this role assignment, with married women able to pay less social security contribution and therefore receive less benefits. Although this option was dismantled in the 1970s following the passage of equal opportunities legislation, little systematic state aid has ensued to assist women's integration into the labour market. Lister (1997) argues that the UK's position in relation to the care of children exemplifies a liberal welfare regime 'in which childcare is seen as the responsibility of the individual parent, and to a lesser extent the voluntary sector and employers, but not the state, to the particular detriment of lone-parent families' (Lister 1997: 183). This is compounded, in turn, by what Leira (1992) refers to as the tensions between wage-earner and carer in the construction of women's citizenship, with the privileging of the former over the latter in 'the hierarchy of work forms, which accords primacy to wage-work, however useless, over other forms of work, however useful' (Leira 1992: 171).

In Australia the two-tier system of welfare divided between social insurance and social assistance is not evident. Generally, only the latter is available. Because of this, the Australian system, though shaped by assumptions about the traditional sexual division of labour, has not been quite as deeply gendered (Orloff 1995) as in Britain and Japan. The unitary system of flat-rate means-tested benefits for those outside the labour market 'does not offer different benefits to the clients of work-related versus family related programmes' (Orloff 1995: 46), thus exposing the unemployed as well as single mothers to stigmatized, residual benefits. In other words, benefit programmes do not reward former wage-earners any more than those who have principally been carers. However, Shaver (1990: 14) argues that 'the fiscal circulation of social citizenship is patriarchal in both symbolic and material effects'. She continues:

> claimants are treated as members of family groups, making provision for dependent members and applying means test to joint income . . . Monies are taxed from individuals, with men paying the largest amount because of their larger incomes. Monies are returned to the same individuals only as members of family groups, with eligibility in ideologies of maternalism, marriage and mutuality. The overall circulation reproduces the breadwinner/dependent relation of traditional family ideology.
>
> (Shaver 1990: 14)

However, the recognition of widespread poverty facing solo-parent households in the 1970s and 1980s led to the extension of targeted support for this group. Combined with other legislative reform, such as the anti-discrimination and divorce law, the establishment of women's policy units and the increasing number of 'feminist bureaucrats' or 'femocrats' employed by the state, strategies for promoting policies to improve the circumstances of women in Australian society (Levi and Singleton 1991) are being put in place. The increased participation of women in the Australian labour force has, according to Castles (1994), meant that they are able

> to acquire the rights that accrue from participation in the occupational welfare system – sickness benefits (although often used by women for family rather than personal need), long-service leave (although far less frequently accrued by women than men because of interrupted careers) and now, progressively, rights to superannuation benefits in old age. Whether formally in terms of equal rights within the benefits system or more positively in terms of sharing the more valuable rights contingent on labour force participation . . . women no longer have a different and lesser status to men in Australia's welfare state.
>
> (Castles 1994: 138)

Nevertheless, the assumptions and influence of the male breadwinner model have influenced the different terms on which women compete in the labour market and has shaped the terms on which the boundaries of women's citizenship have been drawn. It is still the case that assumptions about women's nature, their economic status and the division of labour in the private and public spheres influence policy and affect women's capacities to act as citizens.

Policy logics of race, ethnicity and the nation

The most overt discussion of citizenship has been in relation to race and immigration. Issues relating to the citizenship of ethnic and racial minorities involve all levels of citizenship: civic, political and social. In addition, the relationship between citizenship, ethnicity and immigration has been central in defining identity and nationhood in all the countries. National identity is complex. It is constructed through a number of interrelated components – cultural, ethnic, territorial, political and legal. Bonds of solidarity develop around each of these components and binds together members of a national community. However, it also serves to differentiate between groups – the included and the excluded. It is the demarcation of boundaries that is central to the discovery of national identity. Through demarcation mechanisms, members of a national community are able to mark out who they are, to differentiate between insiders and outsiders, belonging and otherness. So national identity is produced almost through a process of negation, by the exclusion of groups deemed not to belong. This exclusion can take place within territories even for those with the same legal nationality. Ethnic difference, religious affiliation, age and gender are all potential barriers to citizenship. As discussed earlier, full citizenship rights have often been based on the domain of the white full-time male worker. Race and ethnicity have been used as socially constructed markers to regulate group boundaries defining who is included and who is excluded from a given collectivity – citizenship. There are variations in the extent to which immigrants are integrated and accepted in different nation-states, which themselves are the products of different national traditions and political cultures. The acquisition of citizenship and nationality is shaped by the way in which the nation is defined within the different discourses on nationality and national identity in different countries.

The relationship between citizenship, ethnicity and immigration has been central in defining identity and nationhood in all the three countries. These dimensions have played a major role in what it means to be Australian, and in defining Australia's place in the world. Castles *et al.* (1992) have pointed to two distinct processes in relation to Australian nationhood. He refers on the one hand to the dispossessed Australian Aboriginal people whose destruction and exclusion have been sought through physical and cultural genocide, and on the other hand to the labour recruitment, settlement and incorporation of migrant populations. In post-war Australia, for example, the particular configuration of citizenship excluded the indigenous people (Aborigines and Torres Strait Islanders) whose presence preceded colonial settlement and who were never considered a useful source of labour and therefore never incorporated as industrial citizens. In fact, many of the legislative mechanisms explicitly excluded Aboriginal people from accessing social rights such as social security and award wages so that when they did work their conditions were often close to slavery. According to Bryson (1992) it was not until the mid-1960s that the trade union movement intervened to end their exploitation. Even though little concern was shown for immigrants, particularly those of non-British origin, they were at least able to participate in the labour market.

One of the first acts of the New Commonwealth Parliament in 1901 was to establish the White Australia policy through the Immigration Restriction Act, which was to remain in force as the basis for immigration policy until the 1960s. According to Pearson (1995):

> The vision of Australian nationhood set out in 1901 . . . was, of course, racist and strongly committed to the notion of a perpetual British society in the South Pacific. The exclusion from citizenship of Aboriginal peoples showed that the vision of nationhood conceived of no place for the country's original inhabitants because they were of a different and inferior race.
>
> (Pearson 1995: 2)

By 1947 only 9 per cent of the Australian population was overseas-born and only 1 per cent (including Aborigines) was of non-European origin. After this period, though Britain remained the largest single source of immigrants, it was unable to meet population growth targets and the emphasis shifted to non-British, 'white' European immigrants. Maintenance of the White Australia policy involved emphasizing assimilation and cultural homogeneity. For Aborigines assimilation policies were, according to Castles *et al.* (1992: 21), 'a cloak for concealing the desperate socio-economic situation of many blacks, both urban and rural' and an attempt to destroy Aboriginal identity through, for example, the removal of Aboriginal children from their parents under the auspices of the Aborigines Protection Act 1909 (NSW), a practice which continued until the 1970s.

The referendum that occurred in 1967 was, according to Tomlinson (1996: 4) 'the first public recognition of Aboriginal citizenship in their own country' and was followed by a reassertion of Aboriginal identity and political action. There was greater involvement in Aboriginal affairs policy at a national level rather than state level and self-determination and self-management became important policy goals. During the 1970s the Department of Aboriginal Affairs and the Commonwealth Aboriginal Land Rights Act (Northern Territory) 1976 were established and a range of Commonwealth Aboriginal programmes were initiated covering different forms of health and housing provision. This period of political and policy activity represented limited and stuttering progress but an important impetus towards Aboriginal citizenship was established, reinforced through the Mabo Judgment 1992 which recognized Aboriginal land rights. However, it is clear that the 'wage-earners' welfare state' has been unsuccessful in meeting the needs of the Aboriginal population. The unemployment rate of Aboriginal and Torres Strait Islander people is 38 per cent (almost five times the national rate), approximately 30 per cent of Aboriginal and Torres Strait Islander people were considered to be homeless or living in substandard accommodation in 1996 (Healey 1997), and life expectancy is between 15 and 17 years less than for the whole population (Australian Bureau of Statistics 1994). In addition, Aboriginal men and women are massively over-represented in police and prison custodial settings. The Royal Commission into Aboriginal Deaths in Custody, set up in 1987, reported that an Aboriginal person was 29 times more likely than a non-Aboriginal person to be held in police custody.

The issue of 'appropriateness' and the recognition of cultural specificity have emerged as the policy discourse has moved from one of assimilation to multiculturalism and cultural pluralism. The Australian population is now one of the most ethnically diverse in the world. There is a growing awareness and sensitivity to the idea that the policy and provision needs to reflect and incorporate the cultural and psychological needs of the various ethnic communities and Aboriginal people as well as meet their economic and social needs. Funds have been channelled through ethnic organizations for education, welfare and cultural programmes and Aboriginal and Torres Strait Islander people achieved a greater role in decision-making with the establishment of the Commonwealth of the Aboriginal and Torres Strait Islander Commission and 60 regional councils throughout Australia in 1990. However, Aborigines have chosen to distance themselves from the notion of **multiculturalism** and instead to find new meaning in the concept of citizenship through their particular claims as indigenous people with legitimate rights to self-determination and the restitution of land (Fletcher 1994).

In Britain the post-war years saw policies to promote the notion of a tolerant and accommodating 'mother country' maintaining the image of a Commonwealth led and nurtured by Britain. Confronted with a massive labour shortage following the end of the Second World War refugees and prisoners of war, followed by the recruitment of workers from other parts of Europe up to 1957 had gone some way to alleviating the shortage. The Labour and Conservative governments, however, were to turn towards the vast and inexpensive resources of labour available in the Caribbean and Asian subcontinent, to assist with the reconstruction of the British economy. The Nationality Act 1948 formally gave all members of the Commonwealth the full set of rights and privileges associated with British citizenship. This placed them on the same social, political and economic footing as Britons born in the UK. By 1958 about 125,000 West Indians and 55,000 Indians and Pakistanis had arrived as UK citizens under the Nationality Act 1958 and served to

> staff the boom and facilitate white upward (and outward) mobility while keeping wages to a minimum that would have been acceptable to the increasingly unionised white working class.
>
> (Mama 1984: 26)

Although Commonwealth immigrants possessed the equivalent legal rights, Jacobs (1985) describes a system of informal racism operating throughout the welfare state, prohibiting access to welfare rights for black people which, in turn served to reduce the black British to the status of second-class citizens. Since then a series of restrictive and selective immigration and nationality laws has meant that black immigration with a view to settlement has virtually come to an end (Gordon and Klug 1985). The Commonwealth Immigration Acts 1962 restricted the admission of Commonwealth immigrants for settlement to those who had been issued with employment vouchers, eventually reducing the numbers of vouchers and issuing mainly to skilled and professional people. The effect was that the total number of Commonwealth immigrants fell from 115,150 in 1961 to 41,762 in 1963 (Amin 1992). This was clearly a system which sought to 'cream off the most skilled and professional personnel from these countries [the Commonwealth] whilst keeping out their unskilled' (Sivanandan 1976: 354). In addition admission was refused if individuals or members of an individual's family would seem likely to seek 'recourse to public funds' (for example housing benefit and income support). By 1971 immigrant settler labour was, more or less, converted to migrant contract labour as workers could enter the UK only on specific and limited work contracts. The creation of tiers of citizenship was initiated within the concept of 'patrial', defining those who would not be subject to immigration control, deportation and employment restrictions as those persons having one or more parent or grandparent born in the UK. As Gordon and Klug (1985) have argued, those likely to be considered patrials were mostly of British descent and therefore white, while non-patrial citizens of the UK and colonies were most likely to be black. The circumstances of black men and women from the new Commonwealth (for example, the West Indies, India) indicate the flexibility of the 'universal' discourse of the post-war era. Indispensable for economic growth during the 1950s, they found themselves concentrated in inner city areas in poor housing (Jones 1970; Cater and Jones 1979), in the lowest stratum of the labour market and forced to take jobs in Britain below their level of qualifications (Castles and Kosack 1973). According to Sarre et al. (1989) the

> newcomers were not able to exercise any locational choice, but were instead forced to act as a replacement population, settling in areas

where they would not be in direct competition for jobs and housing
with the indigenous population.

(Sarre *et al.* 1989: 7)

Law (1996: 79) emphasizes that 'the differentiation in economic position,
migration history, political participation and perceptions of social citizenship are significant across minority ethnic groups, and they are becoming
increasingly evident'. However, the experience for many people from ethnic
minority groups in Britain has been marked by economic disadvantage, with
low pay and poor prospects in the labour market (Modood 1997) and
'racialized' practices in the delivery of welfare services and provision
(Harrison 1999). In contrast to the post-war era, more recently nations in
Western Europe have vigorously been discouraging immigration. The emergence of neo-racist sentiment has been fuelled by a discourse of race and
immigration which focuses on Europe's inability to integrate 'foreign' populations. Thus in the context of European integration, Balibar refers to the
emergence of differentialist racism where the sociological signifier has
replaced the biological one as 'the key representation of hatred and fear of
the other' (Balibar 1988: 21). According to Balibar (1988) the dominant
theme is no longer biological heredity, but the insurmountability of cultural
difference and the incompatibility of lifestyles and traditions which highlight
the harmfulness of abolishing frontiers and reinforce the maintenance of
'Fortress Europe' (see Bunyan 1991; Webber 1991).[1] These trends are evident in Britain where the breaking down of European frontiers, as well as
the reconfiguration of the UK, have called into question what it means to be
British. Issues around immigration, 'bogus' asylum seekers, ethnic origin
and national identity have taken centre stage.

An array of policy initiatives and legal and constitutional reforms, particularly following the Maastricht Treaty (1992), have created a comprehensive system of immigration controls across Europe. However, the response of
EU governments to the 'problem' of immigration, refugees and 'bogus'
asylum seekers has come mainly from ad-hoc, intergovernmental organizations emerging outside the formal apparatus of the EU. Most notable have
been the TREVI Group of Ministers (1976),[2] the Ad Hoc Group on Immigration (1986)[3] and the Schengen Accord (1985 and 1990)[4] established to
address issues of immigration in the context of law and order, terrorism,
public order and international cooperation on policing (Bunyan 1991). More
recently, the Treaty of Amsterdam (1997) incorporated the Schegen acquis
within the institutional and legal framework of the European Union.

The emerging supranational modes of regulation appear to be coalescing
around the issues of control and security (Geddes 2000), and could be said
to be contributing to an ideological construction of a European identity
involving 'us' and 'other'. The social dimension of the EU (discussed in
Chapter 1) emphasizes the rights of workers through improving working

conditions, health and safety, vocational training, and reinforces an emphasis on the conception of a European citizen as an 'industrial citizen'. Article 8 of the Maastricht Treaty deemed freedom of movement a crucial element of EU citizenship. Any national of EU member states is granted rights to stay in other member states for the purpose of employment and to remain there indefinitely. In 1990 freedom of movement was extended to include other categories of people besides workers. Rights of residence were granted to persons who are nationals of a member state (spouses and dependent children) with certain caveats regarding sufficient resources and without recourse to social assistance. What is important about the features of EU citizenship is that to be included in that category is entirely dependent on a conception of national citizenship, since EU citizenship can be acquired only by individuals holding citizenship in one of the member states. As a result the link between nationality and citizenship is, in the main, reproduced rather than undermined by the current conception of European citizenship. Thus, access to European citizenship, and consequently employment, labour mobility and social benefits seems to increasingly encapsulate a narrowly defined notion of EU nationals. Mitchell and Russell (1996) argue that while a nationalist logic places limitations on the further development of citizenship rights for EU nationals, it is a racist logic that has led to the systematic exclusion of 'cultural aliens' usually from less developed countries.

> The marginalization of this growing category and their deteriorating status is a logical extension of the hostile and unwelcoming attitude towards immigrants which is the hallmark of the European immigrations regime.
>
> (Mitchell and Russell 1996: 66)

The construction of national identity in Japan has been built around notions of racial homogeneity and classlessness. However, as Lie (1996: 43) argues, 'the very construction of modern Japan – indeed of all large modern nation states – entailed the subjugation and integration of disparate peoples'. According to Sugimoto (1997: 169), 'In everyday life, racism and ethnocentrism still remain strong in many sections of the community and the establishment' and there are a variety of minority groups, constituting around 4 per cent of the Japanese population, who are subject to discrimination (see Table 5.2).

Each of these groups' minority status emerges from different historical circumstances. The oldest group of peoples are the Aboriginal Ainus who, according to Sugimoto (1997: 185), have 'for more than 10 centuries . . . suffered a series of attempts by Japan's central government to invade and deprive them of their land and to totally assimilate them culturally and linguistically'. They are perceived as primitive by the majority of Japanese. It was only in 1997 that a new Ainu Law was passed recognizing the Ainu as a distinct race,

Table 5.2   Minority groups in Japan

Group	Population
Burakumin	3,000,000
Resident Koreans	700,000
Resident Chinese	250,000*
Ainu	24,000
Foreign workers	700,000
Illegal foreign workers	300,000**

Sources: Adapted from Sugimoto 1997: 171; *Vasishth 1997; **Foreign Press Centre 1999

and supporting the promotion of Ainu culture and traditions. This replaced previous legislation which was more concerned with assimilating the Ainu through Japanese education (*Buraku Liberation News* 1997). However, it is still the case that the Ainu are treated with 'condescending quaintness' by the majority of the population and 'made showpieces for the tourism industry' (Sugimoto 1997: 185).

Their survival as a separate race and culture is in doubt given their declining numbers and disappearing culture. The Ainu receive very little support from the Japanese government, unlike the Aboriginal population in Australia. However, the Ainu, like the indigenous Australians, have become more vocal politically on Ainu issues. They are also involved in international networks supporting the rights of indigenous peoples while at the same time international organizations such as the United Nations have been assessing country governments' human rights performance in relation to indigenous peoples.

The Burakumin are the traditional outcastes of the caste system dating back to feudal times. The Meiji government (1871–1921) abolished all status discrimination as part of its modernization programme; this did not eliminate prejudice but merely transformed if from the 'institutional discrimination of the Tokugawa period to social discrimination of the Meiji era' and beyond (Neary 1997: 56). The Burakumin share common ethnic and racial origins with the majority Japanese population and represent the largest minority group in Japan. Their outcaste status derives from two main sources. *Eta* refers to those involved in tasks considered to be polluting or contaminating such as the slaughter of animals, and working with leather. The *hinin* (non-human people) refers to beggars, entertainers and those involved with the disposal of the dead. The Burakumin have lived in segregated communities and their exclusion from Japanese society has exposed them to poverty, unemployment and homelessness.

In 1992 there were estimated to be 4603 designated Buraku (Burakumin communities) located mainly in the cities of Kyoto, Osaka and Kobe. However, according to Sugimoto (1997), there are an additional 1000 communities whose status is in dispute, and a more accurate assessment might be nearer 6000 communities, and approximately 3 million people. The debate over the designation of Buraku stems from the nature of the government's strategies to overcome the Buraku 'problem', first instituted in the 1960s, following vociferous and sustained campaigning from Burakumin activists. Measures to eliminate discrimination are targeted on distinct communities and have included the allocation of resources through grants and loans by central and local government to improve the inadequate social conditions in many Burakumin communities (see Neary 1997). They have addressed problems such as inadequate sewerage and sanitation, housing conditions and education. So, while the government is interested in controlling expenditure and limiting the number of designated Buraku communities, Burakumin groups are keen to extend and maximize the amount of support received from local and central government. However, the issue is not quite so clear cut for the community members themselves. While there are clearly benefits to designation, for community members the exposure is also likely to be accompanied by increased discrimination from the wider society.

While the number of Buraku households on public assistance dropped from 76 per thousand in 1975 to 62 per thousand in 1993, this is substantially above the national average of 7.1 per thousand. The same is true of access to higher education. Some 20 per cent of Buraku teenagers will receive higher education, compared to 40 per cent of the population as a whole (Neary 1997). Only 10.6 per cent of Burakumin were employed in enterprises of 300 or more, compared to the national average of 23.3 per cent. Neary (1997) suggests that this is an indication of the continuing discrimination exhibited by larger companies in their employment practices. This discrimination has been perpetuated and reinforced through the Koseki system. The Japanese social system is supported by the notion of Seki, the view that unless one is formally registered as belonging to an organization or institution, one has no proper status in society. The notion of Seki is supported by the Family Registration System – Koseki. The unit of Koseki is the household and a record of each individual's gender, birthplace, date of birth, parents' names, position among siblings, marriage, and divorce are kept in detail for each household koseki and filed in local municipal offices. The system not only highlights 'deviant' behaviour such as divorce, illegitimacy or de facto relationships, all of which could adversely affect the life-chances of all koseki members, but also has provided employers and potential parents-in-law with an opportunity to check the status of potential applicants and marriage partners for their children. The Koseki Law was revised in 1976, prohibiting public access to these records. Information highlighting the location of Burakumin communities was, nevertheless, published and distributed to employers, indicating how entrenched the prejudice is and the unwillingness of employers to employ Burakumin.

The entrenched prejudices against the Burakumin are gradually being eroded, with greater social and geographical mobility, greater incidence of intermarriage, improved income levels and educational attainment. The Burakumin are slowly improving their social conditions and eroding centuries of discrimination. The 'apartheid like' conditions which deprived the Burakumin of the social rights of citizenship available to the majority of the Japanese population are gradually diminishing. In Japan, however, there is a 'new underclass' emerging in the shape of approximately 300,000 illegal workers (Foreign Press Centre 1999) mainly from Asia and Africa. Other foreign minorities include approximately 650,000 resident alien Koreans from both North and South, a product of Japan's colonization of Korea from 1910–45, and some 250,000 Chinese who, despite 'a history of exclusion and exploitation' have managed, according to Vasishth (1997: 136) to achieve 'relative economic success' within Japanese society, at least compared to the Korean population. The vast majority of the Korean population in Japan are second- and third-generation residents who speak Japanese but are still not entitled to Japanese citizenship and are therefore deprived of the full benefits of Japanese society. Japanese nationality law is based on the nationality of the parent, rather than the place of birth and naturalization processes are harsh and discretionary. Koreans may not hold public office and, as alien residents, do not hold resident cards. Up until 1982 Koreans and other permanent residents were unable to join the National Pension Scheme, thus giving them no access to Japanese pension programmes. However, as with the Burakumin, attitudes are changing with much of the impetus coming from the minority groups themselves as from government and the wider society. Sugimoto (1997: 182) points to the changing climate among young Koreans: 'second and third generations, committed permanent residents with interests in Japan, increasingly put priority on the expansion of their legal, political, and social rights'. Nevertheless, discrimination against minority groups in Japan remains strong, supported through a rejection of the notion of difference, a failure to recognize the true extent of cultural and racial diversity in Japan, and the perpetuation of Japanese society as homogeneous, cohesive and middle class (Gordon 1993).

Restructuring and a renegotiation of the social contract

As economic conditions deteriorated from around the mid-1970s, the institutional arrangements of the post-war period which had supported specific configurations of citizenship were increasingly perceived as barriers and impediments to the deploying of new methods of production and consumption, while labour contracts and social legislation have increasingly been seen as responsible for inhibiting effective competition both within nation-states and in the increasingly important international markets. By the mid-1970s Australia and Britain had abandoned Keynesianism and adopted a reconstructed political agenda. The political rhetoric of this period encompassed deregulation, privatization, the efficiency of the 'free market' and rolling back the frontiers of the state. The emergence of this alternative policy discourse has been accompanied by changes in the way citizenship is being constructed. The concern has shifted from social rights to obligation and contract.

A given mode of integration and citizenship configuration will be influenced by the institutional arrangements of previous regimes and will also be a response to pressure from interest groups. In Britain, the erosion of the post-war consensus occurred in the context of rampant inflation in the wake of the oil crisis, and involved the acceptance by the 1976 Labour government of the IMF's prescription of income restraint, cuts in social expenditure and, ultimately the abandonment of Keynesian policy. By the 1980s a major structural reform of the welfare state was underway, linked to an alternative economic doctrine, philosophical tradition and an anti-collectivist orthodoxy. Economic individualism and supply-side economics, as advocated by Hayek (1960) and Friedman (1962), provided the framework for the policy formulations of monetarism, and the rhetoric for the devaluation of the welfare state portraying it as a barrier to economic recovery and the road to 'serfdom' and economic ruin.

Following the victory of the Thatcher government in 1979, government strategy, according to Krieger (1991: 53), involved 'a co-ordinated assault, with electoral appeals, policy agendas, and discourse united to reconstitute common sense, redefine the nation, and shatter traditional Labourist-collectivist solidarities'. The restructuring of relations between state and civil society and the establishment of new forms of intervention were most evident during the Conservative era in Britain when there was the most profound shift towards 'welfare pluralism' (Dean 1999). However, following its election in May 1997, the Blair government has pursued similar strategies indicating, according to Marquand (1998), that New Labour 'has turned its back on Keynes and Beveridge' (quoted in Dean 1999: 221). According to Dean (1999: 221), 'new Labour has combined the economic liberalism of the Thatcher/Reagan orthodoxy, with something approaching socially conservative Christian democracy'. For Tony Blair the 'Third Way' is 'the best label for the new politics which the progressive centre-left is forging in Britain and beyond' (Blair 1997: 1). This new orthodoxy reflects the 'communitarian turn' (Etzioni 1995; Driver and Martell 1997) of the 1980s, emphasizing the institutions of civil society, the family, community and the notion of active membership. It is concerned with the promotion of a just society and the values of equal worth, opportunity for all, responsibility and community. Fundamental to these goals is a rebalancing of the social contract between the state and the individual, between rights and responsibility. For Blair:

the demand for rights from the State was separated from the duties of citizenship and the imperative for mutual responsibility on the part of individuals and institutions. Unemployment benefits were often paid without strong reciprocal obligations; children went unsupported by absent parents . . . The rights we enjoy reflect the duties we owe: rights and opportunities without responsibility are engines of selfishness and greed.

(Blair 1997: 4)

Key policies of New Labour have been Welfare-to-Work and the New Deal through which the government seeks 'a change of culture among benefit claimants, employees and public servants – with rights and responsibilities on all sides . . . Our comprehensive welfare-to-work programme aims to break the mould of the old passive benefit system (Blair 1997: 23). Initially introduced to overcome the problem of unemployment among young people the scope of the New Deal has been extended to include, for example, lone parents and those over 25. According to King and Wickham-Jones (1999):

The policy recast in fundamental fashion Labour's strategy to tackle poverty: previously, Labour administrations and social democrative thinkers had placed much weight on amelioration of general destitution through State-directed public spending programmes. New Labour, by contrast, emphasised paid work, seemingly to the exclusion of other approaches.

(King and Wickham-Jones 1999: 271)

They go on to point out that in contrast to the commitment to universal and unconditional social rights which was central to Marshall's conception of citizenship and to the Labour Party's welfare agenda between 1945 and 1992, conditionality, compulsion and coercion appear to be the hallmarks of the policies of the Blair administration. Sanctions and penalties, such as loss of benefit, will fall on those who either refuse to participate or who are unable to finish the New Deal programmes. The implications of this move towards conditional citizenship are as yet unclear. Dean (1999) argues that in the context of conditional citizenship, one outcome might be that

more citizens will defect from their contract with the State, in the sense that they will 'disappear' into the shadowy world of the informal economy. If welfare reform does not work with the grain of everyday survival strategies the result may be more not less social exclusion.

(Dean 1999: 232)

Similarly, the emphasis on labour market insertion as the means to social inclusion fails to take account of the nature and content of employment and the fact that low pay and casualization characterize large sectors of the labour market today. Drawing on the work of Jessop (1994), Dean argues that the space between the individual and the State is itself 'hollowed out' as it is subordinated to economic forces and made increasingly conditional on the citizen's individual 'stake' in the economy as a paid worker.

(Dean 1999: 225)

Similar trends can be seen in Australia where Keating's Labour government introduced *Working Nation* (Keating 1994), which proposed a different role for social policy and represented a re-evaluation of the social relations of Australian welfare from rights based entitlements towards those based on obligation (Macintyre 1999). It indicated the dismantling of the protective measures which had ensured high levels of employment and maintained the 'wage-earners' welfare state'. According to Michael Jones (1996), strategies of economic rationalism (Pusey 1991) incorporating privatization and deregulation were embraced 'regardless of their effects on employment and wages. Government accepted the case for free trade and extensive structural change in the economy' (Jones 1996: 29). The strength of the trade union movement in Australia and the institutionalized system of state reconciliation and arbitration meant that the eventual outcome, according to Castles (1993: 9), was a 'hybrid and uneasy combination of economic rationalist solutions for freeing up markets and corporatist negotiation to buy-off trade union dissent'.

A central element of *Working Nation* was the 'Job Compact' incorporating a reciprocal obligation between the government to provide work and the recipient to accept any reasonable offer or be subject to penalties (Keating 1994). With the election of a Coalition government in 1996 under the leadership of John Howard, according to Kerr and Savelsberg (1999: 243) it was the more coercive and punitive elements of *Working Nation* which were emphasized and which 'fundamentally re-conceived the relationship between the beneficiary, the state and the community'. The relationship was no longer one of reciprocal obligation with the state providing employment, training and skill enhancement, but instead the state resorted to 'coercive powers to make unemployed people work in some form for their income support, without offering enhancement of their personal capability to re-enter the workforce' (Kerr and Savelsberg 1999: 244).

In Japan the notions of obligation, reciprocity and community have always had a prominent role in welfare. This is exemplified in the system of *minsei-in* (approximately 190,000 volunteer officers operating in communities throughout Japan), usually senior members of the community, who offer advice and support those in need (see Goodman 1998). More recently, however, these elements have become increasingly important. The 1974 oil crisis and a downturn in economic prosperity resulted in the Japanese government 'set[ting] a new course' (Peng 2000: 99) and revising the planned expansion of welfare. As Peng (2000: 99) asserts, 'the policy aim of completing the construction of a western-style welfare state was criticized as having been misguided, and the new theme emphasized a reactivation of the "traditional" family and community ties'. Individual contribution rates were increased for health insurance and pension schemes, pension age was increased from 60 to 65 and eligibility criteria for public assistance were tightened. At the same time tax reforms were introduced to encourage traditional two- and three-generation households to take on a greater share of welfare responsibilities. According to Peng (2000: 100), 'these policies were aimed at strengthening the traditional family arrangements and reasserting the welfare responsibilities of the individual and the family'. Mackie (1988) argues that the

> slogan concerning the 'unique' Japanese family system and . . . calls for 'a Japanese-style welfare state' reflect a desire to make the family shoulder the major burden of care for the aged and the handicapped.
>
> (Mackie 1988: 76)

However, new pressures and contradictions are emerging in the Japanese system of welfare. Although the Japanese economy performed well during the 1980s, by the 1990s the bubble economy had collapsed, accompanied by a reversal of economy prosperity and rising unemployment (though at just over 4 per cent it is still relatively low compared to the older industrial economies of the west). A rapidly ageing population, decreasing fertility rates, the increasing participation of women in the labour market and changing household composition with an increasing number of single and nuclear families, have put the enterprise, family and state dynamic under challenge. Pressures for financial deregulation, the removal or reduction of non-tariff barriers and freer trade have required the Japanese government to open up its domestic economy to international competition. At the same time large corporations faced with the increasing costs of social and employment benefits are reassessing their commitment to company welfare and are employing more part-time and irregular (women) workers in order to maximize profits, reduce labour costs and increase flexibility. In contrast to Australia and Britain, the policy response in Japan has been to reassert the Keynesian strategy of reinflation and increased demand through greater state expenditure on infrastructure and the expansion of welfare (Mishra 1999). Despite the rhetoric the government has, in reality, been 'forced to take on a greater role in both providing and coordinating welfare' (Peng 2000: 106). The Japanese system of welfare is in a state of flux as the balance between the state, the market, the family and occupational welfare, and thus the nature of the social contract between the individual and the state, is being renegotiated. It is the conflicts and contradictions emerging in Japanese society, combined with the political articulation of the interests of minority groups, the increasing visibility of women in the public world of work and politics, and the nature of Japan's participation in the global arena, which will ultimately shape the relations between people and the institutional arrangements of the Japanese system of welfare.

Conclusion

This chapter has considered the nature of the state and the social relations of welfare in a historical and cross-national perspective in order to show that citizenship has been shaped by ideology, historical legacy and social struggle relating to issues of class, race, ethnicity and gender. The boundaries of citizenship interact not only with class struggle, but also with other forms of social power such as racism and patriarchy. The significance and constitution of these social relations change over time and place and such relations are institutionalized through the nation-state and its articulation with the inclusionary and exclusionary boundaries of citizenship. Thus citizenship for some can be partial and discriminatory. As Bovenkerk *et al.* (1990) have argued:

the degree of exclusion and the mechanisms by which exclusion is effected may not differ a great deal from one country to another, but the discourse does. This reflects separate national traditions and sensitivities and this needs to be clearly grasped conceptually and analytically.

(Bovenkerk *et al.* 1990: 487)

The structural and institutional reforms regarding trade unions, the welfare state and supply-side economics and individualism have been most far-reaching in Britain and Australia than in Japan, though the very strength of organized labour and the framework established to support the 'wage-earners' welfare state' in Australia have prevented any substantial dismantling of the institutions of the post-war regime. Nevertheless, all three countries have experienced a renegotiation of the boundaries of citizenship, and a reassessment of the balance between rights and obligation. Both British and Australian governments have emphasized and strengthened the notion of individual obligation and the active citizen, representing a shift in concern from equality to dependency. In Japan, the re-emphasis on the traditional family and community ties is an attempt to reassert patriarchal social relations and redirect caring responsibilities, an approach which has, paradoxically, necessitated an increasing role for the state as it seeks to promote the themes of obligation and reciprocity. The sustainability of these approaches is uncertain as the impact of economic restructuring and global integration, and the implications of the redrawing of the boundaries of citizenship becomes evident. The political and social tensions emerging from unemployment, increasing inequality, homelessness and more general uncertainty in everyday life may provoke pressure for a social contract through which people are enabled to pursue full participation in the norms of society. As the meaning of citizenship becomes more complex and the role of the nation-state is diluted by the increasing number of supranational organizations in a new global order, there is potential for people to find new meanings and interpretations of the concept of citizenship, and alternative sites of struggle through which to achieve their goals.

Notes

1 This caricature emerged with the simultaneous strengthening of external border controls between the EU and the outside world and the reduction of cross-border controls between member states.
2 TREVI Group consisted of Ministers for Home affairs and officials concerned with issues of internal security cooperation, such as combatting terrorism and coordinating police cooperation. European institutions were excluded from this process.
3 The Ad Hoc Group on Immigration was established in 1986. It was based on intergovernmental cooperation and was composed of memberstate immigration policy officials. It dealt with issues relating to asylum, external frontiers, forged papers, admissions, deportations and information exchange (see Geddes for a more detailed discussion).
4 Schengen Agreement signed by five EC governments (Belgium, France, Germany, The Netherlands and Luxembourg). The agreement resolved to secure free movement for people between participating states with the removal of border controls.

Further reading

Bulmer, M. and Rees, A.M. (eds) (1996) *Citizenship Today*. London: UCL Press. This edited collection covers philosophical, theoretical, methodological and substantive concerns relating to the theme of citizenship. It assesses the relevance of Marshall's (1950) original formulation of the concept of citizenship and the extent of its continuing significance today.

Castles, S., Kalantzis, M., Cope, B. and Morrissey, M. (1992) *Mistaken Identity: Multiculturalism and the Demise of Nationalism in Australia*. Sydney: Pluto. This book provides an analysis of the different ways in which the Australian nations and citizenship have been constructed over time. It considers the changing parameters of inclusion and exclusion based upon racial or ethnic origin and the politics and ideologies associated with immigration to Australia. They critically examine the notion of multiculturalism and consider the possibilities and alternatives for constructing Australian national identity.

Henshall, K.G. (1999) *Dimensions of Japanese Society: Gender, Margins and Mainstream*. London: Macmillan. This book explores the organization of the social structure in Japan and the nature of gender relations in constructing social relations. It also draws out the distinctions between mainstream and marginal groups and questions normative assumptions about Japanese society which are prevalent in the west.

Lister, R. (1997) *Citizenship: Feminist Perspectives*. London: Macmillan. This book draws on feminist and political theory to explore the question of citizenship and, in particular, the political and social citizenship of women. It considers the exclusionary as well as the inclusionary aspects of citizenship and relates this to notions of gendered and racialized welfare regimes.

chapter

six

The future of comparative social policy research

Supranational social policy?

Social policy is undergoing a fundamental reassessment as the political, social and ideological conditions of the past have eroded and undermined the foundations on which the welfare state emerged in Western Europe in the post-war period. At the same time the essentialism and universalism embedded in policy discourses and the assumptions of social science research have been reappraised. The reordering of the global hierarchy, the ending of tensions between East and West, increasing heterogeneity in the Third World and the proliferation of global institutions have contributed to a more fluid form of international politics. These developments have highlighted the inadequacies of conventional explanatory concepts and frameworks to capture the complexity and dynamics of the contemporary global political economy.

The factors influencing the direction and discourse of policy research now emerge in a global as well as a domestic context. The range of supranational institutions and organizations which exert pressure and influence on national governments has expanded. The extent of their penetration into the national arena is most evident in the structural adjustment programmes implemented in developing countries, and their role in the transition economies of Central and Eastern Europe. The influence of the World Bank and the IMF is evident in the promotion of the neo-liberal agenda of global capitalism, the UN system is involved with promoting human rights and the ILO with the improvement of the rights of workers. However, it is still too early to talk of a supranational social policy. What is currently in place is a complex, multilayered system of policy formulation in which the nation-state plays a primary role.

Comparative social policy is concerned with exploring phenomena in more than one country, utilizing functionally equivalent, robust concepts, and theoretically informed analysis. It is still the case that the state remains the focus of analysis. However, in contrast to the domestic orientation of the Keynesian era, the conceptualization of the state should incorporate an interconnected and multilevel framework. Within the emerging system of transnational and global relations, there is an increasing recognition of the relevance of this type of research and its role in reconstructing our understanding of the changing global political economy. The extent and nature of future patterns of globalization are difficult to predict. The way in which transnational influences are absorbed and institutionalized varies from country to country and is, in turn, mediated by specific power relations existing at a given time. Cross-national social policy research is able to capture these trends, the dynamics and the impact of these processes in different national contexts.

A global research strategy

The expansion of cross-national comparative research has been facilitated by the proliferation in data sources, international collaboration and new technologies. The increasing sophistication and availability of data as well as greater familiarity with different cultures, practices and intellectual frameworks has the potential to enhance the multilevel cross-national research paradigm and break down the barriers and 'false segregation' between North and South, developed and developing countries. However, rather than encouraging a global research strategy, there is the danger that these developments will merely reinforce the distinctions of the past. The internet, for example, has opened up a range of opportunities in terms of networking with colleagues across the globe and accessing information at the touch of a button. However, the distribution of internet access is extremely uneven and concentrated in OECD countries, particularly the USA. Even within countries there are gross disparities in access, with the typical user being white, professional and male.

The dominance of the more 'highly developed' countries – economically, ideologically and in terms of research – is less marked than in the past. But it is still the case that a substantial amount of data used in cross-national research is provided by institutions whose purpose is to promote the economic interests of its affluent members in an 'unfettered', global marketplace. Although the Eurocentric paradigms of development and modernization which contributed to this distinction have been undermined, it still remains an implicit assumption that the countries of the OECD provide the blueprint for progress. Thus, the ethnocentrism in cross-national social policy research must be overcome not only in terms of breaking down spatial and cultural barriers but also in relation to the concepts used. It is important to reconsider the scope of the term 'welfare' and to go beyond the formal, institutional framework that we refer to as the welfare state. An ideological shift about welfare, increasing demand, the rhetoric of the welfare state in crisis and the influences of the economic orthodoxy of monetarism and deflationary policies have all contributed to a policy environment more obviously recognized as a 'mixed economy of welfare'. Paradoxically, the recognition of a mixed economy of welfare has implications for the development of cross-national social research. It encourages an expansion in the scope of the definition of welfare and therefore facilitates breadth and depth of analysis through a greater recognition of the role of non-state elements in welfare provision. It can provide a framework for a global perspective on social policy which can overcome the 'false segregation' of classification apparent in earlier cross-national social research.

Conclusion

The restructuring of economies, the re-evaluation of the social relations of the welfare, and a redrawing of the boundaries of citizenship have been evident in a number of countries. Yet the recognition of general trends does not imply convergence in the direction of development. Global processes are complex and contradictory. While opening up opportunities for some countries and people, others have been marginalized and excluded from the benefits of the information age. Each nation interacts in its own way with global, regional, national and local arenas. In the same way the nature of the welfare system and the form and content of social rights will vary. Modes of integration are mediated by the power relations of class, racism and patriarchy and shaped by the construction of nation, unity and identity. Historical and contemporary cross-national analysis provides an understanding of the multifaceted and interrelated nature of social divisions, and their spatial expression. It can highlight how the significance and constitution of these social relations changes over time and place and are institutionalized through the nation-state and its articulation with the inclusionary/exclusionary boundaries of citizenship. Thus it can illuminate the complex and diverse processes leading to discrimination and inequality across borders and contribute to the implementation of welfare systems which are appropriate to the social and economic conditions of contemporary society.

Glossary

Citizenship   Membership of a political community, generally assumed to be a state. Thus, the concept incorporates the relationship between the individual and the state and the reciprocal rights and duties embodied in that relationship.

Comparative, cross-national analysis   Explicit and systematic comparison of data from more than one country.

Convergence theory   The logic of industrialization and technological growth leads to convergent patterns of political, economic and social structures regardless of ideological, cultural or historical differences.

Epistemology   Theory of knowledge exploring the different ways in which the world is understood.

Ethnocentrism   The perception that one's own group or culture is superior and of greater significance morally, culturally and racially than others. Thus, ethnocentric attitudes incorporate prejudice towards other groups. For example Eurocentrism refers to the attitude whereby Western European cultural and intellectual achievements are superior to other parts of the world.

European Union (EU)   The European Communities (European Coal and Steel Community (ECSC), EEC and Euratom) were established in 1957 with powers transferred to a single body in 1965. The EU is founded on the existing European Communities, supplemented by the policies of the Treaty of the European Union, signed in Maastricht in 1992 and in force in 1993. Currently consists of fifteen members: the six founder countries (Belgium, France, Germany, Italy, Luxembourg and the Netherlands) having been joined between 1973 and 1995 by Austria, Denmark, Finland, Greece, Ireland, Portugal, Spain, Sweden and the UK. The basic objectives of the EU are to promote economic and social progress through the creation of an area without internal frontiers, the strengthening of economic and social cohesion, and the establishment of economic and monetary union, ultimately including a single currency.

General Agreement on Tariffs and Trade (GATT)   The GATT was established in the mid-1940s to initiate a programme of multilateral negotiations for the mutual reduction of tariff and non-tariff barriers and the improvement of the practices of international trade. Succeeded by the World Trade Organization in January 1995.

Globalization   Multifaceted concept involving economic, social, cultural, technical and political dimensions. Processes of globalization are said to include the expansion of capitalist markets and the growth of international trade and transactions. These developments have been facilitated through advances in information technology and the increasing role of TNCs in world markets. In addition, international, non-profit organizations have grown in number, strength and sphere of influence. State boundaries are being eroded and the sovereignty of the nation-state is in question as its ability to function and act is increasingly constrained by actors and institutions beyond the state. Some commentators believe that external pressures will eventually necessitate the 'downsizing' of the welfare state as nations attempt to attract international capital investment. Contradictory processes are also evident, for example, the parallel processes of globalization and localization, cultural homogeneity and the resurgence of cultural identity and diversity.

Group of 7 (G7)   Intergovernmental organization with representatives from Canada, France, Germany, Italy, Japan, the UK and the USA. G8 includes Russia.

Group of 77 (G77)   Main international forum for consultation and policy coordination between developing countries. It was established in Geneva in 1964 at the UN Conference on Trade and Development (UNCTAD). The interests of the then 77 countries were united around issues of international trade and development issues. The group currently consists of approximately 130 countries from Africa, Latin America and the Caribbean.

Intergovernmentalism   The sovereign state is the key actor within this decision-making arena, enjoying internal and external sovereignty. National interests generally predominate in this process with sovereignty maintained usually through unanimous decision-making with each state given the power of veto.

International Monetary Fund (specialized agency of the UN) (IMF)   The IMF was established in 1946 to foster international monetary consultation and cooperation and exchange stability in order to promote the expansion and growth of world trade. It is also involved with member countries experiencing difficulties in foreign payments. Best-known instrument is the Structural Adjustment Facility set up in March 1986 in order to provide balance of payments assistance to low-income developing countries on concessional terms. Heavily involved in Central and Eastern European countries as well as the republics of the former Soviet Union, it now has 183 country members.

International non-governmental organizations   Non-profit-making transnational organization.

Multiculturalism   Recognition and promotion of cultural diversity. It involves ensuring the protection and maintenance of minority cultures as well as addressing the discrimination, disadvantageous socio-economic circumstances experienced by many minority groups.

Nation-state   Territory and people with clearly defined boundaries. It is a legal and political entity whose boundaries usually correspond with particular cultural, linguistic and ethnic dimensions. The principle of sovereignty refers to the absolute and unlimited power enshrined within the state to demand compliance as defined by law and to exercise coercive force.

Patriarchy   Pattern of social organization in which males achieve and maintain social, cultural and economic dominance over females, and which reinforces power inequality between men and women.

Postmodernism   Debates exploring and critiquing modernity. The modern era is characterized by universalism, essentialism and the belief in scientific rationality. Postmodernism is concerned with diversity, difference and contingency, the deconstruction of knowledge, non-essentialism and anti-reductionism.

Privatization   Sale or transfer of publicly owned assets, such as industries (for example British Rail, British Telecom, British Gas) and housing, into private ownership and control.

Supranational governance   Framework of laws and institutions at a level above the state whose authority extends beyond just one state. Decision-making bodies which influence or set limits on the behaviour of individuals, organizations and governments and supersede or override the sovereign authority of individual states who are constituent members of the organizations involved.

Third World   Originally associated with countries in Asia, Africa, Latin America and the Caribbean to distinguish them from the countries of the first world (capitalist liberal democracies such as Western Europe and the USA) and the second world (the command economies of Eastern Europe and the former Soviet Union). The term was an attempt to assert the positive identity of this region and to emphasize its specific political and economic trajectories which were different from other parts of the world. The term has come to be associated with the negative characteristics of political instability, economic stagnation, extreme social inequality and corruption. It has been criticized for failing to capture the diversity of circumstances existing between countries in this part of the world.

Transnational   Activities and relationships that cross state boundaries.

Transnational corporation (TNC)   Profit-making enterprise operating from a home state with subsidiaries in other host states. Foreign direct investment refers to the acquisition of assets in one country from another. This activity is a key characteristic of TNCs.

United Nations Organizations (UN)   An intergovernmental organization established as an attempt to ensure world peace. The structure and mechanisms of the UN were established in 1945. The institutional framework established a whole range of 'specialized agencies' and regional commissions covering the social and economic activities of the UN. The UN and its specialized agencies have a very wide remit from diplomacy, peace-keeping and fact-finding missions to humanitarian intervention, and activities for refugees and disasters.

Welfare state   Involvement of the government in a range of activities to provide social services and promote social well-being through a set of social and economic policies.

Welfare system   A range of institutions and providers through which welfare activities are provided to promote social well-being. These include the family, the community, the market and the voluntary sector.

World Bank (specialized agency of the UN) (WB)   Established in 1947, its focus has been on social development in countries of the South. It has been involved, with the IMF, in structural adjustment programmes. More recently the World Bank has become concerned with softening the impact of some of the SAPs and promoting strategies for reducing poverty. The Bank has been particularly active in the countries of the CIS and Eastern Europe.

World Trade Organization (WTO)   Established in 1995 as a successor to GATT with wider powers and functions.

Bibliography

Abrahamson, P. (1997) Combating poverty and social exclusion in Europe, in W. Beck, L. van der Maesen and A. Walker (eds) *The Social Quality of Europe*. Bristol: Policy Press.

Abrahamson, P. (1999) The welfare modelling business, *Social Policy and Administration*, 33(4): 394–415.

Adams, N.A. (1993) *Worlds Apart: The North–South Divide and the International System*. London: Zed Books.

Aglietta, M. (1979) *A Theory of Capitalist Regulation: The US Experience*. London: Verso.

Aina, T.A. (1999) West and Central Africa: social policy for reconstruction and development, in D. Morales-Gomez (ed.) *Transnational Social Policies: The New Development Challenges of Globalization*. London: Earthscan.

Ake, C. (1995) The new world order: a view from Africa, in H. Holm and G. Sorensen, *Whose World Order? Uneven Globalization and the End of the Cold War*. Boulder, CO: Westview.

Alber, J. (1981) Government responses to the challenge of unemployment: the development of unemployment insurance in Western Europe, in P. Flora and A.J. Heidenheimer (eds) *The Development of Welfare States in Europe and America*. New Brunswick, NJ: Transaction Books.

Alber, J. (1983) Some causes of social security expenditure developments in western Europe 1949–1977, in M. Loney, D. Boswell and J. Clarke (eds) *Social Policy and Social Welfare*. Milton Keynes: Open University Press.

Alber, J., Esping-Andersen, G. and Rainwater, L. (1987) Studying the welfare state: issues and queries, in M. Dierkes, H.N. Weiler and A.B. Antal (eds) *Comparative Policy Research: Learning from Experience*. Aldershot: Gower and Berlin: WZB.

Albrow, M. (1996) *The Global Age*. Oxford: Polity.

Alcock, P. (1997) *Understanding Poverty*. London: Macmillan.

Allen, J., Cars, G. and Madanipour, A. (1998) Introduction, in A. Madanipour, G. Cars and J. Allen (eds) *Social Exclusion in European Cities: Processes, Experiences and Responses*. London: Jessica Kingsley.

Allen, T. and Thomas, A. (eds) (1992) *Poverty and Development in the 1990s*. Oxford and Milton Keynes: Oxford University Press in association with The Open University.

Amin, K. (1992) *Poverty in Black and White*. London: CPAG (Child Poverty Action Group).

Appadurai, A. (1990) Disjuncture and difference in the global cultural economy, *Theory, Culture and Society*, 7(2/3): 295–310.

Armer, M. (1973) Methodological problems and possibilities in comparative research, in M. Armer and A. Grimshaw (eds) *Comparative Social Research: Methodological Problems and Strategies*. New York: Wiley.

Atkinson, T., Rainwater, L. and Smeeding, T. (1995) *Income Distribution in OECD Countries*. Paris: OECD.

Australian Bureau of Statistics (ABS) (1994) *Special Article – Statistics on the Indigenous Peoples of Australia* (Year Book Australia 1994). Canberra: ABS.

Avramov, D. (1995) *Homelessness in the European Union: Social and Legal Context for Housing Exclusion in the 1990s*. Brussels: FEANTSA (European Federation of National Organisations Working with the Homeless).

Avramov, D. (1996) *The Invisible Hand of the Housing Market*. Brussels: FEANTSA.

Balbo, L. (1987) Family, women and the state: notes toward a typology of family roles and public intervention, in C. Maier (ed.) *Changing Boundaries of the Political: Essays on the Evolving Balance between the State and Society, Public and Private in Europe*. Cambridge: Cambridge University Press.

Balchin, P. (1996) *Housing Policy in Europe*. London: Routledge.

Baldock, J., Manning, N., Miller, S. and Vickerstaff, S. (eds) (1999) *Social Policy*. Oxford: Oxford University Press.

Balibar, E. (1988) Is there a 'Neo-racism'?, in E. Balibar and I. Wallerstein (eds) *Race, Nation, Class: Ambiguous Identities*. London: Verso.

Ball, M., Harloe, M. and Martens, M. (1989) *Housing and Social Change in Europe and the USA*. London: Routledge.

Bartelmus, P. (1994) *Environment, Growth and Development: The Concepts and Strategies of Sustainability*. London: Routledge.

Bauman, Z. (1990) From pillars to post, *Marxism Today*, February: 20–5.

Bauman, Z. (1992) *Intimations of Postmodernity*. London: Routledge.

Beals, R.L. (1954) A review of Miner, *American Anthropologist*, 56: 307–8.

Bebbington, A. and Theile, G. (eds) with Davies, P., Prager, M. and Riveros, H. (1993) *NGOs and the State in Latin America: Rethinking Roles in Sustainable Agricultural Development*. London: Routledge.

Bebbington, A.J. (1997) Reinventing NGOs and rethinking alternatives in the Andes, in *The Annals of the American Academy of Political and Social Science* (554), November. London/New Delhi: Sage.

Beck, U. (1992) *Risk Society: Towards a New Modernity*. London: Sage.

Bell, D. (1974) *The Coming of Post-Industrial Society*. London: Heinemann.

Bertaux, D. (1981) *Biography and Society: The Life-History Approach in the Social Sciences*. London/Beverly Hills, CA: Sage.

Bertaux, D. (1984) The Life Story Approach: A Continental View, *Annual Review of Sociology*, 10: 215–37.

Beveridge Report (1942) Report on the Social Insurance and Allied Services, Cmnd 6404. London: HMSO.

Biersteker, T.J. (1998) Globalization and the modes of operation of major institutional actors, *Oxford Development Studies*, 26(1): 15–32.

Blair, T. (1997) *The Third Way: New Politics for the New Century*. London: Fabian Society.

Booth, D. (1994) *Rethinking Social Development: Theory, Research and Practice.* London: Longman.

Borchorst, A. (1994) Welfare state regimes, women's interests and the EC, in D. Sainsbury (ed.) *Gendering Welfare States.* London: Sage.

Bovenkerk, F., Miles, R. and Verbunt, G. (1990) Racism, migration and the state in western Europe: a case for comparative analysis, *International Sociology*, 5: 475–90.

Boyden, J. (1990) Childhood and the policy makers: a comparative perspective on the globalization of childhood, in A. James and A. Prout (eds) *Constructing and Reconstructing Childhood: Contemporary Issues in the Sociological Study of Childhood.* London: Falmer.

Boyer, R. (ed.) (1986) *Capitalismes Fin de Siecle.* Paris: Presses Universitaires de France.

Bradshaw, J., Ditch, J., Holmes, H. and Whiteford, P. (1993) A comparative study of child support in fifteen countries, *Journal of European Social Policy*, 3(4): 255–71.

Brenner, R. and Glick, M. (1991) The regulation approach: theory and history, *Capital and Class*, 188: 41–120.

Bryson, L. (1992) *Welfare and the State.* London: Macmillan.

Bulmer, M. and and Rees, A.M. (eds) (1996) *Citizenship Today.* London: UCL Press.

Bunyan, T. (1991) Towards an authoritarian European state, *Race and Class*, 32(3): 19–27.

Buraku Liberation News (1997) Law to preserve Ainu culture was passed, July: 97 http://blhrri.org/blhrri_e/news/new097/new09703.htm (accessed 27 July 2000).

Byrne, D. (1997) Social exclusion and capitalism, *Critical Social Policy*, 17(1): 27–51.

Byrne, D. (1999) *Social Exclusion.* Buckingham: Open University Press.

Calhoun, C. (1995) *Critical Social Theory.* Massachusetts, MA: Blackwell.

Callinicos, A. (1992) *Against Postmodernism: A Marxist Critique.* Oxford: Polity.

Cardoso, F.H. and Faletto, E. (1979) *Dependency and Underdevelopment in Latin America.* Berkeley, CA: University of California Press.

Carey-Wood, J. (1991) Leaving home: housing for young people in England and France. Unpublished thesis, University of Bristol.

Carter, J. (1998) Studying social policy after modernity, in J. Carter (ed.) *Postmodernity and the Fragmentation of Welfare.* London: Routledge.

Castells, M. (1998) *End of Millennium.* Oxford: Blackwell.

Castles, F. (ed.) (1982) *The Impact of Parties: Politics and Policies in Democratic Capitalist States.* London: Sage.

Castles, F. (1985) *The Working Class and Welfare.* Sydney: Allen & Unwin.

Castles, F. (1988) *Australian Public Policy and Economic Vulnerability.* Sydney: Allen & Unwin.

Castles, F. (1993) *Families of Nations: Patterns of Public Policy in Western Democracies.* Aldershot: Dartmouth.

Castles, F. (1994) The wage earners' welfare state revisited, *Australian Journal of Social Issues*, 29(2): 120–42.

Castles, F. (1998) *Comparative Public Policy: Patterns of Post-war Transformation.* Cheltenham: Edward Elgar.

Castles, F. and Mitchell, D. (1990) *Three worlds of welfare capitalism or four? Mimeo Graduate Programme in Public Policy.* Canberra: Australian National University.

Castles, F. and Mitchell, D. (1992) Identifying welfare state regimes: the links between politics, instruments and outcomes, *Governance*, 5(1): 1–26.

Castles, S. and Kosack, G. (1973) *Immigrant Workers and Class Structure in Western Europe*. London: Harper & Row.

Castles, S., Kalantzis, M., Cope, B. and Morrissey, M. (1992) *Mistaken Identity: Multiculturalism and the Demise of Nationalism in Australia*. Sydney: Pluto.

Cater, J. and Jones, T. (1979) Ethnic residential space: the case of Asians in Bradford, *Tidjschrift voor Economische en Sociale Geographie*, 70: 86–97.

Central Statistics Office (1997) *Labour Force Survey, 1996*. Dublin: Stationery Office.

Chamberlayne, P., Bornat, J. and Wengraf, T. (2000) *The Turn to Biographical Methods in Social Science: Comparative Issues and Examples*. London: Routledge.

Chambers, R. (1993) *Challenging the Professions*. London: Intermediate Technology.

Clasen, J. (ed.) (1999) *Comparative Social Policy: Concepts, Theories and Methods*. Oxford: Blackwell.

Commission of the European Communities (CEC) (1990) *Community Labour Force Survey: A User's Guide*. Luxembourg: Office for Official Publications of the European Communities.

Commission on Global Governance (1995) *Our Global Neighbourhood: The Report of the Commission on Global Governance*. New York: Oxford University Press.

Cornia, G.A. and Jolly, R. (1987) *Adjustment with a Human Face: Protecting the Vulnerable and Promoting Growth – A Study by UNICEF*. Oxford: Clarendon.

Costello, N., Michie, J. and Milne, S. (1989) *Beyond the Casino Economy*. London: Verso.

Creighton, M. (1997) *Soto* Others and *uchi* Others: Imagining racial diversity, imagining homogenous Japan, in M. Weiner (ed.) *Japan's Minorities: The Illusion of Homogeneity*. London: Routledge.

Crow, G. (1997) *Comparative Sociology and Social Theory: Beyond the Three Worlds*. London: Macmillan.

Cutright, P. (1965) Political structure, economic development, and national social security programs, *American Journal of Sociology*, 70 (March): 537–50.

Dahrendorf, R. (1996) Citizenship and social class, in M. Bulmer and A.M. Rees (eds) *Citizenship Today*. London: UCL Press.

Dasgupta, B. (1998) *Structural Adjustment, Global Trade and the New Political Economy of Development*. London: Zed Books.

Deacon, A. and Mann, K. (1999) Agency, modernity and social policy, *Journal of Social Policy*, 28(3): 413–35.

Deacon, B., Castle-Kanerova, M., Manning, N. *et al.* (1992) *The New Eastern Europe: Social Policy Past, Present and Future*. London: Sage.

Deacon, B. with Hulse, M. and Stubbs, P. (1997) *Global Social Policy: International Organizations and the Future of Welfare*. London: Sage.

Dean, H. (1999) Citizenship, in M. Powell (ed.) *New Labour, New Welfare State? The Third Way in British Social Policy*. Bristol: Policy Press.

Denzin, N. (1978) *Sociological Methods: A Sourcebook*. New York: McGraw-Hill.

Derrida, J. (1970) Structure, sign and play in the discourse of the human sciences, in R. Macksey and E. Donato (eds) *The Structuralist Controversy: The Language of Criticism and the Sciences of Man*. Baltimore: Johns Hopkins University Press.

Desrosieres, A. (1996) Statistical traditions: an obstacle to international comparisons?, in L. Hantrais and S. Mangen (eds) *Cross-National Research Methods in the Social Sciences*. London: Pinter.

Diamond, L., Linz, J. and Lipset, S. (eds) (1988) *Democracy in Developing Countries: Asia*. London: Adamantine.

Dickens, P. (1992) *Global Shift: Internationalization of Economic Activity*, 2nd edn. London: Paul Chapman.

Dierkes, M., Weiler, H.N. and Berthoin Antal, A. (eds) (1987) *Comparative Policy Research: Learning from Experience*. Berlin: WZB.

Dogan, M. and Pelassy, D. (1990) *How to Compare Nations: Strategies in Comparative Politics*. New York: Chatham.

Dominelli, L. (1991) *Women Across Continents: Feminist Comparative Social Policy*. Hemel Hempstead, Herts: Simon & Schuster.

Driver, S. and Martell, L. (1997) New Labour's communitarianisms, *Critical Social Policy*, 17(3): 27–44.

Durkheim, E. (1964) *The Division of Labour in Society*. New York: Free Press.

EC (European Communities) (1992) *Treaty on European Union: The Maastricht Treaty*. Luxembourg: European Communities/Union.

Edwards, M. and Hulme, D. (eds) (1995) *Non-governmental Organisations Performance and Accountability: Beyond the Magic Bullet*. London: Earthscan/ Save the Children.

Eisenstadt, S.N. (1996) *Japanese Civilization: A Comparative View*. Chicago: University of Chicago Press.

Elam, M.J. (1990) Puzzling out the Post-Fordist Debate: Technology, Markets and Institutions, *Economics and Industrial Democracy*, 11: 9–37.

Elder, J.W. (1976) Comparative cross-national methodology, *Annual Review of Sociology*, 2: 209–30.

Escobar, A. (1997) The making and unmaking of the Third World through development, in M. Rahnema with V. Bawtree (eds) *The Post-Development Reader*. London: Zed Books.

Esping-Andersen, G. (1985) Power and Distributional Regimes, *Politics and Society*, 14(2): 223–56.

Esping-Andersen, G. (1990) *The Three Worlds of Welfare Capitalism*. Cambridge: Polity.

Esping-Andersen, G. (1997) Hybrid or unique? The distinctiveness of the Japanese welfare state, *Journal of European Social Policy*, 7(3): 179–89.

Esping-Andersen, G. and Korpi, W. (1984) Social policy and class politics in post-war capitalism: Scandinavia, Austria and Germany, in J. Goldthorpe (ed.) *Order and Conflict in Contemporary Capitalism*. Oxford: Oxford University Press.

Etzioni, A. (1995) *The Spirit of Community*. London: Fontana.

European Commission (1994) *European Social Policy: A Way Forward for the Union*, White Paper COM (94) 333. Brussels: Commission of the European Communities.

Eurostat (1998) *Statistics in Focus: Population and Social Conditions no. 11 – Analysis of Income Distribution in 13 Member States*. Luxembourg: Statistical Office of the EU.

Fadayomi, T.O. (1991) The history of social development in Gambia, Ghana,

Nigeria, in D. Mohammed (ed.) *Social Development in Africa: Strategies, Policies and Programmes after the Lagos Plan*, UK.ACARTSOD Monograph Series. London: Hans Zell.

Farrington, J. and Bebbington, A. (eds) (1993) *Reluctant Partners? Non-governmental Organisations, the State and Sustainable Development*. London: Routledge.

Fernando, J.L. and Heston, A.W. (1997) The role of NGOs: charity, empowerment and beyond (special edition), *The Annals of the American Academy of Political and Social Science*, 554(2).

Ferrera, M. (1996) The southern model of welfare in social Europe, *Journal of European Social Policy*, 6(11): 17–37.

Fletcher, C. (ed.) (1994) *Aboriginal Self-Determination in Australia*. Australian Institute of Aboriginal and Torres Strait Islander Studies. Canberra: Aboriginal Studies Press.

Flora, P. and Heidenheimer, A. (eds) (1981) *The Development of Welfare States in Europe and America*. London: Transaction Books.

Florida, R.L. and Jonas, P. (1991) US urban policy: the post-war state and capitalist regulation, *Antipode*, (23): 349–84.

Foreign Press Centre (1999) *Facts and Figures of Japan*. Japan: Foreign Press Centre.

Foucault, M. (1972) *Archaeology of Knowledge*. London: Tavistock.

Foucault, M. (1980) *Power/Knowledge: Selected Interviews*. Brighton: Harvest Press.

Foucault, M. (1984) *The History of Sexuality, vol 1*. Harmondsworth: Penguin.

Fowler, A. (1985) NGOs in Africa: naming them by what they are, in K. Kinyanjui (ed.) *Non-Government Organizations' Contribution to Development*. Occasional paper no. 50. Nairobi: Institute of Development Studies, University of Nairobi.

Fox Piven, F. and Cloward, R.A. (1984) The new class war in the United States, in I. Szelenyi (ed.) *Cities in Recession: Critical Responses to the Urban Policies of the New Right*. London: Sage.

Frank, A.G. (1967) *Capitalism and Underdevelopment in Latin America*. London: Monthly Review Press.

Frank, A.G. (1978) *Dependent Accumulation and Underdevelopment*. Basingstoke: Macmillan.

Franklin, A. (1989) Owner occupation, privatism, and ontological society: a critical reformulation, Working Paper 62. School for Advanced Urban Studies, University of Bristol.

Friedman, M. (1962) *Capitalism and Freedom*. Chicago: University of Chicago Press.

Friedman, M. and Friedman, R. (1981) *Free to choose*. Harmondsworth: Penguin Books.

Garrett, G. (1998) Shrinking states? Globalization and national autonomy in the OECD, *Oxford Development Studies*, 26(1): 71–98.

Geddes, A. (2000) *Immigration and European Integration: Towards Fortress Europe? European Policy Research Unit Series*. Manchester: Manchester University Press.

George, V. and Wilding, P. (1994) *Welfare and Ideology*. Hemel Hempstead: Harvester Wheatsheaf.

Gershuny, J. (1998) Thinking dynamically. Sociology and narrative data, in L. Leisering and R. Walker (eds) *The Dynamics of Modern Society: Poverty, Policy and Welfare*. Bristol: Policy Press.

Gibbins, J.R. (1998) Postmodernism, poststructuralism and social policy, in J. Carter (ed.) *Postmodernity and the Fragmentation of Welfare*. London: Routledge.

Giddens, A. (1982) Class division, class conflict and citizenship rights, in A. Giddens (ed.) *Profiles and Critiques in Social Theory*. London: Macmillan.

Giddens, A. (1990) *The Consequences of Modernity*. Cambridge: Polity.

Giddens, A. (1992) *Modernity and Self-identity: Self and Society in the Late Modern Age*. Cambridge: Polity.

Ginsberg, N. (1979) *Class, Capital and Social Policy*. London and Basingstoke: Macmillan.

Ginsberg, N. (1992) *Divisions of Welfare: A Critical Introduction to Comparative Social Policy*. London: Sage.

Glover, J. (1996) Epistemological and methodological considerations in secondary analysis, in L. Hantrais and S. Mangen (eds) *Cross-National Research Methods in the Social Sciences*. London: Pinter.

Glynn, A. (1992) The costs of stability: the advanced capitalist countries in the 1980s, *New Left Review*, 195: 71–95.

Goodin, R., Headey, B., Muffels, R. and Dirven, H-J. (1999) *The Real Worlds of Welfare Capitalism*. Cambridge: Cambridge University Press.

Goodman, R. (1998) The 'Japanese-style welfare state' and the delivery of personal social services, in R. Goodman, G. White and H-j. Kwon (eds) *The East Asian Welfare Model: Welfare Orientalism and the State*. London: Routledge.

Goodman, R. and Peng, I. (1996) The East Asian welfare states: peripatetic learning, adaptive change and nation-building, in G. Esping-Andersen (ed.) *Welfare States in Transition*. London: Sage.

Goodman, R., White, G. and Kwon, H-j. (1998) *The East Asian Welfare Model: Welfare Orientalism and the State*. London: Routledge.

Gordon, A. (ed.) (1993) *Postwar Japan as History*. Berkeley: University of California Press.

Gordon, P. and Klug, F. (1985) *Immigration: A Brief Guide*. London: Runnymede Trust.

Gough, I. (1979) *The Political Economy of the Welfare State*. London and Basingstoke: Macmillan.

Gough, I. (2000) Welfare regimes in East Asia and Europe. Paper presented at the Annual World Bank Conference on Development Economics Europe 2000, 'Towards the new social policy agenda in East Asia', Paris, June.

Hage, J. and Hanneman, R. (1977) *The Growth of the Welfare State in Four Western European Societies: A Comparison of Three Paradigms*. Madison, WI: Institute for Research on Poverty.

Hague, R., Harrop, M. and Breslin, S. (1987) *Comparative Government and Politics: An Introduction*. London: Macmillan.

Hallett, G. (1988) *Land and Housing Policies in Europe and the USA: A Comparative Analysis*. London: Routledge.

Hantrais, L. and Ager, D. (1985) The language barrier to effective cross-national research, in L. Hantrais, S. Mangen and M. O'Brien (eds) *Doing Cross National Research*, Cross-national research papers, Aston University, Birmingham.

Hantrais, L. and Mangen, S. (eds) (1996) *Cross-National Research Methods in the Social Sciences*. London: Pinter.

Harrison, M. (1999) Theorising homelessness and race, in P. Kennett and A. Marsh *Homelessness: Exploring the New Terrain*. Bristol: Policy Press.

Harvey, B. (1999) Models of resettlement for the homeless in the European Union, in P. Kennett and A. Marsh (eds) *Homelessness: Exploring the New Terrain*. Bristol: Policy Press.

Harvey, D. (1989) *The Condition of Post-modernity: An Enquiry into the Origins of Cultural Change*. Oxford: Blackwell.

Hayek, F.A. (1960) *The Constitution of Liberty*. London: Routledge and Kegan Paul.

Healey, K. (ed.) (1997) *Poverty in Australia*. Balmain, NSW: Spinney Press.

Heidenheimer, A.J. and Heclo, H. (1983) *Comparative Public Policy: The Politics of Social Change*. Basingstoke: Macmillan.

Henshall, K.G. (1999) *Dimensions of Japanese Society: Gender, Margins and Mainstream*. London: Macmillan.

Hewitt, T. (1992) Developing countries – 1945 to 1990, in T. Allen and A. Thomas (eds) *Poverty and Development in the 1990s*. Oxford: Oxford University Press.

Hill, D.M. (1994) *Citizens and Cities*. Hemel Hempstead: Harvester Wheatsheaf.

Hill, M. (1996) *Social Policy: A Comparative Analysis*. London: Prentice Hall.

Hirst, P. and Thompson, G. (1992) The problem of 'globalization': international economic relations, national economic management and the formation of trading blocs, *Economy and Society*, 21(4): 23–40.

Hodge, S. and Howe, J. (1999) Can the European social model survive?, *European Urban and Regional Studies*, 62(2): 178–84.

Hoekman, B. and Kostecki, B. (1995) *The Political Economy of the World Trading System*. Oxford: Oxford University Press.

Holcombe, S. (1995) *Managing to Empower: The Grameen Bank's Experience of Poverty Alleviation*. London: Zed Books.

Holliday, I. (2000) Productivist welfare capitalism: social policy in East Asia, *Political Studies*, 48: 706–23.

Holm, H-H. and Sørensen, G. (eds) (1995) *Whose World Order? Uneven Globalization and the End of the Cold War*. Boulder, CO: Westview.

Hopkins, T. K., Wallerstein, I. *et al.* (1996) *The Age of Transition: Trajectory of the World-System 1945–2025*. London: Zed Books.

Hulme, D. (1994) Social development research and the third sector: NGOs as users and subjects of social inquiry, in D. Booth (ed.) *Rethinking Social Development: Theory, Research and Practice*. London: Longman.

Hulme, D. and Edwards, M. (eds) (1997) *NGOs, States and Donors: Too Close for Comfort?* London: Macmillan/Save the Children.

Hulme, D. and Mosley, P. (1996) *Finance against Poverty*, vols 1 and 2. London: Routledge.

Ichibangase, Y. (1992) *Creating Welfare in Local Communities* (in Japanese). Tokyo: Rôdô Junpôsha.

IDC (International Data Corporation) (1999) Email correspondence on Internet user data for 1998 for Latin America, South-East Asia and Eastern Europe. Mountain View, California, Prague and Singapore (18 and 30 March).

Institute for Development Studies (IDS) (1996) *The Power of Participation*, IDS policy briefing issue no. 7. http://www.ids.ac.uk/ids/publicat/brief7.html

International Monetary Fund (IMF) (1998) *Social Dimensions of the IMF's Policy Dialogue: IMF Involvement in Social Issues*, IMF pamphlet series no. 47. http://www.imf.org/external/pubs/ft/pam/pam47/pam4701.htm

Iyengar, S. (1993) Social research in developing countries, in M. Bulmer and D. Warwick (eds) *Social Research in Developing Countries*. London: UCL Press.

Jacobs, S. (1985) Race, empire and the welfare state: council housing and racism, *Critical Social Policy*, 5–6(13): 6–40.

Jameson, F. (1984) Postmodernism or the cultural logic of late capitalism, *New Left Review*, 146: 53–92.

Jayasuriya, L. (1991) Citizenship, democratic pluralism and ethnic minorities in Australia, in R. Nile (ed.) *Immigration and the Politics of Ethnicity and Race in Australia and Britain*. London: Sir Robert Menzies Centre for Australian Studies, University of London.

Jessop, B. (1988) Regulation theory, post-Fordism and the State: more than a reply to Werner Bonefield, *Capital and Class*, 34: 147–68.

Jessop, B. (1989) Conservative regimes and the transition to post-Fordism: the cases of Great Britain and West Germany, in M. Gottdiener and N. Komninos (eds) *Capitalist Development and Crisis Theory*. Basingstoke: Macmillan.

Jessop, B. (1990) Regulation theories in retrospect and prospect, *Economy and Society*, 19: 153–216.

Jessop, B. (1992) Changing forms and function of the state in an era of globalization and regionalization. Paper presented to EAPE Conference, Paris, November.

Jessop, B. (1994) The transition to post-Fordism and the Schumpetarian workfare state, in R. Burrows and B. Loader (eds) *Towards a Post-Fordist Welfare State*. London: Routledge.

Jones, C. (1990) Hong Kong, Singapore, South Korea and Taiwan: oikonomic welfare states, *Government and Opposition*, 25(4) Autumn: 447–62.

Jones, C. (1993) The Pacific challenge: Confucian welfare states, in C. Jones (ed.) *New Perspectives on the Welfare State in Europe*. London: Routledge.

Jones, M. (1996) *The Australian Welfare State*. Sydney: Allen & Unwin.

Jones, P. (1970) Some aspects of the changing distribution of the coloured population in Birmingham 1961–6, *Transactions of the Institute of British Geographers*, 50: 199.

Katznelson, I. (1986) Rethinking the Silences of Social and Economic Policy, *Political Science Quarterly*, 101: 307–25.

Keating, P. (1994) *Working Nation: The White Paper on Employment and Growth*. Canberra: AGPS (Australian Government Publication Service).

Kennett, P. (1998) Differentiated citizenship and housing experience, in A. Marsh and D. Mullins (eds) *Housing and Public Policy: Citizenship, Choice and Control*. Buckingham: Open University Press.

Kerr, C., Dunlop, J.T., Harbison, F.H. and Myers, C.A. (1964) *Industrialism and Industrial Man*. Harmondsworth: Penguin Books.

Kerr, L. and Savelsberg, H. (1999) Unemployment and civic responsibility in Australia: towards a new social contract, *Critical Social Policy*, 19(2): 233–45.

King, D. (1989) Economic crisis and welfare state recommodification: a comparative analysis of the United States and Britain, in M. Gottdiener and N. Komninos (eds) *Capitalist Development and Crisis Theory*. Basingstoke: Macmillan.

King, D. and Wickham-Jones, M. (1999) Bridging the Atlantic: the Democratic (Party) origins of welfare to work, in M. Powell (ed.) *New Labour, New Welfare State? The Third Way in British Social Policy*. Bristol: Policy Press.

Kondo, D.K. (1990) *Crafting Selves: Power, Gender and Discourses of Identity in a Japanese Workplace*. Chicago: The University of Chicago Press.

Krieger, J. (1991) Class, consumption and collectivism: perspectives on the Labour Party and electoral competition in Britain, in F. Fox Piven (ed.) *Labour Parties in Post-Industrial Societies*. Cambridge: Polity.

Kwon, H-J. (1997) Beyond European welfare regimes: comparative perspectives on East Asian welfare systems, *Journal of Social Policy*, 26(4): 467–84.

Kwon, H-J. (1998) Democracy and the politics of social welfare: a comparative analysis of welfare systems in East Asia, in R. Goodman, G. White and Huck-ju Kwon (eds) *The East Asian Welfare Model: Welfare Orientalism and the State*. London: Routledge.

Lambert, J. (1991) Europe: the nation state dies hard, *Capital and Class*, 43: 9–24.

Land, H. and Rose, H. (1985) Compulsory altruism for some or an altruistic society for all, in P. Bean, J. Ferris and D. Whynes (eds) *In Defence of Welfare*. London: Tavistock.

Landau, S. (1993) Borders: the new Berlin walls, in R. Miliband and L. Panitch (eds) *Socialist Register*. London: Merlin Press.

Lang, T. and Hines, C. (1994) *The New Protectionism: Protecting the Future against Free Trade*. London: Earthscan.

Langan, M. and Ostner, I. (1991) Gender and welfare. Towards a comparative framework, in G. Room (ed.) *Towards a European Welfare State*. Bristol: SAUS, University of Bristol.

Lash, S. and Bagguley, P. (1988) Labour relations in disorganized capitalism: a five-nation comparison, *Environment and Planning D: Society and Space*, 6: 321–38.

Lash, S. and Urry, J. (1987) *The End of Organized Capitalism*. Cambridge: Polity.

Law, I. (1996) *Racism, Ethnicity and Social Policy*. London: Prentice Hall/Harvester Wheatsheaf.

Leibfried, S. (1991) *Towards a European Welfare State? On Integrating Poverty Regimes in the European Community*. Bremen, Germany: Centre for Social Policy Research, Bremen University.

Leibfried, S. (1993) Towards a European welfare state?, in C. Jones (ed.) *New Perspectives on the Welfare State in Europe*. London: Routledge.

Leibfried, S. (1994) The social dimension of the European Union: en route to positively joint sovereignty?, *European Journal of Social Policy*, 4(3): 239–62.

Leibfried, S. and Pierson, P. (eds) (1995) *European Social Policy: Between Fragmentation and Integration*. Washington, DC: Brookings Institution.

Leibfried, S. and Pierson, P. (2000) Social policy, in H. Wallace and W. Wallace (eds) *Policy-Making in the European Union*. Oxford: Oxford University Press.

Leira, A. (1992) *Welfare States and Working Mothers*. Cambridge: Cambridge University Press.

Levi, M. and Singleton, S. (1991) *Women in 'the Working Man's Paradise': Sole Parents, the Women's Movement, and the Social Policy Bargain in Australia*, working paper no. 1. Canberra: Administration, Compliance and Governability Programme, Australian National University.

Lewis, J. (1992) Gender and the development of welfare regimes, *Journal of European Social Policy*, 2(3): 159–73.

Lewis, J. (1999) The 'problem' of lone motherhood in comparative perspective, in J. Clasen (ed.) *Comparative Social Policy: Concepts, Theories and Methods*. London: Blackwell.

Leys, C. (1996) *The Rise and Fall of Development Theory*. London: James Currey.

Lie, J. (1996) Sociology of contemporary Japan, *Current Sociology* (special issue) 44(1).

Lipietz, A. (1984a) *Accumulation, Crises et Sorties de Crises: Quelques Réflexions Methodologiques Autour de la Notion de Regulation*. Paris: CEPREMAP.

Lipietz, A. (1984b) Imperialism or the beast of the apocalypse, *Capital and Class*, 22: 81–109.

Lipietz, A. (1985) *The Enchanted World: Inflation, Credit and the World Crisis*. London: Verso.

Lipietz, A. (1986) New tendencies in the international division of labour. Regimes of accumulation and modes of regulation, in A.J. Scott and M. Storper (eds) *Production, Work, Territory*. New York: Unwin Hyman.

Lipietz, A. (1987) *Mirages and Miracles: The Crises of Global Fordism*. London: New Left Books.

Lipietz, A. (1989) *Towards a New Economic Order: Postfordism, Ecology and Democracy*. Cambridge: Polity.

Lisle, E. (1985) Validation in the social sciences by international comparison, *Cross-national Research Papers*, 1(1): 11–28.

Lister, R. (1994) 'She has other duties' – women, citizenship and social security, in S. Baldwin and J. Falkingham (eds) *Social Security and Social Change: New Challenges to the Beveridge Model*. New York: Harvester Wheatsheaf.

Lister, R. (1997) *Citizenship: Feminist Perspectives*. London: Macmillan.

Lyotard, J-F. (1979) *Discours Figure*. Paris: Klincksieck.

Lyotard, J-F. (1984) *The Postmodern Condition: A Report on Knowledge*. Manchester: Manchester University Press.

Lyotard, J.F. (1986) Rules and paradoxes or svelt appendix, *Cultural Critique*, 5(2): 207–16.

Mabbett, D. (1998) European and international data sources, in P. Alcock, A. Erskine and M. May (eds) *The Student's Companion to Social Policy*. Oxford: Blackwell.

Mabbett, D. and Bolderson, H. (1999) Theories and methods in comparative social policy, in J. Clasen (ed.) *Comparative Social Policy: Concepts, Theories and Methods*. Oxford: Blackwell.

McGrew, A. (1992) The Third World in the new global order, in T. Allen and A. Thomas (eds) *Poverty and Development in the 1990s*. Oxford: Oxford University Press.

Macintyre, C. (1999) From entitlement to obligation in the Australian welfare state, *Australian Journal of Social Issues*, 34(2): 103–18.

Macintyre, S. (1985) *Winners and Losers*. Sydney: George Allen & Unwin.

Mackie, V. (1988) Feminist politics in Japan, *New Left Review*, 167: 53–76.

McMichael, P. and Myhre, M. (1991) Global regulation vs the nation state: agro-food systems and the new politics of capital, *Capital and Class*, 43: 83–106.

MacPherson, S. and Midgley, J. (1987) *Comparative Social Policy and the Third World*. Brighton: Wheatsheaf.

Madanipour, A., Cars, G. and Allen, J. (eds) (1998) *Social Exclusion in European Cities: Processes, Experiences and Responses*. London: Jessica Kingsley.

Mama, A. (1984) Black women, the economic crisis and the British state, *Feminist Review*, 17: 21–35.

Mama, A. (1989) *The Hidden Struggle*. London: London Race and Housing Research.

Mann, M. (1987) Ruling-class strategies and citizenship, *Sociology*, 21: 339–54.

Mann, M. (1993) *The Sources of Social Power, vol. II: The Rise of Classes and Nation-States, 1760–1914*. Cambridge: Cambridge University Press.

Marchand, M.H. and Parpart, J.L. (eds) (1995) *Feminism/Postmodernism/Development*. London: Routledge.

Marinakou, M. (1998) Welfare states in the European periphery: the case of Greece, in R. Sykes and P. Alcock (eds) *Developments in European Social Policy: Convergence and Diversity*. Bristol: Policy Press.

Marks, G. (1992) Structural policy in the European Community, in A. Sbragia (ed.) *Euro-Politics: Institutions and Policy-making in the 'new' European Community*. Washington, DC: Brookings Institute.

Marks, G. (1993) Structural policy and multi level governance in the EC, in A. Cafruny and G. Rosenthal (eds) *The State of the European Community II: The Maastricht Debates and Beyond*. Boulder, CO: Lynne Rienner.

Marquand, D. (1998) What lies at the heart of the people's project?, *Guardian*, 20 May.

Marsh, A. (1998) Processes of change in housing and public policy, in A. Marsh and D. Mullins (eds) *Housing and Public Policy: Citizenship, Choice and Control*. Milton Keynes: Open University Press.

Marsh, A. and Kennett, P. (1999) Introduction, in P. Kennett and A. Marsh (eds) *Homelessness: Exploring the New Terrain*. Bristol: Policy Press.

Marsh, R. (1967) *Comparative Sociology: A Codification of Cross-societal Analysis*. New York: Harcourt, Brace.

Marshall, T.H. (1950) *Citizenship and Social Class*. Cambridge: Cambridge University Press.

Marzouk, M. (1997) The associative phenomenon in the Arab world: engine of democratisation or witness to the crisis?, in D. Hulme and M. Edwards (eds) *NGOs, States and Donors: Too Close for Comfort?* London: Macmillan/Save the Children.

Massey, D. (1992) A place called home?, *New Formations: The Question of 'Home'*, 17: 3–15.

Mathur, H. (1995) The role of social actors in promoting participatory development at local level: a view from India, in H. Schneider and M. Libercier (eds) *Participatory Development: From Advocacy to Action*. Paris: OECD (Organisation for Economic Co-operation and Development).

May, T. (1997) *Social Research: Issues, Methods and Processes*, 2nd edn. Buckingham: Open University Press.

Midgley, J. (1997) *Social Welfare in Global Context*. Thousand Oaks, CA: Sage.

Miliband, R. (1969) *The State in Capitalist Society*. London: Weidenfeld & Nicolson.

Miliband, R. (1977) *Marxism and Politics*. Oxford: Oxford University Press.

Mishra, R. (1999) *Globalization and the Welfare State*. Cheltenham, Edward Elgar.

Mitchell, D. (1991) *Income Transfers in Ten Welfare State*. Aldershot: Avebury.

Mitchell, M. and Russell, D. (1996) *Immigration, Citizenship and Social Exclusion in the New Europe*. Bristol: Policy Press.

Modood, T. (1997) Employment, in T. Modood, R. Berthoud, J. Lakey *et al. Ethnic Minorities in Britain: Diversity and Disadvantage*. London: Policy Studies Institute.

Morales-Gomez, D. (ed.) (1999) *Transnational Social Policies: The New Development Challenges of Globalization*. London: Earthscan.

Mosley, P., Harrigan, J. and Toye, J. (1995) *Aid and Power: The World Bank and Policy-Based Lending*, 2nd edn. London: Routledge.

Munck, R. and O'Hearn, D. (1999) *Critical Development Theory: Contributions to a New Paradigm*. London: Zed Books.

Mwansa, L-K. (1995) Participation of non-governmental organizations in the social development process in Africa: implications, *Journal of Social Development in Africa*, 10(1): 56–75.

Ndegwa, S. (1996) *The Two Faces of Civil Society: NGOs and Politics in Africa*. West Hartford, CT: Kumarian Press.

Neary, I. (1997) Burakumin in contempory Japan, in M. Weiner (ed.) *Japan's Minorities: The Illusion of Homogeneity*. London: Routledge.

Network Wizards (1998a) *Internet Domain Survey July 1998*. http://www.nw.com (accessed Mar. 1999).

Network Wizards (1998b) *Number of Internet Hosts*. http://www.nw.com (accessed 22 Oct. 1998).

Nua (1999) *How many online*. http://www.nua.ie (accessed 1 Mar. 1999).

NTIA (National Telecommunications and Information Administration) (1998) *Falling through the Net II: New data on the Digital Divide* http://www.ntia.doc.gov/ntiahome/net2/falling.1

O'Brien, M. and Penna, S. (1996) Postmodern theory and politics: perspectives on citizenship and social justice, *Innovation*, (9)2: 185–203.

O'Brien, M. and Penna, S. (1998) *Theorising Welfare: Enlightenment and Modern Society*. London: Sage.

O'Connor, J. (1973) *The Fiscal Crisis of the State*. London: St Martins Press.

O'Connor, J. (1993) Gender, class and citizenship in the comparative analysis of welfare state regimes: theoretical and methodological issues, *British Journal of Sociology*, 44(3): 501–18.

ODI (Overseas Development Institute) (1995) The funding of NGOs, ODI briefing note. London: ODI.

OECD (1988) *Voluntary Aid for Development: The Role of Non-governmental Organizations*. Paris: OECD.

OECD (1993) *Challenge for the Mid-1990s: The Development Centre's Programme for 1993–1995*. Paris: OECD Development Centre.

Offe, C. (1984) *Contradictions of the Welfare State*. Cambridge, MA: MIT Press.

Ohmae, K. (1992) *The Borderless World: Power and Strategy in the Interlinked Economy*. London: HarperCollins.

Orloff, A. (1995) Gender in the liberal welfare states: Australia, the United Kingdom and the United States. Paper presented to the ISA Research Committee 19 Conference, Comparative Research on Welfare State Reforms, University of Pavia, Italy, 14–17 September.

Osei-Hwedie, K. and Bar-on, A. (1999) Sub-Saharan Africa: community-driven social policies, in D. Morales-Gomez (ed.) *Transnational Social Policies: The New Development Challenges of Globalization*. London: Earthscan.

Overbeek, H. (1990) *Global Capitalism and National Decline: The Thatcher Decade in Perspective*. London: Unwin Hyman.

Oyen, E. (ed.) (1990) *Comparative Methodology: Theory and Practice in International Social Research*. London: Sage.

Parsons, T. (1964) *The Social System*. London: Routledge and Kegan Paul.

Pascall, G. (1986) *Social Policy: A Feminist Analysis*. London: Tavistock.

Pateman, C. (1989) *The Disorder of Women*. Cambridge: Polity.

Pearson, N. (1995) An optimist's vision, in N. Pearson and W. Sanders, *Indigenous Peoples and Reshaping Australian Institutions: Two Perspectives*, discussion paper no. 102. Canberra: Centre for Aboriginal Economic Policy Research, Australian National University.

Peck, J.A. and Tickell, A. (1991) *Regulation Theory and the Geographics of Flexible Accumulation: Transitions in Capitalism, Transitions in Theory*. SPA Working Paper 12. Manchester: University of Manchester, School of Geography.

Pederson, S. (1993) *Family, Dependence and the Origins of the Welfare State: Britain and France 1914–1945*. Cambridge: Cambridge University Press.

Peng, I. (2000) A fresh look at the Japanese welfare state, *Social Policy and Administration*, 34(1): 87–114.

Penna, S. and O'Brien, M. (1996) Postmodernism and social policy, *Journal of Social Policy*, 25(1): 39–61.

Picciotto, S. (1991) The internationalisation of the state, *Capital and Class*, 43: 43–63.

Pickvance, C.G. (1986) Comparative urban analysis and assumptions about causality, *International Journal of Urban and Regional Research*, 10(2): 162–84.

Pierson, C. (1991) *Beyond the Welfare State: The New Political Economy of Welfare*. Cambridge: Polity.

Pierson, C. (1998) *Beyond the Welfare State: The New Political Economy of Welfare*, 2nd edn. Cambridge: Polity.

Pierson, P. and Leibfried, S. (1995) Multitiered institutions and the making of social policy, in S. Leibfried and P. Pierson (eds) *European Social Policy: Between Fragmentation and Integration*. Washington, DC: Brookings Institution.

Pollert, A. (1988) Dismantling flexibility, *Capital and Class*, 34: 42–75.

Pooley, S. (1991) The state rules, OK? The continuing political economy of nation states, *Capital and Class*, 43: 65–82.

Potter, D. (1992) Colonial rule, in T. Allen and A. Thomas (eds) *Poverty and Development in the 1990s*. Buckingham: Open University Press.

Pryor, F. (1968) *Public Expenditure in Capitalist and Communist Nations*. Homewood, IL: Irwin.

Przeworski, A. (1987) Methods of cross-national research 1970–1983, in M. Dierkes, H. Weiler and A. Antal (eds) *Comparative Policy Research: Learning from Experience*. Aldershot: Gower and Berlin: WZB.

Pusey, M. (1991) *Economic Rationalism in Canberra: A Nation-building State Changes its Mind*. Cambridge: Cambridge University Press.

Ragin, C. (1987) *The Comparative Method: Moving Beyond Qualitative and Quantitative Strategies*. Berkeley, CA: University of California Press.

Rahnema, M. with Bawtree, B. (eds) (1977) *The Post-Development Reader*. London: Zed Books.

Redclift, M. (1987) *Sustainable Development: Exploring the Contradictions*. London: Routledge.

Rees, A.M. (1996) T.H. Marshall and the progress of citizenship, in M. Bulmer and A.M. Rees (eds) *Citizenship Today*. London: UCL Press.

Rein, M. and Rainwater, L. (1981) *From Welfare State to Welfare Society: Some Unresolved Issues in Assessment*, IIVG-AP 81. Berlin: WZB.

Rimlinger, G.V. (1971) *Welfare and Industrialization in Europe, America and Russia*. New York: Wiley.

Risse-Kappen, T. (1996) Exploring the nature of the beast: international relations theory and comparative policy analysis meet the European Union, *Journal of Common Market Studies*, 34(1): 53–80.

Rist, G. (1997) *The History of Development: From Western Origins to Global Faith*. London: Zed Books.

Robson, W. (1976) *Welfare State and Welfare Society*. London: Allen & Unwin.

Rodgers, J. (2000) *From a Welfare State to a Welfare Society*. London: Macmillan.

Room, G. (1991) *National Policies to Combat Social Exclusion: First Annual Report of the European Community Observatory CRESEP*. Bath: University of Bath.

Room, G. (1992) *Observatory on National Policies to Combat Social Exclusion*, Second annual report. Brussels: DGV.

Room, G. (ed.) (1995) *Beyond the Threshold*. Bristol: Policy Press.

Rosamond, B. (2000) *Theories of European Integration*. London: Macmillan.

Rose, H. (1986) Women and the restructuring of the welfare state, in E. Oyen (ed.) *Comparing Welfare States and their Futures*. Aldershot: Gower.

Rose, M. (1986) The methodology of comparative policy analysis, in S. Mangen and L. Hantrais (eds) *Research Methods and Problems in Comparative Public Policy*, cross-national research papers, Birmingham: Aston University.

Rose, R. (1991) Comparing forms of comparative analysis, *Political Studies*, 39: 446–62.

Rostow, W.W. (1960) *The Stages of Economic Growth: A Non-Communist Manifesto*. Cambridge: Cambridge University Press.

Rustin, M. (2000) Reflections on the biographical turn in social science, in P. Chamberlayne, J. Bornat and T. Wengraf (eds) *The Turn to Biographical Methods in Social Science*. London: Routledge.

Sainsbury, D. (ed.) (1994) *Gendering Welfare States*. London: Sage.

Sainsbury, D. (1996) *Gender, Equality and Welfare States*. Cambridge: Cambridge University Press.

Salamon, L.M. (1994) The rise of the non-profit sector, *Foreign Affairs*, 73(4): 30–43.

Saraceno, C. (1997) The importance of the concept of social exclusion, in W. Beck, L. van der Maesen and A. Walker (eds) *The Social Quality of Europe*. Bristol: Policy Press.

Sarre, P., Phillips, D. and Skellington, R. (1989) *Ethnic Minority Housing: Explanations and Policies*. Aldershot: Avebury.

Sassen, S. (1991) *The Global City: New York, London, Tokyo*. Princeton, NJ: Princeton University Press.

SatelLife (1998) *Healthnet*. http://www.heathnet.org (accessed 9 Nov. 1998).

Sayer, A. (1989) Post Fordism in question, *International Journal of Urban and Regional Research*, 13(4): 666–995.

Schiavone, G. (1997) *International Organizations: A Dictionary*, 4th edn. London: Macmillan.

Schoenberger, E. (1989) Thinking about flexibility: a response to Gertler, *Transactions of the Institute of British Geographers NS*, 14: 98–108.

Schottland, C. (1967) *The Welfare State*. New York: Harper.

Schuurman, F.J. (ed.) (1993) *Beyond the Impasse: New Directions in Development Theory*. London: Zed Books.

Scoones, I. and Thompson, J. (1994) *Beyond Farmer First: Rural Peoples' Knowledge and Extension Practice*. London: Intermediate Technology.

Scott, A.J. and Storper, M. (1992) Industrialization and regional development, in M. Storper and A.J. Scott (eds) *Pathways to Industrialization and Regional Development*. London: Routledge.

Shaver, S. (1990) *Gender, Social Policy Regimes and the Welfare State*, discussion paper no. 26. Social Policy Research Centre, University of New South Wales.

Short, J.R. and Kim, Y-H. (1999) *Globalization and the City*. New York: Addison Wesley Longman.

Silver, H. (1993) National conceptions of the new urban poverty: social structural change in Britain, France and the United States, *International Journal of Urban and Regional Research*, 17(4): 347–68.

Sivanandan, A. (1976) Race, class and the state: the black experience in Britain, *Race and Class*, 17(4): 347–68.

Sivananden, A. (1987) Imperialism and disorganic development in the Silicon Age, in R. Peet (ed.) *International Capitalism and Industrial Restructuring*. London: Allen & Unwin.

Smelser, N.J. (1964) Towards a theory of modernization, in A. Etzioni and E. Etzioni (eds) *Social Change: Sources, Patterns and Consequences*. New York: Basic Books.

Smelser, N.J. (1976) *Comparative Methods in the Social Sciences*. Englewood Cliffs, NJ: Prentice Hall.

Smillie, I. and Helmich, H. (1993) *Non-Governmental Organisations and Governments: Stakeholders for Development*. Paris: OECD.

Smith, S.J. (1989) Society, space and citizenship: a human geography for the 'new times'?, *Transactions of the Institute of British Geographers*, 14: 144–56.

Spicker, P. (1991) The principle of subsidiarity and the social policy of the European Community, *Journal of European Social Policy*, 1(1): 3–14.

Stoker, G. (1995) Introduction, in D. Marsh and G. Stoker (eds) *Theory and Method in Political Science*. Basingstoke: Macmillan.

Sugimoto, Y. (1997) *An Introduction to Japanese Society*. Cambridge: Cambridge University Press.

Swanston, T. (1993) Beyond economism: urban political economy and the post-modern challenge, *Journal of Urban Affairs*, 15(1): 55–78.

Takahashi, M. (1997) *The Emergence of Welfare Society in Japan*. Aldershot: Avebury/Ashgate.

Taylor, C. (1989) *Sources of the Self*. Cambridge, MA: Harvard University Press.

Taylor-Gooby, P. (1988) The future of the British welfare state: public attitudes, citizenship and social policy under the Conservative governments of the 1980s, *European Sociological Review*, 4(1): 1–19.

Taylor-Gooby, P. (1994) Postmodernism and social policy: a great leap backwards?, *Journal of Social Policy*, 23(3): 385–404.

Tendler, J. (1989) Whatever happened to poverty alleviation?, *World Development*, 17(7): 1033–44.

The Times (2000) *Why do the poor still pay the rich?* http://www.thetimes.co.uk/news/pages/tim/2000/04/14/timfeafea02001.html (accessed 14 Apr. 2000)

Thompson, S. and Hoggett, P. (1996) Universalism, selectivism and particularism. Towards a postmodern social policy, *Critical Social Policy*, 16(1): 21–43.

Tickell, A. and Peck, J. (1992) Accumulation regimes and the geographies of post-Fordism: missing links in regulationist theory, *Progress in Human Geography*, 16: 190–218.

Tiffen, M. (1994) More people, less erosion: environmental recovery in Kenya. Chichester: John Wiley & Sons.

Titmuss, R. (1968) *Essays on the Welfare State*. London: Allen & Unwin.

Titmuss, R. (1974) *Social Policy*. London: Allen & Unwin.

Tokyo Metropolitan Government (1997) *Tokyo: Services for Today, Challenges for Tomorrow*. Tokyo: Tokyo Metropolitan Government.

Tomlinson, J. (1996) Citizenship and sovereignty, *Australian Journal of Social Issues*, 31: 2–18.

Townsend, P. (1979) *Poverty in the United Kingdom*. Harmondsworth: Penguin.

Townsend, P. (1993) *The International Analysis of Poverty*. London: Harvester Wheatsheaf.

Toye, J. (1987) *Dilemmas of Development: Reflections on the Counter-Revolution in Development Theory and Policy*. Oxford: Blackwell.

Tricart, J.P. (1991) Note de problematique, working papers of the Social Exclusion Observatory, EC Commission, in D. Robbins (ed.) (1992) *Social Exclusion 1990–1992: The United Kingdom*. Lille: EC Observatory on Policies to Combat Social Exclusion, European Economic Interest Group, Animation and Research.

Tsoukalis, L. (1991) *The New European Economy: The Politics and Economics of Integration*. Oxford: Oxford University Press.

Tvedt, T. (1998) *Angels of Mercy or Development Diplomats? NGOs and Foreign Aid*. Trenton: Africa World Press and Oxford: James Curry.

Ungerson, G. (ed.) (1985) *Women and Social Policy: A Reader*. London: Macmillan.

United Nations (1994) *Statistical Yearbook – 1992*. New York: UN Official Publications.

United Nations Centre for Human Settlements (HABITAT) (UNCHS) (1996) *An Urbanizing World: Global Report on Human Settlements*. Oxford: Oxford University Press.

United Nations Development Programme (UNDP) (1999) *Human Development Report 1999*. Oxford: Oxford University Press.

Vasishth, A. (1997) A model minority: the Chinese community in Japan, in M. Weiner (ed.) *Japan's Minorities: The Illusion of Homogeneity*. London: Routledge.

Veit-Wilson, J. (1998) *Setting Adequacy Standards*. Bristol: Policy Press.

Vivian, J. (1994) NGOs and sustainable development in Zimbabwe: no magic bullets, *Development and Change*, 25: 181–209.

Walker, A. and Walker, C. (eds) (1997) *Britain Divided: The Growth of Social Exclusion in the 1980s and 1990s*. London: Child Poverty Action Group.

Walker, A. and Wong, C-K. (1996) Rethinking the western construction of the welfare state, *International Journal of Health Services*, 26(1): 67–92.

Wall, A. (ed.) (1996) *Health Care Systems in Liberal Democracies*. London: Routledge.

Wallace, H. and Wallace, H. (2000) *Policy-Making in the European Union*. Oxford: Oxford University Press.

Wallerstein, I. (1974) *The Modern World System*. New York: Academic Press.

Wallerstein, I. (1979) *The Capitalist World Economy*. Cambridge, MA: Cambridge University Press.

Warwick, D.P. and Osherson, S. (eds) (1973) *Comparative Research Methods*. Englewood Cliffs, NJ: Prentice Hall.

Watson, S. (1999) A home is where the heart is: engendering notions of homelessness, in P. Kennett and A. Marsh (eds) *Homelessness: Exploring the New Terrain*. Bristol: Policy Press.

WCED (World Commission on Environment and Development) (1987) *Our Common Future* (commonly known as the Brundtland report). Oxford: Oxford University Press.

Webber, F. (1991) From ethnocentrism to Euro-racism, *Race and Class*, 31(3): 11–17.

Weiss, L. (1998) *The Myth of the Powerless State*. Cambridge: Polity.

Weiss, M. (1991) *Industry in Developing Countries: Theory, Policy and Evidence*. London: Routledge.

Weiss, M. (1992) *Industry in Developing Countries: Theory, Policy and Evidence*. London: Routledge.

Wellard, K. and Copestake, J.G. (eds) (1993) *Non-Governmental Organisations and the State in Africa: Rethinking Roles in Sustainable Development*. London: Routledge.

Welsh, H. (1994) The collapse of Communism in Eastern Europe and the GDR: evolution, revolution, and diffusion, in M. Hancock and H. Welsh (eds) *German Unification: Process and Outcomes*. Boulder, CO: Westview.

Wignaraja, P. (ed.) (1999) *New Social Movements in the South: Empowering the People*. London: Zed Books.

Wilensky, H.L. (1975) *The Welfare State and Equality: Structural and Ideological Roots of Public Expenditures*. Berkeley, CA: University of California Press.

Williams, F. (1989) *Social Policy: A Critical Introduction*. Cambridge: Polity.

Williams, F. (1992) Somewhere over the rainbow: universality and diversity in social policy, *Social Policy Review*, 4: 200–19.

Williams, F. (1994) Social relations, welfare and the post-Fordist debate, in B. Loader and R. Burrows (eds) *Towards a Post-Fordist Welfare State?* London: Routledge.

Wilson, E. (1977) *Women and the Welfare State*. London: Tavistock.

Woods, N. (ed.) (1999) *The Political Economy of Globalization*. London: Macmillan.

World Bank (1999) *Entering the 21st Century: World Development Report*. Washington, DC: World Bank.

Index